# The Financial SAMURAI

Also by Aron Viner
Inside Japanese Financial Markets

# The Financial
# SAMURAI

## The Emerging Power of Japanese Money

### Aron Viner

KOGAN
PAGE

First published in Great Britain in 1988 by
Kogan Page Limited
120 Pentonville Road, London N1 9JN

**British Library Cataloguing in Publication Data**
Viner, Aron
  The financial samurai: the emerging power of Japanese money.
  1. Japan. Finance
  I. Title
  332′.0952

  ISBN 1-85091-614-4

Printed and bound in Great Britain
by Billing and Sons Ltd, Worcester.

. . . TO DORIS AND BOB

## ACKNOWLEDGEMENT

Hilary McLellan worked on parts of this book with me. As far as I'm concerned, she was a co-author. However, she declined to be recognized as such.

# CONTENTS

# PREFACE

Like a volcanic eruption bursting dramatically through the surface
of the ocean, the emerging power of Japanese money presages the
appearance of a new system whose final shape cannot yet be gauged.
Indeed, like some new volcanic islands, it may enjoy only a brief
existence before sinking back beneath the waves; or it may be that
we are witnessing the foundation of a new financial continent.

I chose to write this book because, if this island does grow and
become the base of a durable economic force, we in the West need to
understand the implications of that development. Such understanding
will not be easily acquired. The representatives of Japan, the United
States, and the European Community are far, indeed, from mutual
understanding. The gulf that separates Japanese and Western views
shows many signs of deepening rather than disappearing.

Protectionism and anti-foreign sentiments can only be destructive
to all members of the world economy. While technology is swiftly
uniting the separate national worlds of finance into a single global
nexus, political differences and unilateral economic concerns conspire
with cultural biases to undermine free trade.

This book is intended to raise issues and provoke thought. It begins
by exploring the views on both sides of some of the major trade issues
which have resulted in disputes between Japan and the West. Chapter
One offers a Western perspective while Chapter Two provides an
indication of Japanese views. Thus, many of the opinions presented
in these chapters are not mine. My intention is to describe ongoing
trends in Japan's economic relationships with the world. Chapter

Three provides an outline of the historical context and the contemporary framework which will, I believe, influence the unfolding of Japan's participation in the financial sector. I think that these discussions will help to foreshadow and clarify the future financial trends and current financial activities discussed in the book's remaining three chapters.

Chapter Four focuses on a few recent changes in world finance and the implications of those changes. The fifth chapter describes current Japanese approaches to finance and corporate structure within the context of international investment. Chapter Six, the conclusion, considers Japan's preeminent role in the new world of international finance which is now emerging.

# INTRODUCTION

# IS JAPAN POOR?

*Is Japan poor?* Perhaps this is an odd question to pose at the beginning of a book which claims to be about the emerging power of Japanese money. Nonetheless, it is a question taken very seriously by the majority of Japanese economists who are persuaded that in many ways – the ways which matter most – Japan *is* poor.

There is no shortage of evidence to support pessimism about Japan's immediate prospects. The economy has been in a 'growth recession,' albeit a mild one. Economic growth in 1986 declined to 2.6 percent. This was the second lowest growth rate since the first oil crisis in 1973 and a far cry from the double digit growth of the heady 1960s. Although corporate profits recovered dramatically during the second half of 1987 and economic growth will rise significantly above the doldrums of 1986, continued appreciation of the yen could undermine all gains.

Seasonally adjusted unemployment reached 3.2 percent in May 1987, the highest rate since 1953 when statistics were first compiled. In remote locations, such as the northern island of Hokkaido, unemployment exceeded 4.5 percent. But according to the Japanese government definition of unemployment, a person who works as little as one hour per week is considered employed.* By US or EEC methods of calculation, unemployment in Japan would have surpassed 5 percent.

* Part-time employees (who represent 5 percent of the employees of Japan's larger companies) who would like to work full-time are thus not considered unemployed. Unemployment statistics also do not include workers who have been laid off by their companies but continue to receive compensation. Graduating students who are given job offers in August for the financial year beginning the following April are also regarded as employed for statistical purposes.

Many Japanese economists believe that overall unemployment will double during the next several years, and that it will triple in the manufacturing sector.

Mature industries such as shipbuilding, steel, coal, and textiles are closing plants and will fire tens of thousands of workers. 'Rationaliz-ation' efforts by Japanese manufacturers are resulting in increased overseas production, leading to fewer jobs at home. The strong yen seems destined to shatter forever Japan's export-based economy.

Because Japan's corporations gained their wealth primarily through the manufacture of superior and price-competitive products, it has been assumed that they will decline as the high yen (which the Japanese term *endaka*) eliminates their competitive edge. Exports will shrink and corporate losses will consume excess liquidity. As a result, the Japanese manufacturing sector will contract and many sunset industries will dip below the horizon, never to rise again. In Japan this process is known as 'the hollowing out' (*kudoka*) of Japanese industry. Thus, Japan is the apple and the high yen is the apple corer.

Those who have been too busy with immediate concerns to read about Japan, may not know that Japan, the exporter of autos (Toyota) and electronics (Sony), has too many yen ('excess liquidity') and negligible consumer price inflation. Meanwhile, the yen appreciated against the dollar by 40 percent in 1985, the Year of the Ox, and continued strengthening throughout 1986 and 1987. That means that if Japanese assets are considered in terms of dollars many Japanese corporations and financial institutions are exceedingly rich.

Here are just five examples of that wealth, admittedly selected in order to impress.

* THE STOCKMARKET Not only is the Tokyo stockmarket the biggest in the world (in terms of the capitalization of listed companies), but *just one* of the listed stocks (NTT) is worth more than the entire value of all the stocks listed on the West German and Hong Kong Stockmarkets combined. Meanwhile, the provincial Osaka stockmarket (a mere 13 percent the size of the Tokyo stockmarket) ranks number three in the world.
* BANKS. The five biggest commercial banks in the world (in terms of deposits) are Japanese. Japan's postal savings system, which is not a bank at all, holds deposits six times as large as the deposits held by Citibank, North America's largest commercial bank. More than one third of *all* global cross-border assets held by banks belonged to Japanese institutions in 1987. As a result, Japanese banks have become the biggest creditors in the inter-

national banking system, with $1.1 trillion in cross-border assets, an increase of 100 percent over the 1985 level.
* LEADING CREDITOR. Japan is the world's biggest creditor nation. In 1986 its net overseas credits increased by 40 percent over the preceding year, reaching a record $180.35 billion. During fiscal 1986 (ended March 31), Japan's current account surplus reached $93.76 billion, up 70 percent over the year before.
* STOCKBROKERS. Japan is the home of four of the largest securities companies the world has ever seen. The biggest, Nomura Securities Company, is valued on the Tokyo Stock Exchange at $58 billion, far more than the market value of all US securities firms combined. By itself, Nomura has been buying a major portion of the annual US government budget deficit, which it then sells effortlessly to its Japanese clients.
* CORPORATE CASH. Many leading Japanese corporations hold highly liquid assets. Toyota and Matsushita, for instance, each have liquid assets exceeding $12 billion.

You are impressed? Japanese economists are not. They believe that Japan, as the second largest economy in the free world with about 15 percent of the free world's gross national product (GNP), is bound to be the grazing ground of fat corporations and institutions. They perceive Japan's wealth as 'paper riches,' of no value to the Japanese people whose standard of living they consider not comparable to that of their Western counterparts.

Furthermore, they are afraid that the recent appreciation of the yen against the dollar and other major currencies will result in sharply higher world prices for Japanese exports. Thus, the future will be determined by the foreign exchange markets: the higher the yen, the smaller Japan's global market share. Japanese exports will cease to be competitive and the nation and its assets will soon decline.

Japanese economists fear that, as the newly appreciated yen causes the Japanese export market to dry up, the economy will swiftly deteriorate and Japan will return to the struggle for survival that characterized the grim years of postwar reconstruction. Although Japanese consumers have not yet begun to stockpile food for the imminent crisis, few Japanese believe that their nation's economic future is bright.

Many Japanese are convinced that Japan is about to follow the well-beaten path established by Britain and the United States: international trade declines, the government deficit increases, and the economy contracts. Welcome, Japan, to the exclusive club of industrial and financial leaders gone to seed.

American economists, on the other hand, view Japan as a superstar economy hindered by labyrinthine government regulations and anti-quated distribution systems. They argue that if Japan would pause for a moment and modernize (abolish or liberalize its regulatory systems) then the East Asian giant would become what MacArthur meant it to be: a rich and powerful US ally capable of complementing and not competing with the US economy. In a Japan with a truly open market, Japanese consumers could select products manufactured throughout the world on the basis of quality and price.

These economists urge that Japan must reform its restrictive tax system, relax its monetary policies, and open its financial markets. These issues aside, however, they argue that Japan is a supreme capitalist. Japanese manufacturers provide the US with vital products and leading edge technology. At the same time, Japanese investors supply the US economy with indispensable transfusions of cash. Indeed, US interest rates would be substantially higher were it not for Japanese purchases of US Treasury issues.

In the jaded eyes of American economic observers, Japanese industry is *not* being crushed by an overvalued currency. Of course, Japanese companies are faced with a period of major readjustment, a consequence of the recognition that the yen was undervalued during most of the period following the second 'oil shock'. This undervaluation can be demonstrated by a variety of measures of the exchange rate. But, overall, after a brief period of rationalization, the productivity of Japanese industries will be stimulated rather than retarded by the newly appreciated yen. Thus, the Japanese term *endaka* or 'high yen' is a misnomer. The yen is not high – on the contrary, it is at (or perhaps slightly above) sea level.

Some American economists have termed Japan neo-mercantilist. By this they mean that Japan favours exports over imports in a system that concentrates wealth in selected institutions and provides individuals with little opportunity to spend money. Certainly, Japanese policy has distinct echoes of the mercantilist writings of the seventeenth century. A strong national focus on exports, together with the creation of non-tariff barriers that have discouraged imports, has given Japan an economy based on 'adversarial trade'.

Japanese politicians and bureaucrats have been stung by the use of the term 'adversarial'. Nonetheless, for critics of Japan, no epithet better captures her attitude towards trade relations with the West. Ordinarily, when nations conduct trade, all partners benefit. Yet, from the perspective of foreign economists, Japan's economic growth has been achieved at the expense of the economies of the other major industrial nations rather than complementing them. Japan exports manufactured products to the West (reducing the importer's demand for domestically produced goods) but imports little from the West. Japan's surplus in telecommunications trade is an example of this. In 1985 (the most recent year for which OECD statistics are available), Japan exported telecommunications products worth $1.38 billion but her imports in the same sector amounted to just $57.6 million – thus exports exceeded her imports by a factor of 24. Seen from this perspective, Japan has made only a minor contribution to the total volume of world trade.

Although Japan has grown to be a multi-trillion-dollar economy and is the biggest creditor nation, Japanese consumers pay exorbitantly high prices for nearly all commodities. The quality of life in Japan's cities is generally considered to be far inferior to the middle-class urban splendour of North America or Western Europe. A majority of the Japanese population considers itself to be poor. Just ask!

A common phrase in Japan, rapidly becoming a cliché, is 'a rich country but a poor people.' No one can deny that Japan, the nation, is rich. Its hefty surplus on the current account, the magnitude of its foreign investments, the sheer value of its corporations, and its expensive urban real estate all attest to the vast accumulation of physical and monetary assets. Yet, who owns Japan? Who owns Japan's corporations? Who owns the land of Japan? Who owns Japan's overseas investments?

Of course, the Japanese government does own land, as well as a handful of national corporations (rapidly being privatized at great profit). But, with a budget deficit equivalent to 4.1 percent of GNP in 1987 and an aggregate debt exceeding one-third of GNP, the government is scarcely the proud owner of Japan's great liquid wealth. Indeed the Japanese government is chronically short of revenue. Thus, while Japan has an enormous trade surplus, it is all in the private sector.

The vast majority of Japan's major corporations are publicly held. The top 1,860 companies are listed on Japan's stock exchanges, while others are traded over the counter. Yet only 23.9 percent (in 1986) of all the outstanding shares in these corporations are held by individuals. To make matters more perplexing, corporate profits are not redistributed as dividends. Dividends *are* paid to shareholders, but they are based on a tiny percentage of par value and there is little correlation between the sums paid out and the magnitude of corporate profits.

Nor are Japanese workers highly paid in relation to the cost of living in Japan. The average Japanese family must spend roughly 30 percent of its disposable income on food alone. The costs of rent, clothing, education, and other necessities consume another 48 percent of disposable income. Japan's corporate profits are not redistributed to employees in the form of generously high salaries or profit sharing.

Much of Japan's choicest urban real estate is owned by major corporations. Indeed, the current high market value of Japanese stocks is, in part, attributable to the fact that many blue-chip Japanese companies have 'hidden assets' in the form of real estate.

Similarly, Japan's overseas investments are owned by Japanese companies. Japan's wealth is corporate wealth. The five examples of Japanese financial prowess listed above are manifestations of corporate wealth.

Thus, the charge of neo-mercantilism seems justified. Japan, the nation, is rich as a direct result of accumulated corporate surpluses derived from a pattern of trade with other nations that has favoured exports and discouraged imports. The Japanese people have little money to spend and therefore a limited choice about how to spend it. Non-tariff barriers either exclude foreign-made products or inflate their prices to match patterns within the domestic pricing system. For example, Japanese rice (discussed in Chapter 1) costs far more than Southeast Asian rice, but rice imports are banned.

So, is Japan rich or poor? The answer is that the people are poor (at least by consensus and in terms of relative deprivation) and the government is poor (just look at that debt). If there is wealth in Japan, it is the corporations that hold the purse strings. What does this mean for Japan's future?

Today, corporate profits are invested in a range of financial market instruments and in plant and equipment. Recently, the expansion of corporate facilities has focused on the creation of *overseas* factories, offices, and networks. Offshore manufacturing in countries with lower labour costs is already well underway.

For example, in 1987 Matsushita Electric Industrial, Japan's biggest electronics firm, produced 14 percent of its products outside Japan and planned to increase overseas production to 25 percent by 1990. In 1986, the Aiwa Company, another major electronics concern, set up production facilities in Singapore (eliminating 1,000 jobs in Japan in the process) in order to raise the proportion of its output produced overseas from 12 to 50 percent. Unlike Aiwa Company which has focused production in a single country, Canon Inc has spread its factories throughout the West. Canon plants in West Germany, the United States (Virginia), Italy (a joint venture with Olivetti), and France produce a total of 100,000 plain paper copiers per year.

Although only about 3 percent of total Japanese production occurred outside Japan in 1987, this percentage will increase by a factor of between five and seven during the next decade. Furthermore, a hefty portion of Japanese overseas production will be exported to Japan. In the future, much of Japan's import bill will be accounted for by Japanese products produced outside the country.

In 1987 again Japanese investors (primarily corporations and institutions) bought a net $90 billion in foreign securities and spent more than $6 billion on US corporate acquisitions and investments. Indeed, Japanese corporations have become market movers throughout the world. The swelling portfolio of investments held by Japanese corporations as well as the expanding international role of Japanese banks and securities companies is giving these institutions considerable global power.

The contraction of the domestic manufacturing sector will serve to drive the overseas subsidiaries of domestic corporations into new areas promising high return. In 1986 and 1987, many Japanese corporations derived a major share of their profits from activities in overseas (and domestic) financial markets. Japan's major trading houses (the *sogo shosha*) today own financial subsidiaries in Europe. At home, Sony Corporation, the famous producer of acoustic equipment, now operates a life insurance company and will soon be managing its own pension funds. All indications suggest that these trends will continue for quite some time.

Simultaneously, Japan's service sector will expand. In the post-industrial era which is now underway, services will become increasingly more important than manufacturing. The purveyors of products ranging from hamburgers to movie reviews, from mortgages to life insurance, will expand to satisfy domestic demand and will come to represent a growing portion of the economy.

The leaders of the service sector, however, will be financial institutions. Barring a collapse of the Japanese economy, Japan's financial institutions and corporations, *because of the money which they control*, will become forces with an increasingly global influence. Indeed, long before the turn of the century, they will have become the world's most powerful entities in finance, foreign exchange, and trade. As Japan's financial institutions and organizations rise, Tokyo as a world financial centre will rise with them. Inhibiting regulations will be shed, uncovering Japan's new and toughly competitive financial skin.

China, Greece, Spain, England – each had its moment of glory and today each is a second-rate power supported by a wobbly economy. That rich countries become poor and poor countries become rich, although a platitude, is true for all sovereign entities.

The United States, for example, enjoyed its heyday of riches and economic power during the twentieth century. With the approach of a new millennium, America is on the threshold of a new era. Not for much longer will it be the world's dominant financial power or the most technologically advanced nation. The United States is in the process of being superceded by the next global economic power – Japan!

# 1 THE WORLD VIEWS JAPAN

**FROM RICE TO STOCK**

I had been living in Indonesia for nearly two years when I arrived at Tokyo's Narita airport in 1978. I had come to Japan to attend a conference about rice. I thought that rice was one of the most fascinating and important (and appetizing) things in the world. From my point of view, when it came to the growing of rice, the Japanese were inefficient but masterful artists.

I had shown a movie of Japanese farmers transplanting and harvesting rice in several dozen villages in North Sumatra. When they saw the film, Indonesian women sighed, while men exclaimed with awe at the images of excellent yield and automated harvesting. My audiences marvelled when I mentioned that Japanese farmers held more political clout than any other single group in Japan. But when I told them that the Japanese government bought virtually the entire national rice harvest at ten times the Indonesian price, it was suggested (not always politely) that I was spinning a yarn. It was not to be the last time that my statements about Japan evoked such a response.

The day before I was scheduled to leave Tokyo a fateful event occurred. An old school friend, who was then working for a large Japanese securities firm, offered to give me a tour of the Tokyo Stock Exchange. Because my friend was Japanese, I attempted to be Japanese in my phrasing of a refusal. I politely protested that he was very busy and his valuable time could be better spent. He insisted that 'the TSE', as he called it, was the eighth wonder of the world and under no circumstances could I be permitted to leave Japan without witnessing the stock exchange floor during trading hours. 'You're an economist,' he concluded, as though that clinched the matter.

Reluctantly, I agreed to meet my friend in *Kabuto-cho*, Tokyo's Wall Street, the following morning. In the eighteenth and nineteenth centuries, *Kabuto-cho* had been the home of Japan's rice warehouses. In those days, the government collected taxes in the form of rice. Rice trading predated the stockmarket and was the first commodities market in Japan as well as the first futures market in the world. I was intrigued by the historical connection between stock trading and rice trading.

I had been advised that it would be quicker for me to travel by subway from my hotel rather than contend with rush-hour traffic. When I emerged from the depths of the underground, I was certain I had alighted at the wrong station. Surely this motely collection of dingy concrete buildings, main thoroughfares, and narrow streets could not be the centre of Japan's financial district? I wandered past little shops and paused to watch an old woman who sat on the sidewalk repairing shoes. Across the street, a young man wearing a white apron carried a tray of coffee cups into a building. The smell of raw sewage permeated the air and for a second I thought that I was back in Jakarta.

A passerby directed me to the stock exhange building, a seven-storey circular structure, whose Corinthian columns and Grecian facade reminded me of its counterpart in New York. My friend greeted me with a smile and led me inside.

From the visitors' gallery, I looked down upon a thronging melée of at least two thousand people. Men in blue suits shouted and gesticu-lated while men in brown suits shoved their way through the crowds as though intent upon some urgent personal mission. Suddenly, the mass of people seemed to coalesce into a single unit as everyone began to applaud enthusiastically.

'What's happening?' I asked my friend in bewilderment.

'The market just broke 6,000!' he replied excitedly. 'This marks the market's full recovery from the oil shock.'

'How much higher will the market go?' I naively inquired.

'There's no limit,' he grinned. 'The market will break 10,000 in a few years, it will surpass 20,000 even 30,000 within 10 years, 40,000 by the end of the century.'

I knew that my friend's company made the lion's share of its profits from stockmarket commissions and I disregarded his optimistic projec-tions. He had once told me that by accepting a job with a Japanese securities company he had become a minotaur – half bull and half human.

'Congratulations,' I said sardonically. 'You'll get rich.'

'So can you,' he replied. 'Buy electronics: Sony, Matsushita, Hitachi, Toshiba. Or automobiles: Toyota, Nissan.'

I had invested my small savings in US municipal bonds and had no intention of speculating in foreign stockmarkets. Later that day, I left Japan.

Japan, however, did not leave me. Every Monday, reports on the Japanese economy and the Japanese stockmarket arrived in the mail – courtesy of my friend. Soon I found myself following the Japanese stockmarket with mounting interest. I subscribed to the *Japan Economic Journal* and the *Japanese Stock Journal*. Gradually, almost insidiously, Japanese finance became something of a preoccupation while my interest in rice began to wane.

I began to notice bizarre and enigmatic movements in the Japanese stock charts. A particular issue would move along a narrow box range for a long time. Then, suddenly, like a Nijinsky leap, the issue would take off dramatically, increasing in value by as much as 50 percent in a few weeks. Subsequently, as if succumbing to the force of gravity, the stock would drift to the ground. It crossed my mind that advance knowledge of these sudden jumps could make an investor very rich, very fast. The idea intrigued me so much that I telephoned my friend in Tokyo, ostensibly to wish him a happy new year.

'By the way,' I inquired, making my voice casual, 'I've noticed that certain Japanese stocks double in value overnight and then return to previous levels before I can find an explanation for the rise.'

'Nothing new about that,' my friend replied.

'Well, US stocks don't behave that way,' I pointed out.

He laughed.

I tried again. 'I really don't understand what is going on.'

He laughed again. 'Look at it this way,' he said finally, 'climbing Mount Fuji is a good thing to do but everyone can't do it at the same time.'

The telephone call was costing me over a dollar a minute and, on my salary at that time, this could easily have added up to a formidable bill. Nonetheless, a minute elapsed before I could think of a response.

'Who decides who will climb and at what time?' I delicately inquired. Now, it was my friend who paused for a minute before answering.

'The best time to climb Mount Fuji is at night so that you can see the sunrise from the summit,' he clarified. 'We will have to go together when you next visit Japan. By the way, I've just been promoted to section chief.'

'Congratulations,' I said without enthusiasm. 'It's a great way to begin the new year.'

I hung up the telephone feeling perplexed. As usual when dealing with the Japanese, I felt that there was more to this issue than met the eye. I decided to return to Japan for my next vacation.

Some years later, still intrigued by the Japanese, I found myself working for my friend's company in Tokyo. I discovered many interesting things. For example, the odour of raw sewage which I had detected in the vicinity of the stock exchange had a simple explanation. Many of the office buildings were not connected to sewers. Instead, a truck would arrive once each week to pump out the septic tanks located in the basements of the buildings. A comparable situation in Wall Street or in the City of London would be difficult to imagine.

In Japan the juxtaposition of advanced development and Third-world characteristics never ceased to astound me. Nothing seemed to exemplify this odd contrast better than the Tokyo stockmarket. The Tokyo stock exchange utilizes state of the art computer facilities tailored to the trading of shares in some of the most technologically advanced corporations in the world. But at the same time a kind of institutionalized corruption, typical of the Third World, permeates Japan's stockmarkets.

For example, a host of marginal activities (trading on inside information, cornering the float of an issue, spreading false rumours, and systematic pushing of certain stocks in order to fulfil marketing goals as well as government aims) are common practice. These marginal activities are considered illegal and reprehensible in the United States and Europe. They are also illegal in Japan; but there they are ignored by regulatory authorities and condoned by the biggest securities companies. Everyone does it, everyone denies it, and no one discusses it.

## THE WEST VIEWS JAPAN

To the average Westerner, peering over a hazy horizon barely illuminated by the rising sun, everything east of the Urals has for centuries been a vague, homogenous enclave known as the 'Orient'. Europeans or North Americans often cannot even distinguish the very different cultural characteristics of broad ethnic groups such as the Chinese, the Japanese, and the Koreans.

Even today, to many people in the West, Asia remains what it was in the Middle Ages, a *terra incognita* – vast, populous, and exotic.

Europeans have long associated 'Orientals' with treachery and inscrutability, and ever since Attila the Hun invaded the Roman Empire in the 5th century Europe has been wary of the power of the 'yellow peril' erupting from the distant East. Seven centuries after Attila was killed in France, swarms of Mongols mounted on fast horses overran what is today the Soviet Union, inspiring terror and threatening the very survival of Christendom. Another seven centuries later, Tojo invaded Southeast Asia and bombed Pearl Harbor, demolishing the peace and stability of the Pacific.

Westerners have, perhaps fallaciously, come to perceive Asians to be more devious, dangerous, and destructive foes than their European counterparts. It is widely believed that 'Life is cheap in Asia' and that Asian wars are fought by different rules from those of the West. Thus, while European warfare was conducted in terms of set-piece battles between opposing armies, in which victory was determined by superior strength and skill, in Asia more emphasis was placed on cunning in battle rather than on strength. For example, Genghis Khan's cavalry sometimes feigned retreat and then turned back, rapidly surrounding and destroying the opposing forces. Marco Polo, a European witness, reported that 'In this sort of warfare, the adversary imagines he has gained a victory, when in fact he has lost the battle.'

As recently as the Vietnam War, popular American sentiment regarded guerilla tactics as inappropriate. For years American generals unsuccessfully used classic European strategies in combating the Vietcong's more effective techniques of concealment and suprise. US troops were often deployed in a manner more appropriate to European terrain than to a jungle environment and did not conform to the recognized patterns of attack and withdrawal indigenous to the region.

Strategies of international trade are analogous to military strategies. European nations expect their trading partners to conform to agreements (often unwritten) regarding acceptable and unacceptable practices. On the other hand, Asian nations may utilize the most effective method, regardless of the expectations, needs, or desires of their trading partners.

In war, surprise and the confusion it inspires can be instrumental in achieving victory. Some of the most dazzling military victories in history have been the result of surprise attacks, and, sometimes, the more shocking the surprise the more rapid the victory. In trade, however, surprise attacks are still seen by Western nations as underhand and illegal. Although such tactics may yield a crucial advantage, they are not ordinarily adopted in the West, where trading partners are regarded as allies rather than opponents.

Today, many Americans and Europeans are firmly convinced that 'Orientals' play by different rules: they ignore agreements, reciprocate only when convenient, and invade markets with inexpensive products. Asian commodities like the textiles produced by cheap labour in Hong Kong, the VCRs built in Taiwanese sweat shops and semiconductors mass-produced in efficient Japanese factories, are seen as invading Western markets like cancerous cells that destroy the ability of indigenous industry to grow and prosper. Dumping, or predatory pricing, is sometimes viewed as an East Asian creation designed to kidnap market share for native producers. Thus Japanese silicon chips are viewed as the modern equivalents of barbarian Huns or Mitsubishi Zeros.

## MADE IN JAPAN

Today, of course, the West is no longer as ignorant about the East as it was a century ago. Advances in cartography and printing have provided us with an abundance of accurate and colourful maps that enable the man or woman in the street to pinpoint the location of Taiwan, South Korea, and Outer Mongolia. Television, documentaries and package tours have filled in the gaps in popular knowledge of the Far East.

Nothing, moreover, concentrates attention as sharply as the immediacy of danger and as Japanese manufactured products began to rival those of the US in the early 1970s, there emerged a desire to learn the rules that govern business operations in Japan. Books about Japanese management techniques and Japanese industrial production proliferated. The idea that Americans (or Europeans) should emulate Japanese methods has been proposed by a number of prominent American writers as an obvious method of defending domestic interests against foreign threats.

The Japanese ability to manufacture products which are better and cheaper than those of their competitors in the West has become a major issue in the late 1970s and 1980s. The benefits of such Japanese institutions as 'lifetime employment,' consensus decision-making, and quality control circles (an American invention) have been popularized in the United States, at least since 1979. Innovative US companies and managers have attempted to replicate certain features of Japanese corporate organization with varying degrees of success.

But the Japanese still remain more adroit at using their own production and management techniques then we Westerners, despite a proliferation of English language books and commentaries on the subject. By the 1980s, Japanese corporations dominated world production of products ranging from cars to semiconductors and from VCRs to ball bearings.

But while Japanese manufacturers freely opened factories in the United States and Europe, foreign companies wishing to open plants in Japan encountered barriers. The Ministry of International Trade and Industry (MITI) often excluded foreign direct investment by insisting that it be confined to minority participation in joint ventures with Japanese corporations. Japan's protected industries thrived by freely combining the benefits of production *and sales* in Japan with unrestricted opportunities abroad. Thus, Japanese success was seen, at least in part, to be a product of unfair advantage.

Many Western producers disappeared as a direct result of overwhelming Japanese competition. In the wake of their collapse, tens of thousands of unemployed American and European workers expressed mounting animosity toward Japan.

So great was the anti-Japanese sentiment that during a demonstration one group of American auto workers took sledgehammers to a Japanese car which was ritualistically demolished and subsequently buried. Other hostile workers expressed their anger more directly by killing Chinese Americans, whom they mistakenly identified as Japanese; those who were brought to trial were given sentences that were extremely lenient considering the magnitude of the crime. It is against this sort of background that legislators in the United States began to draft a whole series of protectionist bills aimed against Japan. In fact, American legislators with an eye to their public, had been becoming increasingly vehement in their expression of anti-Japanese sentiment. In this kind of atmosphere, with tempers already running high and protectionism in the air, a single incident was enough to ignite a conflagration. In the spring of 1987 a company little-known in the United States, Toshiba Machine, provided the spark which set the tinder aflame.

## OF MITI AND SUBMARINES

There is a marginal area where the separate activities of trade and war meet before they again diverge. In this grey, ill-defined area the sale of military equipment can itself have great political impact or be seen as an expression of political alignment. Victory in war is often determined by access to appropriate military hardware. Thus, the sale of weapons-related technology is never apolitical.

Manufacturing companies and governments sell weapons and the machinery to manufacture weapons to the highest bidder. Although generally a legitimate sector of world trade, a portion of the sale of weapons and related equipment occurs on the black market. Sometimes private corporations illegally sell classified equipment and information to an enemy. When this is done by individuals they may be condemned as traitors. There is no term to describe a company that engages in such activity.

Between December 1982 and June 1984, Toshiba Machine Company, one of the world's largest machine-tool makers (50.08 percent owned by the Toshiba Corporation, Japan's second largest general electrical machinery producer) shipped some model MF–4522 milling machines to the Soviet Union. Under a contract with a Soviet trading concern (*Techmashimport*), numerical controllers (computers that guide the milling machines) were provided by the Norwegian arms maker, Kongsberg Vaapenfabrikk, and were attached to the Toshiba machines prior to shipment.*

In June 1984, after the machines had been shipped by Toshiba Machine, a special computer program was given to the Soviets by Toshiba Machine as the concluding portion of the package. The deal was arranged by C. Itoh, one of Japan's major trading houses.

This series of apparently routine transactions would have gone unnoticed by the press were it not for an April 1987 report presented to the US Congress by the Central Intelligence Agency. Perhaps not coincidentally, the report was released several days before President Reagan was scheduled to meet Prime Minister Nakasone in Washington.

The CIA had prepared its report as a result of the disturbing discovery that for a period of time (unspecified) a number (undisclosed) of Soviet attack submarine had been evading US detection with unprecedented success. Subsequent investigations determined that the computerized milling machines that Toshiba Machine had sold to the Soviet Union were not ordinary. Technologically superior to anything available in the USSR, the machines enabled the Soviet navy to build ultra-quiet submarine propeller blades. It was these blades that allowed Soviet attack submarines to evade detection so successfully that, according to Representative Duncan Hunter, they can now approach to within ten minutes missile flying time of the mainland United States.

Transfer of the milling machines to the Soviet Union was a violation of regulation IL 1091 of the Coordinating Committee on Multilateral Export Controls (Cocom), a Paris-based monitoring entity created by the United States and sixteen allies, including Japan. Fully aware that the sale constituted an illegal diversion of high-technology goods to the USSR, Toshiba Machine executives misrepresented the machine tools' capabilities in their application for export permission from Japan's Ministry of International Trade and Industry (MITI). Toshiba also invited a team of Soviet technicians to visit the Toshiba Machine plant in Japan in order to examine and test the milling machines. Subsequently, Toshiba Machine employees went to the USSR and assembled at least one machine in the Baltic Ship Yard, outside Leningrad.

---

* As this book goes to press, recent revelations have indicated that Kongsberg Vaapenfabreikk shipped 140 numerical controllers (and necessary software) to the Soviet Union. Many of these shipments preceded Toshiba Machine's illicit sales of nine-axis milling machines to the USSR.

The US response to the revelation was sharp and rapid. Five members of Congress introduced a bill banning all imports from Toshiba Corporation and its Norwegian accomplice. The US Defense Department delayed the award of several electronic contracts (including a $100 million plan to supply the Air Force with 90,000 lap-top computers made by Toshiba Corporation) until the Japanese government conducted a satisfactory investigation of Toshiba's role in the debacle. The Pentagon also objected to Japanese government supervision of exports to the USSR and other Soviet-bloc nations.

The sanctions on the part of Congress and the Pentagon seemed to have the desired effect, initially at least. On the very day on which Reagan and Nakasone met in Washington, Japanese police searched all offices and factories belonging to the Toshiba Machine Company. MITI lodged a complaint with police against Toshiba Machine for violating a domestic ban against the exportation of strategic equipment to the USSR. MITI also ordered a review of all outstanding export applications for computers, certain machine tools, and semiconductor manufacturing equipment valued at more than 100 million yen ($710,000).

The effectiveness of this last move was, however, moot. The export control inspection staff of MITI's Office of Security Export Controls consisted of 42 people (subsequently increased to 63 and, at the end of 1987, to 100), who were responsible for reviewing roughly 200,000 licence applications per year. The size of the staff is, perhaps, an indication of the importance that MITI attached to export controls.

Several weeks later, Japanese police arrested two senior Toshiba Machine Company executives, the chief of the materials division and the vice-director of a machine technology division, and charged them with violating Japan's foreign exchange and foreign trade control laws. Under Japanese law, a three year statute of limitations prevented the government from charging the men with the illegal exportation of the machine tools and they were therefore charged only with the sale of the computer programme. Although details regarding the computer programme are classified, it is known that it was indispensable to the production of the propeller blades. The maximum penalty for the executives, if convicted, would be three years in prison.*

The Pentagon praised the quick Japanese government action and congratulated MITI and the police. Stephen Bryen, Deputy Undersecretary of Defense for Trade Security Policy, commented that the Japanese government's vigorous role in the investigation represented

* Several months later, four additional employees of Toshiba Machine and three employees of Wako Koeki (a Tokyo based trading firm) were arrested, bringing to nine the total number of individuals liable to be prosecuted.

'positive evidence that Japan views this problem with the same seriousness as we do.' This public statement, designed to encourage Japan to strengthen its monitoring of strategic exports, was only a veneer that barely masked hostile US sentiment. The actions of Toshiba Machine Company had violated US security and, according to the US government, neutralized a critical part of America's anti-submarine technology, undermining a vital area of the NATO defence system.

Two months later, in June 1987, Japanese investigators announced that further milling machines, had reached the Soviet Union in addition to the four 200-ton machines which the CIA had mentioned in its report to Congress. Apparently another four machines, of even greater technical sophistication, had been sent to the USSR in the Spring of 1984, and it was said that these machines should enable Soviet attack aircraft carriers to attain higher speeds and improved manoeuvreability. This new revelation left little doubt in Washington that the Toshiba Corporation, parent of Toshiba Machine, knew about the orders. It was assumed that large and repeated sales to the USSR would have routinely come to the attention of the directors of Toshiba Corporation.

The revelations continued. Following Japanese press reports that Toshiba Machine Company had shipped half-a-dozen propeller milling machines to the USSR before 1980, the firm admitted that it had begun selling the milling equipment to the Soviet Union in 1974. According to a Pentagon report released on 28 July 1987, the Soviet Union started a programme to reduce propeller noise in 1979 and by 1981 had already acquired five-axis propeller milling machines which used numerical controls produced by Kongsberg.

The indictment was a damning axe: Toshiba Machine Company had knowingly given the USSR critical technology that was immediately used against the defences of the United States and other Japanese allies. Not stopping there, the company had permitted Soviet experts to visit its factory and scrutinize the equipment. Subsequently, Toshiba Machine had sent its own employees directly to a Soviet shipyard in order to ensure that Soviet engineers would successfully adapt the technology to their attack submarines. C. Itoh, one of Japan's biggest trading houses, had arranged at least some of the deals with full knowledge of the implications and illegality.

Given the gravity of the crime, what penalties were meted out to the corporations responsible?

* Toshiba Machine Company, which had provided the technology, was barred from shipping goods to the Soviet bloc and China for a year. This could cost the company as much as ¥5 billion ($36

million) in sales – about 5 percent of total annual revenue. However, the revenue gained from the Soviet deal was not confiscated from Toshiba Machine. Indeed details of the profits deriving from the transaction were not officially announced – the National Police Agency (equivalent to American's FBI) did, however, state that the USSR paid *triple* Toshiba Machine's list price.

* C. Itoh, the trading firm which arranged the deal for the Soviet Union, was asked in a letter from MITI to 'refrain' from selling machine tools to Soviet bloc countries and China for three months.
* Wako Koeki (a small Tokyo trading company devoted exclusively to trade with communist countries) which reportedly served as an intermediary between Soviet KGB agents (representing the trading firm *Techmashimport*) and Toshiba Machine, received a written reprimand from MITI.*
* Toshiba Corporation, the owner of Toshiba Machine, was not penalized.
* The president of Toshiba Machine voluntarily resigned. Meanwhile it remains to be seen whether the employees of Toshiba Machine who are alleged to be legally culpable will be convicted.

American congressmen regarded the penalties as exceptionally mild. After all, barely a month after MITI imposed its sanctions on Toshiba, the American Securities and Exchange Commission (SEC) extracted a $25 million fine from Kidder Peabody, an investment banking firm responsible for several insider trading infractions. From the US perspective, the Japanese punishments did not fit the severity of the crimes. Perhaps as a result, the Senate Banking Committee, led by Senator Jake Garn, prepared an amendment to an impending bill intended to prohibit the entire Toshiba group (and the Norwegian Kongsberg group) from participating in the US market for two to five years. In addition, the US was authorized by a new bill to demand compensation from Japan (and Norway) for the enormous cost of developing methods to detect the quieter Soviet submarines.

Anger over the episode mounted steadily in the Senate and the House of Representatives. The Toshiba Corporation's failure to acknowledge culpability and the Japanese government's light-handed response added fuel to the flames of resentment in Washington. On 1

---

* In December 1985, a former employee of Wako Koeki informed officials at Cocom's Paris headquarters that the firm had illegally exported equipment. Although Cocom notified MITI officials, the ministry either did not investigate the allegations or failed to discover information about Toshiba Machine's actions. Six months later, the Pentagon provided MITI with similar information. Yet, again MITI failed to uncover or disclose information regarding Toshiba Machine.

July, 1987, two months after the initial revelations, ten Congressmen assembled on the lawn of the Capital and flattened a Toshiba radio with sledgehammers.

That same day, the Senate, by an overwhelming majority (92 to 5), approved an amendment to the Omnibus Trade Bill which required import penalties against the Toshiba Corporation and Norway's Kongsberg Vaapenfabrikk. Under the terms of the bill Toshiba and its Norwegian accomplice would be prohibited from exporting their products to the United States for a period ranging from two to five years. The import ban, applying to the entire Toshiba group, would, it was estimated, cost Toshiba sales of more than ¥400 billion ($2.75 billion) per year, substantially reducing (or eliminating) the firm's pretax profits for fiscal 1988.

In addition, the legislation would require the US government to seek civil damages. Estimates of the cost of regaining US anti-submarine capability range from $20–40 billion. Meanwhile, the US Commerce Department temporarily suspended Toshiba Corporation's licence to buy American high-technology products in bulk.

Less than 24 hours after the Senate bill was approved, Prime Minister Nakasone sharply criticized Toshiba Machine for exacerbating trade tensions between Japan and the United States. Although the criticisms were addressed to Toshiba Machine Company, they also applied to the parent. In Japan, as elsewhere, a parent corporation must take responsibility for the delicts of its subsidiaries. In Japan, however, the form of such responsibility is often amorphous.

Shortly after Nakasone's statement the president and chairman of the Toshiba Corporation resigned because they felt 'gravely responsible for straining the already strained Japan-US relations further.' They carefully noted, however, that Toshiba Corporation had no role in its unit's illegal sale of machinery and that their resignation was not a response to the Senate vote. Toshiba Machine, they pointed out, was an independent subsidiary and not a division of Toshiba Corporation. Nonetheless, their resignation was viewed by the Senate as a positive, though merely cosmetic, gesture.

By way of partial compensation, Toshiba officials offered to assist the Defence Department in its efforts to develop new technologies to counter the Soviet advantage. In addition, Toshiba engaged Price Waterhouse, one of the Big Eight US accounting firms, and several American law firms to establish the exact relationship between Toshiba and Toshiba Machine. In this way, Toshiba Corporation hoped to demonstrate to the United States that it could not have known about or prevented Toshiba Machine's illegal sales and that it should not be held accountable by the US for the independent subsidiary's actions. At about the same time, Toshiba Corporation initiated a massive advertising campaign intended to apologize for damage caused by its subsidiary.

Released in September 1987, the Price Waterhouse report confirmed Toshiba Corporation's claim that it had no prior knowledge of Toshiba Machine's shipments to the USSR. Simultaneously, Toshiba Corporation announced a detailed 'Strategic Products Control Programme', under which a separate management group would monitor exports by the parent firm and its subsidiaries. In addition, Toshiba's export compliance programme would verify the authenticity of prospective buyers and would conduct spot inspections of the subsidiaries. Employees guilty of any infraction (including unreported knowledge of infractions) would be severely punished. In this way, Toshiba hoped to prove its determination to ensure that future breaches of Cocom regulations by any part of the Toshiba group would be impossible.

While Toshiba was announcing these reforms, the upper house of the Japanese *Diet* rubber-stamped an export control law that had already been approved by the lower house. This law increased from three to five years the maximum prison term for violators and recognized intent as a crime. The law, which was designed primarily to dilute American anger and encourage the US Senate to modify its sanctions against Toshiba Corporation, had the effect of tightening controls on Japan's strategic exports to communist countries; it was, however, vague regarding necessary arrangements for cooperation among the ministries to ensure full enforcement.

Meanwhile, in the US, it soon became clear that not all interest groups were prepared to stand by and see Toshiba tarred and feathered. A group of the biggest and most politically powerful American corporations (including IBM, Honeywell, Motorola, General Electric, AT&T, Hewlett-Packard, Rockwell, United Technologies, and Xerox) began lobbying against the congressional efforts to exclude Toshiba from US markets. These companies were supported by the American Electronics Association, the Computer and Business Equipment Manufacturers Association, the Business Roundtable, and the National Association of Manufacturers.* Toshiba's electronic components, these companies and associations announced, were so vital that without them billions of dollars of corporate profits and many jobs would be endangered.

In support of these lobbying efforts, Toshiba brought the general manager (an American) of the company's facility in Lebanon, Tennessee, to Washington. There he argued that sanctions against Toshiba would 'cripple' all of Toshiba's American operations, including its plans to export US-made products to Japan. As a result, Toshiba's

* As reported by *The New York Times*, 14 September, 1987.

4,200 American workers could find their jobs at risk and potential US exports to Japan (which would, of course, contribute to a reduction of the trade imbalance) could be lost.

American dependence upon Japan's second largest electric machinery producer was revealed to be complex and considerable. Lobbyists announced that, without imports from Toshiba, many US companies would be obliged to abandon product lines or market areas. The Toshiba Corporation – with $17.8 billion in annual sales and hundreds of overseas subsidiaries – maintained supply contracts (including sole-source arrangements involving custom-made components) with virtually every major electronics concern in the United States. Many US companies were engaged in original equipment arrangements whereby Toshiba made products that were marketed under the labels of the American importer. Thus, for example, some televisions sold under the Sears label are produced by Toshiba. A *New York Times* editorial observed that 'when Congressional grandstanders lash out at Japan, they lash out at America too.'*

It is worth pointing out that although the US Senate was appalled by the Japanese government's lenient action towards the Toshiba Corporation, the limited export bans imposed on Toshiba Machine and C. Itoh were *the strongest* penalties ever meted out to Japanese companies guilty of violating foreign trade control laws. Indeed, the imposition of such bans has been so rare that many who followed the case had no doubt that the relatively harsh penalties were designed to appease American anger. Thus, when the public memory of the case begins to wane, the two arrested Toshiba executives may receive mild sentences.

What can we learn from this case? That the Japanese government is a mild disciplinarian and a lackadaisical overseer of international trade practices? That Japan has little concern for the strategic interests of its allies? That ultimately Japanese regulators turn a blind eye to exports while paying vigorous attention to imports? That only American anger can prompt the Japanese government to investigate or remedy trade infractions?

Certainly assumptions like these have become a part of Western folklore which could be summarized as follows. A beast, Japan Inc, inhabits Japan. A pragmatic union of government and industry, the beast uses its corporate arm to satisfy government interests while it uses its government arm to fulfil corporate aspirations. Meanwhile, a single institutional brain weighs alternatives and makes decisions.

---

* 'Bashing Toshiba, Hurting America,' *The New York Times*, 15 September, 1987.

Foreign businesses which fall prey to this beast are faced with decline and obsolescence, for free market economies are no match for the synergy of government and business which is the essence of the beast. With a ruthless gleam in its eye, the beast goes out and eats foreign markets for lunch while terrified foreign businesses can do little more than cower and ponder what the beast is planning to eat for dinner.

## THE BEAST

Chalmers Johnson, in his insightful book *MITI and the Japanese Miracle*, writes that the Ministry of Commerce and Industry (MCI) and the Ministry of Munitions (MM) 'were once such fearsome agencies that it was said the mere mention of their names would stop a child from crying.'* MCI (the Ministry of Commerce and Industry) became the MM (Ministry of Munitions) in November 1943 and two years later, under the guidance of Occupation experts, the MM became MITI (the Ministry of International Trade and Industry). Today, under its new title, the institution still has a fearsome reputation: the mere mention of MITI may no longer stop Japanese children from crying, but it is not unknown for foreign adults to burst into tears at the sound of it.

MITI has been termed 'the "reincarnation" of the wartime MCI and MM.'† Indeed, a majority of the prewar bureaucrats in the Ministry of Commerce and Industry continued to work in the Munitions Ministry and were not purged during the reorganizations instituted by the Occupation.‡ As a result, the same officials who dictated Japan's controlled wartime industrial policies formulated and implemented Japan's postwar industrial policies. *Not until 1976 did MITI have a vice minister who had not worked in the Munitions Ministry.* The importance of this smooth administrative continuity cannot be underestimated.

The economic and political orientation of the bureaucrats who determined Japan's industrial policies did not significantly change after the War. Thus, *wartime* industrial policies, under which the systematic development of strategic industries went hand in hand with the careful protection of key domestic industries, continued to dominate MITI's *postwar* thinking. In a nutshell, Japan's wartime economic nationalism became the philosophy of its postwar economic recovery.

The fundamental principles of Japan's economic nationalism during

---

* Chalmers Johnson. *MITI and the Japanese Miracle*. Stanford: Stanford University Press, 1982, p. 33.
    † *Ibid.*, 33,
    ‡ A notable exception was the wartime Prime Minister, Tojo, who simultaneously served as the Minister of Munitions, the Minister of the Army and the Chief of the General Staff.

the Munitions Ministry's heyday (1943–1945) entailed, of course, the absence of free trade. Japanese technology, currency and labour were rarely permitted to move out of Japan. Simultaneously, various industries were forced into mergers which resulted in the creation of monolithic agglomerations. Thus, for example, the MM demanded that the Mitsui Bank merge with the Dai Ichi Bank to form the Teikoku Bank, one of four large bankholding companies which controlled corporate lending in Japan. The Munitions Ministry also decided which corporations would receive massive funding from the banks.

During the decades which followed the end of the Occupation and the realization of Japan's economic 'miracle', MITI played the vital role of determining which industries would receive favoured government support and subsidies. Thus, MITI, a political entity, became the central actor in the development of Japan's postwar economy.

In assessing the role of MITI in Japan's postwar economic development, Johnson concluded that 'the real equivalent of the Japanese Ministry of International Trade and Industry in the United States is not the Department of Commerce but the Department of Defence, which by its very nature and functions shares MITI's strategic, goal-oriented outlook.'* However, MITI's powers and influence have been even more wide-ranging than those of the US Defense Department. Unlike the Pentagon, MITI has the authority to influence (through 'administrative guidance' and other means) the development of entire industrial sectors. In addition, many ministers of MITI, (including such well known politicians as Kakuei Tanaka, Masayoshi Ohira, Yasuhiro Nakasone, and Noboru Takeshita) became prime minister.

The power exercized by MITI during the postwar era was the culmination of Japan's state-controlled economic development which began under the auspices of the Meiji Restoration in 1868. Japan emerged from feudalism in the late nineteenth century, not as a free market economy, but rather as a unique instance of centrally planned capitalist development. This combination of the kind of central planning now associated with communist bloc countries with the elements of a free market system was extraordinarily successful.

Strategic industries (mining, chemicals, shipbuilding) were carefully nurtured and directed by the central government. Financial institutions were especially created in order to function as conduits of funds from individual savers to vital industrial sectors. The MCI had the power to determine not only which industries would grow most rapidly but also which corporate entities would thrive. Thus, for

* Johnson, *MITI and Japanese Miracle*, p. 21.

instance, the government gave ships to Mitsubishi to ensure that it would grow strong.

The economic development of modern Japan (excluding the war years) has been based upon the integration of the political and economic systems in such a way that neither the political nor the economic sectors have controlled the nation. In this unique political economy – a product of modern economic and political constraints – ultimate authority to dictate national policies does not rest with politicians, bureaucrats or corporations.

All of Japan's institutions, industries and organizations support the Japanese political economy as delicately as the surface of water can support a floating needle. Just as water molecules provide a cohesive skin which can sustain the weight of a carefully-placed needle, so Japanese groups, ranging from politicians to gangsters, *through their cohesion*, support a precisely balanced political economy that denies any individual institution or interest group a firm grasp.

From this system to the fallacious concept of Japan, Inc is just a short step. The term Japan, Inc is often used to evoke an image of unfair (and somehow illicit) collusion between the Japanese government and Japanese business. In the eyes of Japan's most extreme opponents in the United States, Japan, Inc embodies the applied consensus of Japan's political factions, ministries, industrialists, and special interest groups. All these groups are believed to band together in order to promote Japan's interests at the expense of those of her trading partners. This degree of cooperation, which surpasses the worst nightmares of antitrust regulators, is perceived as the secret of Japan's economic power. As is often the case, the reality is less complex but more profound than the myth.

The legacy of the totalitarian Munitions Ministry which frightened away children's tears, was inherited by MITI, and it is true that MITI has wielded exceptional power and that its close relationship with political factions has been evinced time and again (for example, by the electoral successes of its retired ministers). Nonetheless, throughout the postwar era, neither MITI nor the prime minister (nor any faction) has possessed the power to command particular industries to take actions. MITI can strenuously suggest mergers, but industries that choose to reject its suggestions, can do so – and flourish. Thus, for instance, MITI's attempts to force a series of mergers in the automotive industry (see below) were systematically ignored by all of Japan's car manufacturers. Similarly, Prime Minister Nakasone was powerless to enforce the details of the semiconductor agreement which Japan signed with the United States in 1986 (see discussion below).

No segment of the Japanese political, economic, and financial systems has ultimate judicial authority over other segments. Of course, laws exist which are enforceable, and action is occasionally taken against individuals or corporations guilty of a breach of those laws. However, the power to flout official orders and demands is found at every level of the Japanese social and political system. As a result, all of Japan's major groups (the *Diet*, the ministries, the industrial organizations) possess the power to insidiously weaken the nation.* In this sense, Japan is the precise inversion of a totalitarian state. The inverted structure, however, is perpetually teetering on the edge of instability. Consensus is the gyroscope that enables the nation's navigational system to work.

## IS ALL OF JAPAN A STAGE FOR A PUPPET SHOW?

*Bunraku*, a traditional Japanese performing art, can be illuminating to anyone interested in Japan. Dating back hundreds of years, *bunraku* is a theatre in which puppets enact great human dramas written for them by some of Japan's finest literary figures.

Each puppet, half life-size, is manipulated by the movements of three puppeteers. The process of manufacturing the puppets is an art requiring years of apprenticeship and the puppeteers undergo an even longer training; it takes thirty years for them to achieve full mastery of their art.

The heads of *bunraku* puppets are painted in lifelike colours, possess eyes that move in all directions eyebrows which move up and down, and noses capable of subtle motion. The puppeteers appear on stage dressed entirely in black and wearing translucent black hoods as they control (in order of their expertise) the movements of the head, arms, and legs of the puppet. These shrouded puppeteers are ignored by the audience, which chooses to see only the colourful puppets.

Devotees of *bunraku* insist that when the three puppeteers work in perfect synchrony, the puppets seem to mystically acquire an existence and a reality independent of the puppeteers. Thus, each *bunraku* puppet, pulsating with life and independent will, appears to transcend the triad of shadowy puppeteers which determines its actions.

Group consensus, which Americans believe to be the keystone of Japanese organizational behaviour and corporate structure, is not fully understood in the West. It is, however, a very simple concept and can be illustrated by means of *bunraku*. The collective agreement of a corporate or bureaucratic entity, like that of the *bunraku* puppeteers, is a well-crafted fabrication.

Japanese institutions, no less than their counterparts elsewhere, are

* Karel G. van Wolferen argues this point eloquently in his article, 'Japan Problem,' *Foreign Affairs* (Winter 1986).

composed of individuals committed to differing objectives and opposing strategies. Those individuals are often more concerned with their personal careers than with corporate objectives. It is quite wrong to suppose, as many Westerners do, that Japanese employees naturally work together toward a common goal with no regard for their own self-interests.

On the contrary, consensus has to be manufactured through guided discussion and socially-imposed compromise. In order to be implemented, the group consensus, like the *bunraku* puppet, must be skillfully manipulated. *Bunraku* is the only puppet theatre in which each puppet is controlled by more than one puppeteer, and it is the tension created by different puppeteers pulling limbs in different but complementary directions that gives the vibrancy of life to the puppet. Similarly, group consensus gains its strength and effectiveness from the balanced resolution of opposing forces.

Because few individuals can have their precise wishes implemented by corporate policy, all individuals are forever striving to achieve a consensus that maximizes the realization of their own personal goals. In this way, group consensus becomes an artful compromise among a group of individuals with disparate desires and objectives. When directed perfectly, the group consensus, an artificial construct, achieves a compelling autonomy. Although it does not wholly represent the ideas or aspirations of any single individual, it reflects a consolidation of individual perspectives and goals.

The *bunraku* puppet theatre is a telling metaphor for many other aspects of Japanese business, including Japan, Inc. Japan, Inc is a magnificent puppet, dressed and outfitted for economic battle. However, just as a puppet is devoid of activity without its puppeteers, so Japan, Inc has no existence outside the sphere of particular regulatory and corporate activity.

Japan, Inc has neither an office nor a staff. Three puppeteers, shrouded but visible, use masterful and harmonious manipulations to give Japan, Inc the illusion of life. MITI, the Chief Handler, controls the head and right arm, while corporate presidents, the Left Handler, control the left arm. Simultaneously, macroeconomic constraints, a key determinant of industrial policy, function as the Leg Handler and help set the rhythm of movement.

Through 'administrative guidance,' MITI (like all other Japanese ministries) has used its authority to issue directives, warnings and suggestions to corporations within its jurisdiction. MITI has imposed mergers on declining or fledgling industries in order to promote strength. It has channelled considerable volumes of government funds into 'strategic' industries in order to nurture growth. Finally, it has used administrative restrictions to limit the importation of goods that would compete with domestic products.

The careful orchestration of MITI policies and corporate actions with economic constraints has resulted in Western perceptions of a concrete entity: Japan, Inc. That entity, however, has no more reality than a character portrayed by a *bunraku* puppet. The puppet's character and goals are a fiction. When the puppeteers are not busy manipulating the puppet's limbs, the puppet becomes an inert cultural artifact.

## TRADE TENSIONS: SMILES ARE NOT ENOUGH

From soda ash to supercomputers, from steam coal to semiconductors, Japanese manufacturers and institutions have been reluctant to the point of unyielding resistance to import products from the United States and Europe. Japanese companies simply prefer to buy from those domestic vendors with whom they have long-established relationships. Thus, for example, although no barriers prevent the importation of soda ash (used in making glass and ceramics), Japanese firms refuse to increase their foreign purchases of this mineral.

In hundreds of meetings during the 1980s, US and European trade negotiators attempted to persuade MITI that it must force Japan's companies to stop favouring other Japanese companies. Despite repeated assurances of cooperation, MITI delivered few concessions.

In 1986, mounting anger in Britain and the United States led to open threats of retaliation. Margaret Thatcher threatened to revoke the licenses of Japanese financial institutions in London unless Japan opened its financial markets to British institutions. In the United States, the Senate prepared a trade bill involving mandatory retaliation against trading partners with large trade surpluses who did not meet demands to remove domestic barriers to imports. The Toshiba scandal served to burnish the impending protectionist trade bill to a lustre.

Mutters of dissatisfaction became grumbles of discontent. It was signalled unequivocally that MITI's shillyshallying could be tolerated no longer. In response, MITI sent Makoto Kuroda its Vice-minister and top negotiator, to London and Washington.

Using 'an often condescending tone of voice, a cocky demeanour, and mocking laugh,'* Kuroda expressed the view that 'the Japanese market is more open than those of the US and the European Community, and Japan continues to make efforts to approach a completely open market.'† Speaking in London, he commented that, 'It is not the Japanese way to reciprocate by using the same level of

* Damon Darlin, 'Japan's Trade Negotiator Irks Americans, His Pugnacious Style Takes Washington Aback,' *The Wall Street Journal*, 3 April 1987, p. 24.

† Quoted from a 15 April 1987 editorial written by Makoto Kuroda and published in *The Financial Times*.

nonsense to describe the [trade] situation.'* Offering few conciliatory statements and no concessions, Kuroda confirmed views in Washington and London that Japan did not take its trading partners' problems seriously.

## TIED AID AND TRADE

Japan's trade with the Third World has a predominantly complementary character. Usually, Third-world nations export raw materials and import Japanese technology – from radios to rubber factories. Because Japanese exports do not compete directly with Third-world products, trade friction between Japan and non-industrial nations such as India, Indonesia, or Ghana is not intense. When disputes do arise it is usually because of Japan's import controls, particularly those applied to agricultural products. Philippine mangoes, for example, cannot be imported into Japan because they are treated with a banned pesticide. Other imports, such as rice, are banned on principle.

One issue that has inflamed Third-world passions against Japan has been aid. Many Third-world nations have insisted for years that although Japan's foreign aid is the third largest in the world (after the United States and France), the total is small in relation to its massive GNP – 0.29 percent in 1986.

In 1985, despite promises to the contrary, Japanese aid declined by 12 percent. The following year, in response to a torrent of complaints from trading partners in the Third World and elsewhere, Japan increased its official development assistance by 49 percent over the 1985 level. These statistics, however, are calculated on a dollar basis (the OECD measures official overseas development aid in terms of US dollars). In yen terms, increases in Japan's bilateral aid have been far less impressive than the 1986 growth rate would suggest.

Furthermore, the geographic distribution of Japan's bilateral aid correlates with Japan's trading interests. Forty-four percent of government-to-government aid in 1986 was directed to China and the Philippines; another 34 percent was allocated to other nations in Asia, only a tiny 11 percent found its way to Africa, and just 8 percent went to Central and South America. Under outside pressure, this skewed pattern of allocation will be changed during the next several years.

Even more disturbing to the governments of developing nations than the question of allocation has been Japan's widespread use of *tied aid*. A tied loan is a foreign loan whose proceeds are applied to purchases of goods or services in the lending nation. In 1986, for instance, Japan lent India roughly $75 million at 3.25 percent interest.

* Quoted by the *Financial Times*, 'Tokyo's chief negotiator still hopeful trade barriers can be avoided,' 13 March 1987.

The loan was to be used for a telecommunications project. However, the terms of the loan stipulated that the funds could be used only to buy equipment in Japanese or Third-world markets. Needless to say, Third-world markets are rarely capable of competing with Japan's technological suppliers. In any case, the terms of the loan also required all consulting services to be provided by Japanese firms.

Dozens of similar loans given by Japanese lending institutions to Third-world governments have forced recipients to spend the borrowed funds on Japanese consultants and to buy Japanese products. In this way, tied loans have served to increase Japan's growing trade surpluses. To make matters worse, following the appreciation of the yen, recipients have often found themselves obliged to pay unnecessarily high prices for Japanese goods financed with Japanese loans.

All industrial nations extend low-interest tied loans to Third-world borrowers and classify such loans as aid. Critics argue, however, that because Japan's interest rates are relatively low, Japanese tied loans are not aid at all. In addition, the close relationships among Japan's consultants, suppliers and bureaucrats assure that Japanese loans to Third-world nations help to fulfil the sales quotas of Japanese manufacturers.

The Japanese government's International Cooperation Agency (ICA) is responsible for coordinating technical assistance to developing nations. In 1986, two ICA officials were alleged to have accepted bribes from Japanese companies in exchange for arranging contracts on aid projects throughout the world. This scandal confirmed frequent allegations that Japanese foreign aid is intended only to promote the international business of Japanese corporations. In this way Japanese foreign aid was used as a method of sweetening export financing rather than providing grants for development.

In March 1987, under strong US pressure, the OECD agreed to a set of rules which would limit the use of tied aid and other subsidized loans. Although, Japan and Switzerland expressed considerable reluctance to adopt new rules that would increase the cost of their foreign aid programs, change was in the air. Finally, in May 1987, yielding to pressure to recycle a portion of its growing surplus, the Japanese government announced plans to increase overseas development aid to more than $7.6 billion a year by 1990. Grant aid to the most impoverished developing countries (the 'fourth world') would reach $500 million during the three-year period preceding 1990, while $20 billion of Japan's payments surplus would be recycled to developing nations. All funds, it was promised, would be provided on an untied basis.

However, there was one catch: a large portion of the funds were to come from Japan's private sector (city banks) and the private sector had not been consulted.* Not surprisingly, Japanese banks balked at the suggestion that they should lend money to such high-risk borrowers. Nonetheless, the vague silhouette of a new Japan, leading the world in multilateral lending if not bilateral loans, began to appear in late 1987. Whether the silhouette will turn out to be a fleeting shadow or a substantial presence remains to be seen. Meanwhile, developing countries continue to be wary of Japanese lending.

The apprehensions of developing countries, however, are small in comparison with the near-hysteria that has characterized the response of leading industrial nations to Japan's massive exporting machine. Countries whose exports compete directly with Japanese products rather than complementing them, are apt to perceive Japan as a threat to indigenous industry. They consider it Japan's responsibility to alter its trading practices with all nations. Their negotiators make strong demands which would be inappropriate if voiced by Third-world diplomats.

In test cases, such as *telecommunications* and *semiconductors*, Japanese negotiators gracefully agreed with their trading partners that a 'problem' existed while simultaneously denying that Japan was responsible for implementing change. These two cases – each of which has recently threatened to explode into an international controversy – exemplify the problems and frustrations encountered by Japan's trading partners. They are presented in this chapter in order to portray American and European views of trade with Japan. It is assumed that other Japanese trading partners have encountered similar problems and hold roughly similar views. There is certainly little evidence to contradict this assumption.

## THE WORLD IS LISTENING: THE CASE OF TELECOMMUNICATIONS

In the industrialized nations telecommunications is one of the most protected of all industries, accounting for a hefty portion of their GDP – telecommunications services and equipment account for an estimated 5 percent of total GDP in the United States, 3 percent in Europe, and 3 percent in Japan.†

State-owned telecommunications monopolies frequently operate or supply a small number of officially sanctioned producers and foreign competition is not welcome. In the United States, for example, where

* Of the $20 billion, about 40 percent is to be provided through multilateral development banks. The balance will take the form of loans from Japanese financial institutions, including the city banks and Japan's Export – Import Bank.

† Borrus, Michael. 'Japanese Telecommunications: Reforms and Trade Implications.' *California Management Review* 28 (3), Spring 1986, p. 44.

non-American firms are prohibited access to the airwaves, there are only three foreign competitors and in France, a state-owned monopoly controls every sector of the telecommunications industry. Similarly, telephone monopolies (one domestic and one international) have dominated the telecommunications sector in Japan.

For more than thirty years, Kokusai Denshin Denwa (KDD) was Japan's sole international telephone carrier. During the 1980s, the costs of international telephone calls in Japan have been more than double comparable rates in North America and Europe. Recognizing the need to modernize the industry, and anticipating an enormous increase in demand, the Telecommunications Business Law of 1984 promised to open the market. In 1985, Japanese authorities authorized the establishment of a second international telecommunications carrier. Legislation permitted the 'second KDD' to have up to one third foreign ownership.

Japan's Ministry of Posts and Telecommunications (MPT), which regulates the telecommunications industry, has long maintained an intimate relationship with KDD. Retiring senior bureaucrats at the MPT have often been given jobs at KDD. This is common practice in Japan where the institution of *amakudari* ('descent from heaven') provides a means for government regulators to move (down) from their ministries into top positions in the industries which they formerly regulated. The current president of KDD, for example, is a retired MPT bureaucrat. While recognizing that its monopoly must inevitably be eroded, KDD and the MPT were strongly motivated to minimize future damage to KDD's profitability.

Following Japan's 1985 legislation, Cable and Wireless, a medium-sized UK telecommunications firm which had been engaged in creating a global network based on fibre optic technology (the 'Global Digital Highway'), saw an opportunity to construct a trans-Pacific cable linking Alaska with Japan. Although Cable and Wireless was not a prominent international firm (it evolved by creating telephone networks in British colonies), the US Defense Department and the National Security Council supported its plans for a new fibre optic cable route which was regarded as a possible component of the Strategic Defense Initiative plan ('Star Wars').

With this new network in the forefront of its strategy, Cable and Wireless organized a consortium, International Digital Communications (IDC), consisting of Japanese and US corporations and capitalized at ¥360 million ($2.5 million). The largest shareholders in IDC were the Japanese trading company, C. Itoh (20 percent), Cable and Wireless (20 percent), Toyota Motor Company (10 percent), and California-based Pacific Telesis International (10 percent). Additional participants included Merrill Lynch and the Industrial Bank of Japan.

This consortium, which was initially the only bidder for the second KDD, gave sole ownership of the fibre optic cable linking Japan and the US to Cable & Wireless and the US firm, Pacific Telesis. Furthermore, as a major shareholder, Cable and Wireless would be assured a substantial management role. In addition to the plan for the trans-Pacific cable, it was also proposed that a satellite air station should be constructed with operational centres in Tokyo and Osaka.

Japan's Ministry of Posts and Telecommunications (MPT) did not disguise its opposition to the presence of a foreign telecommunications carrier on the board of directors of the second KDD. Ignoring the new legislation, the MPT pointed out that none of the industrialized countries permits its international telecommunications companies to have foreign managing ownership. Therefore, Japan was simply conforming to established international practice.

At the same time, the MPT officially argued that the construction of a new cable was superfluous in light of existing capacity and projected long-term demand. Furthermore, the MPT maintained that it was unacceptable that the second KDD become a part of Cable and Wireless's independent international telecommunications system.

In this way, the Ministry dismissed the practicality, the utility, and the acceptability of C&W's participation in a new Japanese telecommunications venture. Not surprisingly, the MPT quietly encouraged the creation of a *second* consortium to bid against IDC and the foreign presence it represented.

With the word 'Japan' featuring prominently in its name, the second consortium, International Telecommunications Japan (ITJ), was capitalized at ¥1.2 billion ($8.5 million) and consisted exclusively of Japanese companies (no foreign participation was allowed): Matsushita Electric Industrial Co, five big trading houses, the Bank of Tokyo and 48 major firms (all representing potential customers). Instead of planning the creation of a new trans-Pacific cable, ITJ proposed renting existing cable and satellite capacity from KDD and AT&T – more money for KDD.

Cable and Wireless responded to the Ministry's rejection of the cable proposal by arguing that growth of the Japanese international telecommunications market had been stunted for years as a result of KDD's exorbitant prices and that the proposed cable would be vital to Japan's communications infrastructure if it was permitted to expand in a new era of widespread deregulation. Furthermore, Cable and Wireless pointed out, the liberalization of the financial sector would lead to a dramatic increase in the use of international communications. Cable and Wireless forecast a threefold increase in Japan's telecommunications market during the next decade (from $1.5 billion in 1986 to $4.5 billion in 1995), while the Keidanren (Federation of

Economic Organizations) forecast a nearly sixfold increase by 1995 (to about $9 billion). Led by Cable and Wireless, the IDC urged the Ministry of Posts and Telecommunications to approve licenses for both consortia.

In response, the MPT, insisting that the Japanese international telecommunications market could not support three companies ('excessive competition'), pressured the two consortia to merge. Using a negotiator from Keidanren, the MPT succeeded in persuading all Japanese members of the two consortia to consent to a merger. Under MPT direction, the Japanese participants also agreed that foreign participation in the new telecommunications company would be reduced to a maximum of 3 percent per company and that all foreign management participation in the second KDD would be prohibited.

Shunjiro Karasawa, the Minister of Posts and Telecommunications, quoted in the Japanese press, described Cable and Wireless as 'greedy' for insisting upon a 20 percent share of the second KDD and a management role. Needless to say, the proposal for the construction of a new cable was quashed.

Cable and Wireless replied that if the new consortium used KDD satellite and cable capability it would not be a legitimate competitor of KDD. The governments of Britain and the United States were infuriated by the merger agreement. They stated that there could be no doubt that the agreement, representing collusion between the Japanese government and private industry, was designed to exclude foreign companies from gaining legitimate entry to Japan's markets.

Vociferous letters of objection were sent to Prime Minister Nakasone from the British prime minister and the American president. The then US secretary of commerce (the late Malcolm Balridge) sent a scathing letter to Karasawa. Five days later the US Senate passed a resolution demanding immediate and 'appropriate' action.

The Japanese government responded that the promise to allow one-third foreign ownership of the new telecommunications company had not been broken since each of eleven foreign companies would be given a 3 percent share. Nonetheless, as a direct result of foreign complaints, the largest Japanese shareholders in the newly merged consortia agreed to grant Cable and Wireless as well as Pacific Telesis shares equal to those of the six top Japanese partners. In addition, the two foreign firms were granted a management role and were permitted the opportunity to conduct a study of the feasibility of building a trans-Pacific cable.

The British Prime Minister, Margaret Thatcher, announced that her government considered the Cable and Wireless bid to be a *test case*, demonstrating the degree of openness of the Japanese market. She asserted that the outcome of the dispute could strongly influence the future of British–Japanese trade relations and suggested that Japanese access to British financial markets would be severely curtailed unless the Japanese government honoured its 1985 legislation providing for one-third foreign ownership of a new telecommunications company.

In this way, the issue of Cable and Wireless's participation in the Japanese telecommunications market became the occasion for a bitter trade dispute between the UK and Japan. Britain's £3.7 billion balance of trade deficit with Japan was always in the background as discussions proceeded.

In the US, senator John Danforth, who was coauthor of legislation intended to penalize Japan for trade infractions, announced in March 1987 that 'the Japanese by their actions are doing more to ensure passage of telecommunications reciprocity legislation than anything I could do.'* The Danforth-Bentsen bill is designed to make mandatory US retaliation against nations violating international telecommunications agreements.

Encouraged by the US government, Cable and Wireless, as well as Pacific Telesis, rejected the Japanese proposal. Subsequently, at the Venice Summit, Prime Minister Nakasone stated that Japan had no objection to the granting of separate licenses to each of the two consortia. Despite this conciliatory gesture, the Ministry of Posts and Telecommunications continued its attempts to force a merger between the two groups. By August 1987, roughly one year after the dispute began, the telecommunications issue promised to explode into a 'three-continent trade dispute,' embroiling Japan with both the US and the UK.

Under these circumstances, the MPT finally yielded to the accumulated pressure of threatened punitive trade measures from Britain and the US. In late September 1987, the Ministry agreed to license the IDC to launch a new telecommunications service in Japan beginning in 1989. Thus, Cable and Wireless, with the vehement support of the British and American governments, won a major battle against the bias of a Japanese ministry.

Cable and Wireless's 16.83 percent share in the IDC, together with the creation of other segments of its 'Global Digital Highway,' will make it the first private sector company to control an independent global telecommunications system. It will be perfectly positioned to become a world leader in the telecommunications industry of the 21st century.

And so the tale ends. Foreign pressure saved the day. But the governments of the United States and Britain were not impressed by

* Quoted by *The Wall Street Journal*, 19 March 1987, p. 4.

the MPT's final acquiesence to their demands. As they saw it, industrial and political leaders in the West had been given further evidence that Japan will not open its domestic markets to foreign competition without enormous and prolonged political and economic pressure.

## JAPAN ACCUSED: THE CASE OF THE US SEMICONDUCTOR INDUSTRY

In 1986 Fujitsu Ltd, a major Japanese electronics firm and the world's largest producer of semiconductors, offered approximately $200 million to buy 80 percent Fairchild Semiconductor, a subsidiary of Schlumberger Ltd. Schlumberger accepted the offer and Fairchild executives were excited by the opportunities offered by Fujitsu. Fairchild had been a founder of the US semiconductor industry, and although it was by now something of a faded flower its acquisition would greatly strengthen Fujitsu's presence (in both production and sales) in the US semiconductor market.

The US Defense Department objected. Fairchild, the Pentagon export control office pointed out, is a major supplier to the Defense Department with contracts worth about $150 million per year. As the only producer of a chip that is central to the electronic guidance and fire control systems of F-16 jets, Fairchild is vital to US security. The takeover of Fairchild by Fujitsu would make America's best fighter aircraft dependent on Japan. The Pentagon maintained that permitting the US Air Force to become dependent on an 'economically aggressive power' was intolerable.

The term 'economially aggressive' was key to the Pentagon's opposition. Schlumberger, the parent of Fairchild, was itself controlled by foreign (French) interests. Thus, the Defense Department in effect expressed the view that of two US allies, one was more trustworthy than another.

Subsequently, the proposed merger was postponed by an unusually lengthy US Justice Department anti-trust investigation. Critics accused the government of obstructing the consummation of the deal.

The Fujitsu-Fairchild case revealed that there is no US policy regarding foreign investment in strategically sensitive industries. The fact is that Japanese companies already own dozens of small Silicon Valley companies and many others receive research financing from leading Japanese electronics groups. Moreover, US companies have not been prohibited from involving foreign allies in the development of potentially sensitive defence technology – National Semiconductor, for example, signed a long-term agreement for the development of advanced chips with NMB, a major Japanese producer of semiconductors. Similarly, Motorola and Toshiba have been cooperating in the development and manufacture of microprocessors.

The thorny problem of foreign involvement in defence-related technology was not addressed by the US Department of Commerce. Instead, a House of Representatives committee proposed the establishment of presidential powers to block all foreign investments threatening national security. Meanwhile, it was rumoured that in private meetings US representatives pressured MITI to demand that Fujitsu withdraw its takeover bid.

On 10 March 1987, Fujitsu announced that it would not permit 'emotional trade issues' to interfere with its acquisition plans. Then, just one week later Fujitsu withdrew its bid without explanation. Opponents of Japanese acquisition of US chip manufacturers exulted. 'Fujitsu got the message that the US government is not going to allow legal rape and pillage of the US semiconductor industry,' remarked Wilfred Corrigan, former president of Fairchild and current president of LSI Logic, a semiconductor producer.*

Not to be thwarted in their determination to cooperate, Fujitsu and Fairchild formulated an agreement for the joint development of new technology, joint manufacturing in both the US and Japan, and the exchange of rights for current and future products. The practical effects of this agreement differed little from those that would have resulted from the abandoned merger.

In early 1987, the Fairchild-Fujitsu merger was widely perceived as a test case of US trade policy. Appropriately, the outcome mirrored US policy regarding Japan. Vague and unresolved US trade positions resulted in small modifications of Japanese plans. The lack of resolution paved the way for new misunderstandings and increased trade friction. The Fujitsu-Fairchild episode demonstrated that the establishment of limits on foreign investments could do little to reduce the flow abroad of critical US technology.

The growing realization in America that Japan (and other allies) have access to specialized technology vital to US defence promises to become a key and unresolvable issue in the burgeoning trade conflict. Six weeks after the Fujitsu takeover plans were aborted, the Toshiba Machine scandal was revealed to Congress by the CIA. It is probable that the Defense Department already knew of the Toshiba's sale of the computerized milling machines to the USSR when it first opposed Fujitsu's bid for Fairchild.

As this book is being written, in the Summer of 1987, the semiconductor industry has come to the forefront of the trade controversy between the United States and Japan. As a result of the 'failure' of a semiconductor trade agreement signed by the two nations in 1986, 100 percent tariffs were imposed on selected Japanese imports in April

---

* Quoted by *The Financial Times*, 'Japan voices concern at blow to Fujitsu,' 18 March 1987.

1987. Although some of those tariffs were lifted before the year was out, the episode will remain as a reminder that US anger (although perceived as irrational) is like nitroglycerin: it explodes under pressure or on exposure to sudden heat.*

In 1986 and 1987 the fact that the three biggest semiconductor manufacturers were Japanese entities, and that an additional three Japanese producers ranked among the world's top ten, led to widespread concern that the entire industry would fall prey to Japan. In many respects, the controversy that has surrounded the microchip industry is an expression of deep-seated fears in the US (and Europe) that Japan can destroy crucial indigenous industries almost at will. The history of the semiconductor industry in the US and Japan, and the subsequent achievement of market dominance by Japan, provide a framework within which current Western views of Japanese industrial production and international negotiations can be explored.

The integrated circuit (IC) was invented in 1959 by Jack Kilby, an American working for Texas Instruments. This discovery roughly coincided with the Soviet launching of the first man-made satellite, *Sputnik*. Partly as a result of American fears of lagging behind the Soviet Union in key defence-related technologies, Texas Instruments was given government contracts to develop ICs for the Minuteman missile program. The highest priority was placed on the development of production techniques that would yield large numbers of reliable ICs.

Not long afterward, Jean Hoenni of Fairchild Industries developed a photolithographic method (the planar process) for etching IC designs on specially treated silicon wafers. NASA subsequently gave Fairchild contracts to develop computer facilities for the Apollo spacecraft. In this way, the novel inventions of American engineers conjoined with the needs of the US government (defence and space programmes) led to the birth and rapid growth of the American semiconductor industry. Subsequent American developments, including the invention of the microprocessor and electron beam lithography, resulted in exceptional technological advances. By 1970, the US was the unrivalled leader of a multibillion dollar semiconductor industry.

Although the Japanese corporation NEC licensed the use of planar technology from Fairchild, throughout the 1960s, the Japanese semiconductor industry lagged behind that of the US. Because Japan did not have a significant defence industry or space programme, Japanese corporations were not given the vital infusions of research funding received by their American counterparts.

---

* As this book goes to press in the Autumn of 1987, $164 million of the original $300 million in sanctions remain in effect

Through administrative guidance in the mid-1970s, however, MITI directed a number of Japan's leading electronics corporations to produce dynamic random access memory chips (D-rams). Special funding and procurement contracts assured that the fledgling production sector would flourish.

During the following decade, from 1976 to 1986, a steadily growing and highly competitive Japanese semiconductor industry emerged. Japan's leading electronics firms cooperated in research projects funded by MITI while simultaneously competing in domestic and international markets. One of the products of the collaborative research and keen competition was a reduction in production costs, and this, in turn, led to a growth in Japan's total share of the world's semiconductor market.

By 1980, Japanese electronics firms held 40 percent of world market share in D-rams. During the next few years, this market share more than doubled, reaching 90 percent in 1986.

In 1984, with semiconductor demand exceeding supply, it became apparent to MITI that an impending world slump in computer sales would lead to a glut of semiconductors in global markets, and thus to a decline of prices and profit margins. Fearing that Japan's semiconductor industry would be damaged, MITI advised the nine leading Japanese semiconductor manufacturers to increase their capital spending by 80 percent (to $2.7 billion) over the 1983 level. Increased spending was subsidized by MITI and by Japanese banks which extended loans at rates far below those prevalent in the US.

As a direct result, Japan's investment in chip-making surpassed that of US commercial producers for the first time. During the next three years, Japan's chip-makers invested more than 25 percent of sales into new plant and equipment, compared with less than 15 percent invested by their American counterparts. Thus, as world demand for semiconductors declined, Japan's production of chips increased and Japanese manufacturers were in a position to corner a larger market share during this critical period.

The strategy worked. Japanese manufacturers successfully *expanded* their total share of world IC markets from 33 percent in 1980 to 48 percent in 1987. During the same period, the US share of world markets *contracted* from 52 percent to 39 percent.

Meanwhile, the unit cost of 256-kilobit D-rams (which are used in virtually all computers) plummeted from an average of $10 in 1984 to less than $2 at the end of 1986. Despite the decline in cost and the parallel decline in profit margins, Japan's semiconductor manufacturers continued to increase production, dumping excess supply in Asian markets. Losses (an estimated aggregate total of $1 billion in

1986) accrued by the manufacturers were easily absorbed by their parent corporations, some of the biggest electronics firms in the world.

During the period 1985–86, four of the six American producers of 256-kilobit D-rams discontinued producing the chips for commercial sales. As a result of stagnant world demand, declining prices, and Japanese dumping, the US semiconductor industry lost more than $1 billion in 1986 alone. Layoffs resulted in the loss of 60,000 jobs during the period 1984–1986. At the same time, the US share of the world market for 256-kilobit D-rams, declined to 10 percent compared to more than 80 percent for Japan.

In 1986, imports from Japan represented 14 percent of total US semiconductor sales. The lion's share of this $1.2 billion piece of America's semiconductor pie was purchased by IBM which found it more cost effective to import 256-kilobit D-rams than to assume the cost of manufacture. (It is noteworthy that a portion of the Japanese imports were in fact produced by Texas Instruments' highly successful Japanese facilities.) In this way, Japan's chip-makers (which were *losing* money) helped IBM to reduce the cost of its computers and to increase its revenue. Thus, while Japanese semiconductor manufacturers seized nearly one-seventh of the US market, the American electronics firms which purchased their products reaped the benefit in the short term at least.

Not surprisingly, US semiconductor producers objected to Japanese encroachment in their territory. They quickly pointed out that 'once again' Japanese manufacturers were using predatory pricing to increase their market share in Europe and Asia. It is by no means novel for US manufacturers of all types of products to object to imports and to contend that dumping in third markets undermines their fair competitive advantage. In this particular case, however, the semiconductor companies had a strong ally: the Pentagon.

Because semiconductors are an essential component on all advanced weapons and detection systems, the Defence Department feared that US defence strategies would become dependent upon foreign suppliers. A Defense Department task force warned that 'US producers are increasingly becoming incapable of producing the highest technology products with sufficient quality in high volumes and with the timeliness required to achieve profitability by American capital market standards.'*

In mid-1986, the US Defense Department proposed a 'defence semiconductor initiative' intended to restore US chip-making capability to its former preeminence. In grandiose terms, the new initiative claimed

* Quoted by Louise Kehoe, 'Pentagon takes initiative in war against chip imports,' *Financial Times*, 27 January 1987.

to be designed to prevent a Japanese 'takeover' of the entire US semiconductor market. Curiously, the special initiative bore a striking resemblance to methods traditionally used by MITI.

The Defense Department suggested the creation of a semiconductor industry cooperative manufacturing project – named Sematech by the Semiconductor Association. In addition, the establishment of a semiconductor manufacturing technology institute run by Sematech was seen as vital. The proposed project called for special government research funding with $50 million earmarked for defence applications of new technology and $1.3 billion available to Sematech over a six-year period. Special antitrust exemptions were also proposed so that Sematech would not become an illegal monopoly.

The Defense Department also suggested that various Japanese competitive advantages (such as the lower cost of capital and the freedom from shareholder pressures that facilitated long-term planning) be matched by special US government protective policies. Charles Sporck, the president of National Semiconductor, told congressional representatives that Sematech 'represented a response to the Japanese challenge, a recognition that, in order to remain competitive internationally, we need to achieve a far higher degree of cooperation among ourselves.'

The idea behind the Defense Department's proposal is that Sematech should create and manufacture future generations of memory chips, tailored to the needs of US defence strategy, as well as commercial technology. In this way, Sematech would ensure that foreign semiconductor producers and scientists would have as little role as possible in the US defence system.

At the time of writing, it is not known to what extent the US judiciary will find the creation of a government-sponsored cartel an acceptable method of rescuing America's semiconductor industry from foreign competition. Nonetheless, in the spring of 1987 the Semiconductor Industry Association, strongly supported by IBM, unanimously approved the creation of Sematech. 'Sematech plans to produce its first chips by the second half of 1988 and to achieve parity with Japanese manufacturing technology by 1990,' Sporck forecast.*

The future of Sematech aside, the Pentagon firmly believed that without immediate government intervention, America's chip business would soon collapse. This catastrophe would leave the entire US defence establishment at the mercy of foreign chip-makers. In such a case, it was argued, the US defence system could swiftly lose the technological edge upon which its superiority depends. This bleak

---

* In the event, Sematech proceeded smoothly from conception to birth. Congress appropriated $100 million of Pentagon funds for 1988 and in January Sematech arranged to set up its base of research in Austin, Texas.

scenario was whispered into ears located in the White House. The ears listened.

Like the Pentagon, many US congressmen believed that Japan stood poised, like an executioner with rifle aimed, to destroy a strategic American industry. Such leading Japanese electronics firms as Toshiba, Fujitsu and NEC were named by US Officials as culprits involved in the widespread dumping of integrated circuits in Hong Kong and Southeast Asia.

American trade representatives negotiated, cajoled, and threatened. Finally, on 31 July 1986, the US signed a semiconductor trade agreement with MITI. This agreement was intended to remedy all of the perceived inequities in the pricing of Japanese chips outside Japan and help US chipmakers gain a larger share of Japan's domestic chip market.

The agreement specified minimum prices,* set by the Commerce Department, for D-rams and erasable programmable read-only memory chips (Eproms) sold outside Japan. US trade representatives hoped that these minimum prices would eliminate the dumping of semiconductors in third-country markets at prices less than half of the producers' manufacturing costs. In return for Japan's acceptance of the accord, the US agreed to waive punitive duties against Japanese producers for dumping semiconductors in the US.

President Reagan praised the agreement as the 'landmark pact' which would serve as a model for trade cooperation between the two nations. Just six months later, in early 1987, the agreement became the platform for US protectionist legislation. If the accord was to be remembered as a 'landmark pact', it became clear it would only be because it served to reinforce the US conviction that Japan could not be trusted to abide by agreements.

For their part, Japanese industrialists and bureaucrats expressed the unofficial view that the US was a heavy-handed, bumbling producer outrageously demanding that Japan compensate for its inadequacies. Officials at MITI responded to American accusations that the agreement had been breached with denials ('we are implementing the agreement in good faith') *and* counter-allegations that US chip-makers were themselves dumping chips in third markets, thus discounting the minimum price levels set by the agreement.

It was scarcely a surprise that the semiconductor accord did not work. It was unworkable before the ink was dry on it.

The minimum prices set in the semiconductor accord were more than

---

* Termed 'fair market value,' the minimum prices were intended to reflect each Japanese manufacturer's cost of production plus an 8 percent profit margin.

double those prevalent in the Japanese domestic market. As a result, American computer manufacturers were required to pay substantially higher prices for their chip supplies than competing Japanese manufacturers who produced their own chips in-house. Not surprisingly, US electronics firms objected to the accord.

Furthermore, the price requirement obliged Japanese semiconductor producers to sell their chips at prices far above production costs. For example, the actual production cost of a 256-kilobit D-ram was roughly $1.15 in early 1987 compared to a sales price of $1.50. However, the agreement compelled Japanese manufacturers to sell the chips for $2.50. Although this resulted in their share of some markets being reduced, it led to an increase in their overall profits.

It did, however, confront Japanese producers with the problem of how to dispose of their rapidly accumulating chip inventories. The largest producers (NEC Corp, Hitachi Ltd, and Fujitsu Ltd) ignored MITI's administrative guidance and continued dumping their excess chips in the familiar Asian markets. Soon, other Japanese producers followed the example set by the industry leaders.

There was, of course, no increase in Japanese imports of US chips. In fact, Japanese imports of US-made semiconductors declined. In the agreement, Japan had acceded to US demands that its chip imports should be doubled to 20 percent of domestic consumption (from 9.5 percent in 1986) by 1991, but this provision, even more than other aspects of the agreement, was unenforceable. Because the Japanese corporations which use chips also manufacture them, the need for imports in the Japanese electronics market is slight.

The semiconductor agreement may have been contrary to principles of free trade, this did not prevent US trade respresentatives and congressmen from fuming at Japan's failure to fulfil the accord's provisions. Phrases such as 'flagrant disregard' and 'continued and intentional violations' filled the Washington air and 'protectionism' became a buzzword. Punitive legislation was on the way.

On 30 March 1987, in a move generally acknowledged as symbolic, President Reagan unilaterally imposed 100 percent tariffs (to become effective two weeks later) on selected Japanese electronic products* valued at $300 million. The products chosen either used semiconductors as component parts or were produced by the same firms alleged to be dumping chips. Designed to compensate the US for business lost through Japanese violations, the tariffs were based on the Administration's calculations of aggregate annual losses.

Representing a mere 0.1 percent of total Japanese electronics sales

* The companies concerned included, Hitachi Ltd, Toshiba Corp, Fujitsu Ltd, NEC Corp and Oki Corp.

in the US in 1986, the $300 million of imports covered by the tariff was a minuscule portion of Japan's total exports to the US. But this was the first time that the Reagan Administration had formally retaliated against Japan on a trade issue, and it was hoped that the tariffs would shock Japan into enforcing the semiconductor accord while simultaneously forestalling congressional demands for protectionism.

Following the announcement of the US sanctions, MITI ordered Japanese chip-makers to cut output. Subsequently, Japanese firms reduced the production of 256-kilobit and 1-megabyte D-rams by roughly one-third.

MITI claimed that the production cut was intended to address US allegations that Japan was flooding world markets. However, Japan controlled 90 percent of the global market in 256-kilobit computer memory chips as well as a major portion of 1-megabyte global production. As a result of the production cuts, US computer manufacturers found it difficult to fulfil their production quotas, and they were forced to turn to grey markets in their quest for semiconductors. The American firms (including IBM and Hewlitt-Packard) lodged complaints with MITI. (Later, following President Reagan's partial removal of the tariffs, MITI allowed Japanese chip-makers to increase output.)

The MITI cut was perceived by US computer manufacturers as *retaliation* against the US sanctions. They believed that MITI hoped that its action would lead them to put pressure on Congress for a repeal of the sanctions.

Japan's semiconductor producers are vertically integrated with electronics groups (Fujitsu, Toshiba, NEC, Hitachi) and exist primarily as providers to the equipment divisions of their parent companies. The profits or losses of the semiconductor units are not stated in annual reports of the parent companies.

The massive capital of the parent companies permits the semiconductor subsidiaries to manufacture product lines and to implement plans *independently of short-term market conditions*. The parent companies subsidize losses, invest capital for research, and advise the subsidiaries regarding world market conditions.

The funding provided by the parent companies is likely to become increasingly vital. As a result of the decline in world semiconductor demand, 40 percent of global semiconductor production capacity, and more than half of US production capacity, was not used in 1986 and will rapidly become obsolete. Furthermore, while the cost of a semiconductor plant was $100 million in 1986, it is predicted to rise to $650 million within a decade.* Japan's rich electronics groups are well-positioned to fund costly semiconductor production – particularly because the lion's share of output is used in-house. Their position sharply contrasts with that of the small, liquidity-starved US semiconductor manufacturers.

Although supplying the parent company is the *raison d'être* of Japan's semiconductor manufacturers, they are also aggressive in pursuit of sales throughout the world. The competition for international market share forces them to maximize cost effectiveness, to stay on the leading edge of technology, and, perhaps most importantly, to maintain a constant level of production.

In the United States, by contrast, most semiconductor producers are not subsidiaries of highly diversified electronic conglomerates. Those which are (such as the semiconductor subsidiaries of IBM and AT&T) produce exclusively for in-house consumption. Consequently, America's chip-makers are obliged to shape product lines, marketing, and long-term strategy on the basis of short-term profits.

Because the US semiconductor industry was moulded by the needs of the defence and space programmes, it focused on the production of high-grade chips. The emphasis placed on the production of these expensive and specialized chips meant that the American industry had priorities very different from those of Japan's semiconductor industry, which concentrated on the mass production of commercial chips. Japan's chip producers, driven by commercial forces, succeeded in mass-producing chips of a quality equal to or better than those of their US competitors – and at lower prices.

As a result, US chip-makers were destined to fall victim to Japan's subsidized and aggressively-marketed mass-produced chips. Nonetheless, America's weakness may very well prove to be its strength. Many market insiders believe that custom-made chips, particularly a category termed application-specific integrated circuits (ASICS), are the products of the future. Already the fastest growing sector of the chip industry, ASICS promise US semiconductor firms a field in which they are strongly suited to competition with their Japanese counterparts.

The tale is not over, of course; micro-chips will continue to be a bone of contention in US–Japanese relations. It still remains to be seen whether or not growing Japanese dominance of the semiconductor industry will emerge as one expression of Japan's economic influence. Will Japanese corporations control vital segments of the American defence and aerospace industries by virtue of a predominant market share? Or will Sematech save the day?

* Louise Kehoe, 'Semiconductors, Facing hard realities,' *The Financial Times*, 18 December 1986, p. 17.

## NEGOTIATIONS, THREATS, AND LEGISLATION

There are three techniques, often used concurrently, which can be employed to persuade a trading partner to alter a trade policy or activity. *Negotiations* involving political pressure can offer incentives or disincentives for change. *Threats* to close a market through tariff or non-tariff barriers can coerce private firms or sovereign bodies to alter policies. *Legislation* can establish regulations and tariffs capable of altering the flow of goods and capital.

Negotiating with Japan has been a confusing and often frustrating undertaking for many of its trading partners, especially those from the West. Japanese government negotiators offer candidly-phrased and conciliatory statements in fluent English, French, and German. These high-ranking negotiators (often vice ministers) are urbane and usually express a deep understanding of US and Common Market trade problems with Japan. They agree with their foreign counterparts that Japan's markets require deregulation and internationalization.

Having met with these foreign trade representatives, Japan's trading partners initially believe that their positions have been accepted and that change is imminent. Later, when no change of policy occurs, disappointment with Japan increases. Have the high-ranking Japanese negotiators deliberately misrepresented Japan's trade policies? No.

Westerners believe that statements and policy are causally linked. It is assumed that an official statement that a system requires change and will be changed means that change will be implemented. In Japan, that is not the case.

In Japan, words are words. They are exchanged to express sympathy and understanding, to promote goodwill, and to demonstrate a relationship. For the Japanese the exchange of words, like the exchange of diplomatic gifts, is important to international relations. But they do not regard policy as a matter of diplomacy; they see it as a product of complex internal relationships, traditions, and exigencies that cannot be affected by the words of negotiators. Thus the job of Japan's sophisticated and articulate representatives is to lubricate Japan's relationships with its allies. They are not expected to institute policy or justify such policy.

This makes negotiating with the Japanese a difficult task. Other governments, frustrated by the ineffectiveness of their negotiations with Japan, have resorted to threats in order to induce change.

In 1987, as mentioned above, Prime Minister Margaret Thatcher threatened to revoke the licenses of Japanese financial institutions in London unless Japan immediately opened its financial markets and telecommunications market to British firms. Had these threats been implemented, approximately 5,000 British citizens employed by

Japanese financial institutions would have faced unemployment. Indeed, *The Financial Times* reported that two British traders who were about to accept jobs with Daiwa Securities Company in London refused the offer for fear that Daiwa's London operations could be closed.

In short, had Margaret Thatcher implemented her threats, the British Government would have thrown out the baby with the bath water. Had Japan's banks been sent packing, British nationals would have been sacrificed on the altar of protectionism.

This illustrates the point that protectionism is a double-edged sword, an impractical political weapon that damages the wielder as much as the victim. Then, while both parties lie bleeding, the cause of the problem remains unscathed.

While not oblivious to the problems of launching protectionist legislation, US legislators in 1987 perceived no other avenue of communication with Japan. Convinced that the Japanese government was refusing to consider American problems, they decided that the only meaningful message they could send to Tokyo would be one involving economic hardship. They believed that through the infliction of deprivation Japan could be forced to change its closed and nonreciprcal policies. Thus, the Omnibus Trade Bill was based on the assumption that it was necessary to punish Japan like a recalcitrant child who won't share his toys and is sent to bed without dinner.

## 'BLAMING IS NOT ENOUGH: WE MUST ACT OR PERISH'
American legislation is often based on the views of constitutents rather than sound economic considerations, rendering trade bills political rather than economic devices. As a result, international political statements are often hidden beneath the mask of economic policies.

The US Congress has the power to launch a trade war through its legislation. Ironically, it does not desire that outcome. By unspoken consensus, US senators and congressmen do not want to damage the prospects of American companies. Nevertheless, a full scale trade war with America's biggest trading partner (namely Japan) could have no other effect. Thus, it is tragic that trade legislation has become the medium for the expression of American anger and frustration.

# 2 JAPAN VIEWS THE WORLD

## A HOT SUMMER

It was a hot July day in 1987. I was talking with a Japanese government official in a bustling bar near Dupont Circle in Washington DC.
He was speaking with vehemence and as he spoke he rattled the ice
in his glass for emphasis.

'In Japan, subsidiaries are not liable for defaults on loans by the
parent company and parent companies exercise little control over
subsidiaries. That is the Japanese system.

'Toshiba Machine is an *independent company*, with its own listing
on the Tokyo Stock Exchange. It happens to be half-owned by the
Toshiba Corporation. That does not mean that the Toshiba Corporation participates in the daily business of Toshiba Machine. To hold
the Toshiba Corporation culpable for the crimes of a few employees
at Toshiba Machine is like holding an umbrella responsible for the
rain.

'The Senate and Congressional response to Toshiba Corporation
is just one more instance of "Japan bashing". Vengeful American
politicians with little understanding of Japanese corporate structure
are interested only in impressing their constituents with bold anti-
Japanese statements. By acting this way, they antagonize the
Japanese people and increase anti-American sentiment in Japan.

'Over and over again, the US Senate has held a gun to our head
and made demands. When we ask what we get in return, they say,
"We won't pull the trigger if you accede to our terms."

'Now congressmen, *representatives of the American people*, pulverize
a Japanese radio while parading a hangman's noose in front of tele-

vision cameras on Capitol Hill. What are we Japanese to think? America wants to fan the occasional sparks of trade friction into the flames of trade war.'

'Well,' I said, 'Americans think that the Japanese care so little about the United States that they're willing to endanger US national security just to make some extra money. The Toshiba sales involved the most serious leak of technology to the Soviet Union in decades.'

He appeared to be unconvinced. 'The technology loss,' he said, 'is deplorable, and those guilty of breaking the law will be punished. But the US response is equally deplorable and misguided.'

I attempted to be diplomatic. 'If Japan had a tough espionage law,' I pointed out, 'which would result in harsh punishment for the culprits, then perhaps US anger would not have been as great.'

'It was the United States which eliminated Japanese espionage laws!'* he replied indignantly. 'And can we even be certain that Toshiba's technology *was* used to manufacture acoustically superior submarine propeller blades? Where is the evidence? It's quite possible that European companies sold multi-axis milling machines to the Russians long before Toshiba Machine.'

A waitress brought us a fresh round of drinks and then disappeared behind a throng of customers. Mopping his brow with a handkerchief, the government official continued.

'A strong argument could be made that the sale of VAX computers to the communist bloc by a number of European companies was a technology loss of far graver importance. Yet there was no popular outcry. No protectionist trade bills were drafted in order to retaliate against those countries.

'The same is true today. American senators and congressmen are not using Norwegian sardine cans for their primitive rituals of public destruction. If Toshiba Corporation is seen as responsible for the actions of Toshiba Machine, why isn't the Norwegian government, which owns Kongsberg Vaapenfabrikk, also ridiculed in the same way?'

I had no reply and my interlocutor nodded. We both knew that Washington was angry with Japan and that the episode we were discussing was a catalyst not a cause. We left the bar and walked out into the sweltering heat of the Washington summer.

'Americans do not like to be surpassed in any activity.' The bureaucrat smiled grimly and continued. 'The United States wants to punish Japan because Japan has succeeded where America has failed. While the Japanese fund profligate American spending, the Senate blames the entire US budget deficit on Japan.'

---

* During the American Occupation.

He hailed a cab, which pulled to the curb. 'It is that kind of economic nonsense that angers us Japanese.' With these words, he got into the taxi and disappeared.

## JAPAN VIEWS THE WEST

For more than two-and-a-half centuries (1603–1868) Japan was ruled by the Tokugawa shogunate. Under a harsh and inflexible policy of seclusion (*sakoku*) initiated in 1634, foreigners were prohibited from visiting the Japanese archipelago and travel abroad by Japanese was a capital crime.

By 1639, Japan had been so successfully isolated from the world that even European missionaries abandoned attempts to visit and proselytize. Western ships rarely came within the vicinity of the islands – with a single exception: once each year a Dutch trading vessel, travelling from the East Indies, would anchor at Deshima, an island in Nagasaki harbour.* Throughout most of the seventeenth and eighteenth centuries, Japan was regarded, by those few Europeans who knew that it existed, as an impoverished and insignificant group of islands in the general area of China.

In the late eighteenth century and early nineteenth centuries, Western ships began to visit Japanese territorial waters with increasing frequency. A number of unsuccessful attempts to negotiate trade agreements in Japan were followed in 1853 by Commodore Matthew Perry's forceful delivery of a letter from the president of the United States to the Japanese Emperor (the 'emperor' to whom he delivered the letter was actually the shogun). This initiated a period in Japanese history termed *bakumatsu*, the end of the shogunate.

Ever since the hot summer days of 1853, when Perry arrived in Japan to propose 'that the United States and Japan should live together in friendship and have commercial intercourse with each other', foreigners have been hammering at the doors of Japan. 'Unfair treaties' signed with France, Germany, and Holland during the nineteenth century were humiliating reminders that, as a nation among nations, Japan was not in a position of strength.

Fourteen years before Perry landed in Japan, the first Anglo-Chinese war had begun. The example of neighboring China was a compelling warning to the Japanese. Great Britain, capitalizing on the degeneracy of the Ch'ing dynasty, forced China to permit the importation of opium. The effects of widespread opium addiction came to symbolize the consequences of having dealings with the West.

Like an addict with glazed eyes, an emaciated body, and a mind

* Chinese traders also anchored at Deshima.

focused solely on the infusion of a drug, China became a frail victim of Western power. Chinese wealth (in the form of silver coinage) was drained as inevitably as the vitality of a drug abuser. Not surprisingly, Japan was suspicious of the suggestion that it could 'live together in friendship' with the United States. Western nations were dangerous 'friends.'

Unlike China, Japan was small and homogenous and had a militarist tradition which had not been diluted by intelluctual élitism. Japan could arm itself with advanced weapons and deflect the Western expansionism that was inspired by delusions of 'manifest destiny'. The new Meiji regime (which replaced the Tokugawa shogunate in 1868) recognized the urgent need to study and adopt European manufacturing techniques. Only with European technology could Japan replicate European weapons.

In 1870, the Ministry of Industry was born. The new ministry encouraged (through subsidies and credit) the development of all private enterprises with military application. A half-century after the signing of unequal treaties, the Ministry of Industry had achieved its goals.

No longer was Japan a sword-wielding, agriculturally based country cringing at the sound of foreign cannon. Japan had armed itself and had become a world-class military power, strong enough to smash Russian forces in a war.

In just one generation Japan learned and mastered diverse Western technologies – from arms manufacture to mining, from telegraphy to textiles. As the result of Japanese ingenuity, organization, and collective concentration, Japan became the only Asian power in a world dominated by the West.

The stories of Japan's birth as an industrial nation in the early twentieth century and of its phoenix-like emergence from the ashes of war have justifiably become present-day folktales. During the 1960s and 1970s, Japanese manufacturers applied to radios and automobiles the same skills which had previously produced outstanding military hardware, and had soon carried the peaceful application of technological research and production to unprecedented heights.

But despite her industrial strength, Japan remained vulnerable. Japan is a nation poorly endowed with natural resources, and as the Japanese economy was modernized and the twentieth century advanced, she necessarily became ever more dependent upon the use of a wide range of mineral and agricultural resources.

During the 1980s, Japan imported 100 percent of her aluminum, nickel, wool, raw cotton, and corn; more than 95 percent of Japan's oil, iron ore, copper, tin, and soybeans were also imported. Furthermore, the bulk of such products as natural gas, lead, wheat, coal, zinc, and lumber had to be purchased from Western and Asian trading partners. Thus, by becoming a part of the modern world, Japan became dependent upon the world's supplies.

Because Japan is an island nation with a strategic dependence on mineral resources, the spectre of blockade and tariffs perpetually haunts Japanese minds when they consider their political relations with their trading partners. Indeed, were it not for the pressure to procure oil, perhaps Japan would never have annexed Manchuria in 1932.

In 1970, Japan's most important trading partner was the United States, which then bought 31 percent of all Japanese exports. However, American attitudes toward Japan were subtle, complex and potentially threatening.

Although the American occupation of Japan had ended in 1952, the United States still held Okinawa, which it had annexed in 1945. During the late 1960s and early 1970s, US government representatives had complained increasingly about the degree of Japanese government protection of industry. They claimed that competition was allowed only in those areas in which US (or European) corporations could not compete effectively with Japanese industries. In a high-handed manner, oblivious to Japan's unique problems, US trade representatives publicly blamed Japan for its trade surplus with the United States.

Then, in 1971, Japan was rocked by the two 'Nixon Shocks' which seemed to show the nation's leaders that the United States could not be trusted to act in Japan's best interests. The 'Nixon Shocks' served as a crude reminder that Japan prospered under the economic and military umbrella of the United States.

The first 'Nixon Shock' was economic. The United States placed 10 percent tariffs on all imports and simultaneously permitted the dollar to float in the international exchange markets. The Administration also demanded that Japan revalue the yen and demolish so-called protectionist barriers in order to open its market to American trade.

These actions and demands on the part of the United States were outrageous. America's unfavourable trade balance was the result of inflation: the Federal Reserve Bank had printed too much money so that the government could pay for the Vietnam war. As a result of the inflation, American products were not cost competitive in world markets. To compound this problem, American businessmen were too parochial. Only by learning the intricacies of marketing in Japan, could US corporations hope to find a niche in the Japanese economy. To take just one obvious example, while Japanese businessmen conducted business in English in the United States, American businessmen did not even attempt to learn Japanese.

The second 'Nixon Shock' was political. In July 1971, President Nixon announced that he would visit Peking the following year. This decision, although not in itself harmful to Japanese interests, stunned the *Diet* and the foreign ministry. The United States, Japan's major ally, had announced a reversal of a critical aspect of its Asian foreign policy without consulting or even forewarning the prime minister of Japan. This move was insulting and potentially dangerous. What would be the new design of US foreign policy? How would Japan be affected? Apparently, the United States government was indifferent to the effects of its actions on Japan.

The Nixon Shocks raised the perennial postwar questions: could Japan depend upon the United States for military protection in the event of a global crisis? If forced to choose, would America put US cities at risk in order to protect Japan? It seemed unlikely. Thus President Nixon provided proof that Western nations could not be trusted.

More evidence that Japan's national interests were at the mercy of the whims of foreigners soon followed. The 'Oil Shock' of 1973 further stimulated consciousness of the vulnerability of Japan's economy. The United States, Japan's so-called protector, could do nothing to alleviate Japan's oil deficiencies which led to the bleeding of the economy and a decline in GNP. That fickle nations such as the United States and Saudi Arabia could dictate, through trade practices, the growth and health of Japan was unacceptable. The Japanese must hold their destiny in their own hands.

Easier said than done. The desire to maintain an autonomous political economy within the expanding nexus of global interdependencies became ever more difficult to realize during the 1970s and 1980s.

Fifteen years after the 'Nixon Shocks', in 1986, the intensity of Western pressure to change Japanese trade and monetary policies had not decreased. Political pressure (particularly American and British) for the immediate elimination of 'barriers' to foreign participation in all of Japan's markets ignored the unique features of Japan's regulatory structure.

The arguments put forward by the US and the EEC regarding market 'reciprocity' ignored the fact that Japanese domestic institutions were no more free than foreign institutions to do as they pleased. For example, the number of institutions authorized to conduct trust banking in Japan was limited to eight. Japan could not be expected to grant a trust banking licence to every foreign financial institution that demanded one.

When Japanese institutions seek overseas opportunities, they readily conform to the customs of the localities in which they conduct business. Japan does not demand that foreign legal and political systems grant it special treatment, and the Japanese, in turn, expect foreign institutions seeking access to Japan's markets to reciprocate by conforming to Japanese law and tradition.

Today, foreign governments threaten retaliation unless Japan burns its regulations and invites immediate access to every market sector. Are these threats any different from Perry's gunboat diplomacy? The more things change, the more they remain the same.

## MADE IN JAPAN

How can a resource poor nation with no military strength other than a small self-defence force hope to control its future in a bellicose world? Is there more than one answer? The Japanese solution in the postwar era has been the power of exports.

Japan's only hope of being an independent world power was to trade its exports for vital resources and foreign exchange. It would not be correct to suggest that government decisions consciously dictated the direction of growth. There was no master plan for the nurturing of a modern Japanese industrial economy. It is, however, true to say that MITI encouraged the resuscitation and subsequent cultivation of choice industrial sectors.

The first products manufactured in the bombed-out shells of buildings in Osaka and Tokyo were crude consumer items intended for Japanese customers. As the nation was rebuilt, factories multiplied like rabbits.

Japan's earliest exported products were not a shining success. Although they were priced competitively, their reliability was often questionable. 'Made in Japan' became a synonym for 'second-rate' in the United States and elsewhere.

The first Japanese product to gain international recognition as an example of unsurpassed quality was the Nikon camera which reached the West via American soldiers returning home from the Korean War. In 1958, the development of the single lens reflex camera ultimately catapulted the Japanese camera industry far ahead of West German producers.

Fifteen years after the war, Japanese products ranging from inexpensive transistor radios to colourful Hawaiian shirts flooded global markets. Total quality control was an American concept (invented by W. Edwards Deming), which the Occupation authorities introduced during the late 1940s; but it was Japanese manufacturers who developed the concept into an art. Blue collar workers voluntarily formed 'circles' devoted to improving the quality of the products which they helped to make.

Twenty years later, the phrase 'Made in Japan' had acquired an altogether different connotation. Japanese products rivalled the finest in the world. By the late 1970s, the Japanese watch industry, for example, had surpassed its famous Swiss competitor.

Akio Morita, the chairman and co-founder of the Sony Corporation, titled his memoirs *Made in Japan*. For him, and for other Japanese industrialists of his generation, the success of Japanese exports was the realization and the proof of Japanese superiority.

It is significant that Morita's autobiography begins with World War II and not with his own birth or the birth of Sony. Japan, at the end of the war, was a country in disarray whose only asset was its people. The war marked a great turning point for the people of Japan. A martial tradition which dated back to prehistoric times had ended. The bitterness of defeat was tasted by every Japanese individual.

Like a caterpillar concealed in a cocoon, Japan during the late 1940s and 1950s appeared to the West to be accomplishing little. In fact, under the leadership of a prescient bureaucracy and devoted industrialists, the country was quietly developing a new form. The outside world was stunned when the butterfly emerged from its cocoon.

At last, Japan was able to show its true colours. By the late 1960s Japan had become an awesome producer and exporter of all types of manufactured products of superb quality and rare ingenuity. The 1970s saw the consolidation and confirmation of Japanese manufacturing prowess. By the late 1980s, Japan had become too successful for its own good, and was embroiled in severe trade friction with other nations.

Japan's trade problems in the 1980s were bittersweet to Japanese industrial leaders. Although trade conflicts were to be avoided at almost all costs, the existence of such conflicts was proof that Japan was the world's paramount producer. Superior ingenuity and competence were alone responsible for Japan's economic success. Could there have been a better comeback?

## THE GREAT TRADE IMBALANCE

The West has become vulnerable to the superiority and low price of Japanese products. Japanese manufacturers have precipitated bankruptcies and industrial restructuring in the United States and the EEC. Not all foreign producers can compete with Japanese products. However, in a capitalist world where free trade flourishes, the best man wins.

Many countries now have balance of trade deficits with Japan. The United States, however, has the largest deficit and the worst attitude. America blames Japan for its massive trade deficit. Such blame is misplaced.

The United States alone is responsible for its deficits. The $60 billion

1986 US trade deficit with Japan is not the result of Japanese trade restrictions or pricing. If Japan demolished every alleged barrier and were completely open (more open than any nation in the world has ever been), American companies would not seize much new market share in Japan; at best the total US trade deficit of $170 billion would shrink by $10 billion.

If, for instance, the Japanese market in meat were deregulated, Australia would underprice American beef, depriving American farmers of that market. Would the United States then accuse Australia of dumping meat in Japan? If the Japanese ban on rice imports were abolished, China and other Asian producers would underprice American rice. Would Washington then demand that Japanese consumers buy more expensive American rice in order to satisfy US farmers?

Japanese financial and trade policies have not been the causes of the more than $100 billion rise in US trade deficits during the period 1980–1986. For America's trade deficit has mushroomed against all of her major trading partners in Europe, Latin America, and Asia, and the ratio of the US trade deficit with Japan to the aggregate US trade deficit was roughly the same in 1987 as it was in 1980.

The cause of the expansion in magnitude of the US trade deficit is to be found in America's domestic policies and the patterns of private-sector savings and spending. If the United States wants to see its deficit with Japan and the rest of the world shrink it must reduce the domestic gap between savings and investment while maintaining a stable dollar.

Unfortunately, rather than considering these concrete actions, American legislators ignore macroeconomic fundamentals and blame their woes on Japan. Legislation which should focus on methods of resolving America's domestic problems is instead aimed against Japan, the modern-day scapegoat for Western failure.

## RIDING THE OMNIBUS

The Omnibus Trade Act of 1987 (approved by the Senate on 21 July) was intended to give American legislators the opportunity to take public action against Japan and other countries perceived as 'adversarial' partners in US trade. Through its more than 100 amendments, filling a thousand pages, the bill offered American politicians broad scope to retaliate against alleged inequities in Japan's trade practices. The bill was designed to limit presidential discretion on trade issues because the Administration has usually failed to retaliate against Japan and other nations.

For example, a telecommunications amendment* would authorize

_____
* Originally the Danforth telecommunications bill – S 596.

negotiations to open foreign telecommunications markets to US products and would require retaliation if the negotiations failed. Such a requirement could potentially be used as a lever to pry open global telecommunications markets which are, in any case, deregulating of their own accord.

Prominent among the trade bill's amendments was a 2–5 year import ban to be imposed on all products manufactured by the Toshiba Corporation and Kongsberg Vaapenfabrikk. In addition, the bill contained a series of proposals intended to force Japan to open its markets or buy more American products. Among these proposals was a move to investigate restrictions preventing American construction companies from participating fully in the construction of the proposed Kansai International Airport (discussed later in this chapter).

Other amendments required the President to take corrective measures in certain circumstances. If oil imports were to exceed 50 percent of demand, for example, then an oil import fee (or tax incentives) would be established in order to stimulate domestic drilling activity. Again, the authority to ban foreign investment if it threatens national security would enable the president to prohibit Japanese investors from purchasing US real estate. One such amendment, which would have required disclosure of foreign investment, was, however, rejected.

The Omnibus Trade Act was fashioned by American legislators into a house of horrors, containing every protectionist demon and troll which legislative imaginations could contrive. Not since the Smoot-Hawley tariff of 1930, have America's law-makers succumbed to anti-foreign mass hysteria on such a scale.

Ignoring the hard fact that Japanese imports of American products rose dramatically during the first half of 1987 and that Japanese exports to the United States decreased, Washington preferred to stick to their delusions. Refusing to examine real macroeconomic evidence, legislators instead invented their own microeconomic world and in so doing responded only to their own misconceptions.

## HOW TO CUT THE TAIL OFF A DOG
Imagine the highest ranking representatives of the United States Treasury visiting a sovereign nation and a vital American ally and forcefully demanding, in public, that that nation's financial system be restructured instantly. Seem far fetched? Imagine further that the country has the second largest economy in the free world and that the US Secretary of the Treasury himself calls a press conference in its capital city in order to slam his fist on a table and declare that if no action is taken the forces of protectionism in the US will get the upper hand.

It happened in March 1984. The US Treasury Secretary, Donald

Regan, and the Treasury Under-Secretary for Monetary Affairs, Beryl W. Sprinkel, made a trip to Tokyo. They did not visit Japan in order to view the cherry blossoms. Indeed, by arriving during the first several days of spring, they missed the full blossoming of the cherry trees. They did, however, arrive during the final days of the Japanese government's fiscal year. They had travelled halfway around the world in order to meet with their counterparts at the Japanese Ministry of Finance and to demand that Japan expand its tiny Euroyen market and swiftly deregulate all of its financial markets.

In Tokyo later that year, Beryl Sprinkel virtually commanded that Japan deregulate its financial system immediately and totally. 'The only way to cut the tail off a dog is with a single chop,' he informed the director general of the Banking Bureau of the Ministry of Finance.

Why should the structure of Japanese financial markets prompt such harsh and pressing US demands? What was at issue for the United States and Japan?

## THE IRON GRIP OF THE REGULATORS: THE CASE OF FINANCE

It is not possible fully to comprehend and appreciate the unique regulatory structure of Japanese financial markets without some idea of the historical conditions which influenced their development. Although it is impossible to present an adequate survey of Japanese financial history in a dozen pages, a brief sketch can nonetheless provide an indication of the unusual conditions which preceded the emergence of Japan's financial markets.

Little is known about Japan's early currency. The evolution of a monetized economy based on universally accepted exchange developed as the result of obligatory population movements. During the Tokugawa era, the feudal lords (*daimyo*) were required to live in Edo (Tokyo) with their families during alternate years. This requirement was imposed by the shogunate to reduce the likelihood of insurrections or revolution. Throughout the seventeenth and eighteenth centuries, Edo was probably the most populous city in the world with a population of 1–1.5 million. The continuous migrations in and out of Edo by the élite contributed to the development of a monetized economy. By the late eighteenth and nineteenth centuries most transactions were conducted in currency.

Gold, silver, and copper coins of varying weights and issuance circulated throughout the archipelago. Exchange brokers, specializing in dealing in the coins, provided the populace with an easy means of conversion from one medium to another. In Osaka, ten large currency dealing firms (known as the 'Big Ten') became so powerful that they functioned as what may have been Japan's first monetary authority. By the end of the Tokugawa era, debased metallic currency circulated freely in the national markets and paper money (*hansatsu*) issued by the *daimyo* circulated regionally.

Although Tokugawa Japan was devoid of modern financial institutions such as security firms, savings banks, life insurance companies and long-term credit banks, rudimentary financial institutions did exist. Exchange brokers and credit cooperatives (*mujin*) as well as organized guilds of money lenders were the precursors of modern financial institutions. But with the exception of simple, short-term bills of exchange, there were no fungible financial instruments nor were there securities. Most financing existed in order to provide loans to the extremes of the social strata: the ruling élite and small rural farmers.

At the beginning of the Meiji era, the price of gold in Japan was below, and the value of silver above, international market levels. As a result, gold poured out of Japan while silver flowed in. At this time, the Mexican silver dollar circulated widely in Japan as a trading currency. When the 'yen' was introduced in 1871 it was set at parity with the Mexican silver dollar. (The Mexican silver dollar was equal to one US dollar, and as a result an exchange rate of ¥1 = US$1 obtained.) The difference between domestic and world prices of gold and silver did not at first result in problems of valuation between the 'yen' and the currencies of other nations nor did it lead to other obvious disparities. Why this should have been the case is a mystery.

By the late 1890s, however, the yen had steadily depreciated against world currencies because of its linkage to the price of silver. In 1897, Japan adopted the gold standard. During the first decade of the twentieth century, the first significant sales of Japanese securities to foreigners occurred. These securities consisted largely of bonds to finance the Russo-Japanese War (1904–5) and small quantities of corporate stock.

The Japan of 1860 was divided into 262 autonomous feudal domains, each ruled by a feudal lord (a *daimyo*). The power of the shogunate which had loosely united these domains through a central government based in Edo, was rapidly eroding. In 1868, following a series of small civil wars (the Choshu Wars), the shogunate collapsed. A revolutionary government with the emperor (*Meiji*) as its figurehead established a new regime in 1868. The era inaugurated by the new government, known as the Meiji Restoration (1868–1912), was characterized by processes of modernization and industrialization which took place with unprecedented rapidity.

The new government was immediately faced with the critical problem of quickly establishing total centralized control of the 262 separate kingdoms, each *daimyo* representing a potential source of rebellion. The successful solution to this problem assured the development of modern Japanese finance.

In 1869, each *daimyo* was made governor of his former domain and was allotted an income consisting of 10 percent of the taxes (paid in rice) collected from the domain. At the same time the central government assumed the debt burden and financing of all local governments. The stipends that the *samurai* class (about six percent of the total population) had formerly received from the *daimyo* were initially maintained by the government and then substantially reduced.

In 1876, the government terminated the tithing of taxes to the *daimyo* and instead commuted their annual payments into one-time monetary pensions in the form of government bonds. This single reform had a profound effect on Japan's financial structure. Virtually overnight, the government had created a new financial instrument, that dwarfed all existing, non-monetary financial vehicles. This had indeed been its intention. Faced with the unique problem of creating a modern financial and industrial infrastructure able to compete with the West, the government arrived at perhaps the only solution possible. In a time when foreign loans – if available – were onerous and indigenous banking capital was small, it was necessary to establish a group of investors who: (1) possessed great non-liquid wealth in the form of government paper; (2) had little immediate or direct means of liquidating the government-issued debt; (3) were accustomed to wielding vast political power; (4) had been stripped of *de facto* political power; and, (5), had little means of acquiring political power through government. The government's hope was that the major recipients would use the bonds as capital to create financial and industrial enterprises.

Several types of bonds were issued, all saleable after September 1878. Most of the bonds bore interest at 7 percent. Subsequently the government made a vast distribution of bonds, representing an estimated 5 percent of national wealth, to roughly 400,000 samurai.*

The government's intention was partially realized. National banks were capitalized with ex-*daimyo* and some former *samurai* owning blocks of stock that they had acquired by tendering their bonds. The promulgation of the National Bank Act in 1872 led to the establishment of five national banks between 1873 and 1876, all of which were authorized to issue notes (redeemable in silver or gold) with

* See Raymond W. Goldsmith, *The Financial Development of Japan, 1868–1977*, p. 23.

government bonds as collateral. Some bonds were effectively monetized through acquisition by the banks.

The National Bank Act was a failure. Few notes were issued and most recipients of bank notes immediately chose to convert them to metal. In April 1876, a revision of the Act rendered bank notes inconvertible. As a result, the Japanese banking system (modelled on the US system) was firmly established by the end of the 1870s. By 1879, when the government halted the creation of national banks, a total of 151, all note issuing institutions, had opened their doors in Japan and filled the nation with paper yen. In 1882, the Bank of Japan, a central bank based on the structure of the *Banque Nationale de Belgique*, was created and became the sole note issuing body. By this time, inflation was rampant.

In 1885, the national banks had assets equal to an estimated 15 percent of the national product.* At first, former *daimyo* and *samurai* contributed the bulk of banking capital. Eventually, however, the deposits of landowners and small entrepreneurs represented a large portion of national banking assets. Following American and European models, a variety of financial institutions, ranging from commercial banks to insurance companies to a postal savings system were opened. Thus, during the first two decades of the Meiji era, all the elements of modern Japan's financial system were created.

Yet the established families were reluctant to gamble their capital by investing in expensive and risky industrial ventures. The enormous expense of funding the formation of factories and the training of labourers had no appeal to merchant families accustomed to a long risk-averse tradition. Instead, the government was forced to borrow from the same former feudal lords whose wealth it had increased through the issuance of bonds. Meanwhile, privately held capital was invested in trade and banking – including the extension of loans to the government – and not in industry.

Under the Meiji régime, leading families which had been given the special honour of extending loans to the shogun, under the Tokugawa shogunate, became directors of banks and the founders of industry. These families, the holders of the largest accumulations of privately owned wealth, wielded a burgeoning economic power. It was a power linked with the central government and inseparable from it; much of the wealth of these families took the form of government debt, either direct loans or bonds. Thus, the financial power of the former feudal nobility moved firmly into the banking sector, favouring lending above

* *Ibid.*, 25.

industrial investment. In this way, bank capital far exceeded industrial capital.

This posed a serious dilemma for the Japanese government. Though vast and populous, neighbouring China had been overrun by European occupiers and Western military might had recently pressured the former shogun to capitulate to foreign trade demands. That Japan might suffer the same fate as China seemed an imminent possibility in the world of the late nineteenth century. The solution to the problem was obvious but not easily obtainable: an army and navy capable of defeating a Western invasion force. The creation and continued support of modern armed forces required the immediate development of such key areas as shipbuilding, heavy industries, and mining.

Merchant families were unwilling to invest in untried, capital-intensive and risky industrial ventures and the new government was in no position to force powerful financial figures to cooperate with its plans. The central government itself was therefore obliged to undertake the task of funding a rapid industrialization which would ensure Japan's security against foreign military invasion (and the more insidious invasion of imported industrial goods).

Virtually overnight, the Meiji government became the biggest and most diversified entrepreneur in the world. The government nationalized all shipyards and iron foundries and hired foreign instructors to train personnel in the latest techniques. Technical institutes were established and staffed with foreign specialists. Japanese students were sent abroad for technical training. Similarly, transportation, communication, mining, and engineering were nurtured and developed with state funds and foreign instructors.

In short, Japan entered the modern industrial world in accordance with a master plan whose paramount purpose was the maximization of military advantage. Some strategic industries, targeted by the government as being the most crucial, developed so rapidly that in less than thirty years many were on a par with the West.

During the 1870s the government's Ministry of Industry became involved in all key military industries from the production of weapons and shipbuilding to railroads and telegraphs. Factories producing machine tools, bricks, cement, glass, and other materials were built in Tokyo. Railways linking key centres and opening domestic markets were constructed, and telephone and telegraph lines were rapidly erected.

To ensure the success of the few private strategic industries in Japan, the government heavily subsidized those ventures which it considered necessary. In 1874, for example, it gave Iwasaki Yataro, the founder of the Mitsubishi Company, a gift of thirteen ships and subsequently allowed his company to buy more, government-owned ships at a price far below cost. The Mitsubishi company was also given a substantial annual cash subsidy. Similarly, the Mitsui Company was given a portion of the textile mills and mines which had been confiscated from the shogun by the new state. Through government gifts and subsidies, four large 'houses' (Mitsui, Mitsubishi, Sumitomo, and Yasuda) and five lesser ones (Dai-Ichi, Kawasaki, Furukawa, Tanaka, and Asano) acquired, at formidable discounts, the vast holdings that were to become the core of Japan's military–industrial complex.

During the 1880s Japan's industrialized sector began to consolidate and became increasingly profitable. The handful of speculators who had purchased industries at extraordinarily low prices controlled a major portion of Japan's new industrial structure. Mitsui, Mitsubishi, Sumitomo, Yasuda and Dai-Ichi, which had each accumulated a range of crucial industries grouped like satellites around private banking enterprises, emerged as giant conglomerates, termed *zaibatsu* ('financial cliques').

Mitsui and Sumitomo, the two largest *zaibatsu*, developed from merchant families which had risen to prominence during the Tokugawa period. Other major *zaibatsu*, such as Mitsubishi, Yasuda, and Dai-Ichi, were created by entrepreneurs during the first twenty years of the Meiji Restoration. By the turn of the century, the *zaibatsu* had achieved predominance in Japan's domestic and international trade. In 1900, for example, Mitsui alone accounted for an estimated 10 percent of all Japanese imports and 20 percent of all Japanese exports.*

The *zaibatsu* and other business concerns were not the evolutionary result of a capitalist tradition. Instead, they were the product of a new state superimposed upon a society whose business past had been based on a system not unlike that of Europe's medieval guilds. In Tokugawa Japan, businessmen cooperated in associations which fixed prices and set production limits. The style of monopolistic cooperation which had characterized Tokugawa enterprise persisted in Meiji Japan. Thus, for example, in 1885 Mitsubishi and Mitsui merged their competing steamship lines into a single corporation, the Japan Mail Line (*Nippon Yusen Kaisha*). Cartels in industries such as cotton spinning were established.

An essential feature of the system was that the *zaibatsu* structured their diversified industries as interlocking combines in which the *zaibatsu*'s own private bank became the 'main' bank of member

* *Ibid.*, 63.

companies, providing most of their financing, while the member companies in turn cooperated in all areas of manufacturing and sales. During the first decades of the twentieth century, the *zaibatsu* grew through the vertical integration of manufacturing and raw materials acquisition and through horizontal expansion into other areas. By the late 1930s, war with Russia and the Manchurian invasion had stimulated the growth of strategic industries, further strengthening the *zaibatsu*.

In August 1946, a special commission, created by the Occupation authorities, began the task of overseeing the dissolution of the *zaibatsu* combines which were viewed as having been instrumental in involving Japan in the war. In an attempt to democratize Japanese industrial structure, the commission purged hundreds of corporate officers and prohibited corporate officials from serving more than one corporation at a time.

During the Occupation, senior representatives from the former Big Three *zaibatsu* – Mitsui, Mitsubishi, and Sumitomo – met frequently in private restaurants. The content of the discussions among these executives is, of course, unknown. What is well known is that they considered strategies of cooperation and consolidation that would facilitate the restructuring of the firms that had once been the core industries of the *zaibatsu* conglomerates.

The *zaibatsu* banks, which had not been dismantled, played a central role in the reorganizations which were to occur during the years following the end of the Occupation in 1952. By becoming the centre of new enterprise groupings, based on the prewar holding company structures, the banks were able to adopt the role of primary lender to all member companies.

Following the reopening of the stock exchanges in 1949, the banks and the companies which clustered around them (in a loose postwar version of the holding company structure) purchased small volumes (from 0.5–3 percent) of each other's stock. The resulting interlocked cross-shareholding made the banks both creditors and shareholders in the member companies. It also sealed control of the corporations within the group. Termed *keiretsu* these new conglomerate groupings became an intrinsic part of postwar Japanese business and finance.

By 1960 the four great prewar *zaibatsu* (Mitsubishi, Mitsui, Sumitomo, and Yasuda) had been reincarnated as postwar *keiretsu*. The three biggest maintained their former names while Yasuda became Fuyo (Fuji). In addition, the Sanwa and Dai-Ichi banks each became the centre of massive corporate groupings.

By 1980, 190 major Japanese corporations were core companies within the six groups. The six giant *keiretsu*, together with their related and dependent companies, accounted for an estimated 50 percent of all capital stock in Japan.

In the absence of holding companies, the *keiretsu* maintained 'presidents' clubs.' So, for example, the Mitsubishi *keiretsu's* 'Friday Club' (*Kinyo Kai*) includes the presidents of 28 core companies led by the Mitsubishi Corporation, the Mitsubishi Bank, and Mitsubishi Heavy Industries (see Table 3–1). In precisely the same way, the 'Monday Club' (*Nimoku Kai*) of the Mitsui *keiretsu* consists of three leading companies (including the main bank and the trading company) and twenty other core companies. Much the same situation obtains for the 'White Waters Club' (*Hakusui Kai*) of the Sumitomo *keiretsu*.

The major shareholders of each company belonging to a particular *keiretsu* are group members. For example, the five largest shareholders in Mitsubishi Oil are the Mitsubishi Corporation (20 percent), Tokio Marine and Fire Insurance (5 percent), Mitsubishi Bank (5 percent), and Mitsubishi Trust & Banking (4 percent). This type of interlocked cross-shareholding (beneficial shareholding) is a characteristic component of *keiretsu* groupings and serves to insulate each company from outside control.

The chairmen, presidents, and directors of many companies within a *keiretsu* are the retired or seconded executives of the leading companies within the *keiretsu*. In addition, the main bank, at the core of the *keiretsu*, is the primary lender to each of its *keiretsu* colleagues. During the 1970s, and particularly during the 1980s, the key role of the main bank began to break down, but the *keiretsu* groupings still remain strong today.

Working in conjunction with Japan's corporate structure, a highly segmented financial system fuelled the extraordinary economic growth of postwar Japan. Large commercial banks based in cities ('city banks') provided short-term lending to Japan's leading corporations. These banks were prohibited from selling, issuing, and underwriting bonds. Long-term credit banks were allowed to issue debentures, but were prohibited from taking deposits (other than from borrowers or government). Small, specialized financial institutions accepted deposits and channelled these deposits to the city banks. Trust banks and insurance companies managed pension funds while securities companies sold stocks and managed investment trusts. Thus, rigid distinctions were established between the banking and securities industries, between banking and trust business, and between long-term and short-term finance.

Stable interest rates and relatively low inflation helped the Japanese savings rate to become the world's highest. During the era of double-digit growth, Japan's specialized banking enclaves smoothly

## CORE MEMBERS OF THE MITSUBISHI KEIRETSU
## (THE KINYO KAI)

---

*Leading companies*

Mitsubishi Corporation
Mitsubishi Bank
Mitsubishi Heavy Industries

*Finance*

Mitsubishi Trust & Banking
Meiji Mutual Life Insurance
Tokio Marine and Fire Insurance

*Chemicals*

Mitsubishi Gas Chemical
Mitsubishi Petrochemical
Mitsubishi Chemical Industries
Mitsubishi Plastic Industries
Mitsubishi Monsanto Chemical

*Steel & Metals*

Mitsubishi Metal
Mitsubishi Steel
Mitsubishi Aluminium

*Electric and Machinery*

Mitsubishi Electric
Mitsubishi Motors
Nippon Kogaku
Mitsubishi Kakoki

*Real Estate and Construction*

Mitsubishi Estate
Mitsubishi Construction
Mitsubishi Mining and Cement

*Petroleum*

Mitsubishi Oil

*Transportation and Warehousing*

Mitsubishi Warehouse & Transportation
Nippon Yusen

*Others*

Kirin Brewery
Mitsubishi Paper Mills
Mitsubishi Rayon
Asahi Glass

---

channelled bank deposits to those industrial sectors which were judged by the government to be the most vital to the national economy.

In 1964 Japan became a member of the Organization for Economic Cooperation and Development (OECD). This marked the beginning of Japan's gradual elimination of capital controls and financial regulations. As Japan's domestic and international direct investments increased, international financial transactions were slowly deregulated. The decline of Japan's economic growth rate led to a parallel decline in lending opportunities for domestic banking institutions, motivating them to look to overseas capital markets.

In December 1980 the Foreign Exchange and Foreign Trade Control Law was revised. Free, at least in principle, the new law allowed Japanese funds to flow abroad without formal restriction. Long-term capital outflows grew from about $10 billion in 1981 to $86 billion in 1986. By 1984, Japan was the world's largest single supplier of cash and by 1985 had surpassed Opec to become the world's number one creditor.

The unprecedented wealth of Japan's banks and securities companies gave them a strong voice at the Ministry of Finance when they articulated their demands for greater freedom in the financial markets. Meanwhile, domestic investors – particularly corporations – ceased to be satisfied with Japan's traditionally low interest rates and the narrow range of financial instruments available.

As this pressure for greater freedom built up, the Japanese government was also confronted with the need to do something about its own massive debt – largely a consequence of the 1973–74 oil 'shock' – which was scheduled to become due in increasing volumes during the middle and late 1980s. The total value of outstanding government bonds had grown from ¥10 trillion in 1974 to more than ¥134 trillion in 1985. The need to rollover this mountain of maturing bonds promised to require vast leverage that would force up domestic interest rates.

The most myopic of regulatory authorities at the Ministry of Finance could read the writing on the wall. 'Weighed, weighed, counted, and divided.' Japan's segmented financial system could not continue in its current state. Internally, institutions and corporations were demanding systemic change, and, to make matters more pressing still, US financial markets were being liberalized and American authorities were howling for comparable changes in Japan.

Modern Japanese finance originates with the allied Occupation when US experts reorganized the country's industrial structure and introduced the concept of commercial banking. It is therefore not surprising that during the 1970s and 1980s deregulation in the United States was watched carefully in Japan. The abolition of interest rate ceilings and the disintegration of the Glass-Steagall Act (discussed in Chapter 4) served to introduce an intense competitiveness to American finance. These precedents were used to justify Treasury Secretary Regan's vociferous demands that Japan liberalize its financial sector. Regan's aim was twofold: to allow US banks to participate in a broad range of financial services in Japan and, more important (from the US perspective), to force the yen to become far more international.

The US Treasury Department believed that the yen was substantially undervalued against the dollar. It regarded this undervaluation as the direct result of Japan's closed markets and the provincial character of the Japanese economy.

A weak yen gave Japanese products an unfair competitive advantage in world markets. This, in turn, served to increase the US balance of trade deficit with Japan. In 1983, $22 billion of the $70 billion US trade deficit was with Japan. The US Treasury argued that strengthening the yen was the most effective way to diminish this trade imbalance.

Regan urged the Japanese government to 'internationalize' its currency in order to strengthen the yen. In 1984, barely 3 percent of Japan's imports and 42 percent of its exports were priced in yen. The yen represented less than 4 percent of the reserves of the world's central banks, compared with roughly 71 percent held in dollars and nearly 12 percent held in deutsch marks. Although a massive market in Eurodollars had thrived for two decades, a market in Euroyen was virtually nonexistent.

Regan argued insistently that the deregulation of Japan's interest rate structure was now imperative. From the American point of view, it was vital that foreign institutions be allowed to participate in Japan's domestic financial markets on an equal basis with domestic institutions. Regan also demanded that the tiny market in Euroyen bonds be expanded. American officials believed that the global use of the yen would grow substantially if Japanese and foreign entities were permitted to issue yen-denominated bonds outside Japan.

Regan threatened that if Japan failed to open the Euroyen market, so paving the way for a more international yen, the Japanese banks would be the targets of new US trade sanctions. Regan and his fellow negotiators referred to legislation proposed by Senator Jake Garn, then chairman of the Senate Banking Committee. If approved, the Garn bill would have allowed US regulators to review the status of US banks in particular foreign markets when evaluating banking applications. Thus, if Japanese regulators failed to give fair treatment to US banks operating in Japan, American regulators could retaliate by refusing to approve the applications of Japanese institutions to establish banking operations in the US or to acquire American banks.

Representatives at the Ministry of Finance flatly rejected the US formulations regarding Japan's domestic financial controls. They dismissed as spurious any suggestion of a correlation between financial market regulation and the dollar's strength against the yen. Instead, they asserted that the US Treasury was obfuscating the issue by ignoring the key influence of the US budget deficit. The dollar's strength against the yen was the direct result of high US interest rates which were, in turn, the product of burgeoning US government debt. The abolition of Japan's domestic financial market controls would have little impact on the international use of the yen. Ministry officials pointed out that key imports, such as oil, were denominated in dollars not yen.

According to officials, the US government was deliberately confusing three distinct areas:

1 The relationship between the yen and the dollar on the exchange markets
2 The provincial character of the yen
3 Opportunities for foreign financial institutions in Japan

As a result, American concerns regarding the overvaluation of the dollar against the yen were being intertwined with pressures to allow US corporations to raise funds in the Euromarkets and to participate in Japan's promising domestic financial markets.

Furthermore, Japanese economists were quick to point out, there was no necessary correlation between reserve currency status and the appreciation of a particular currency. American demands that the yen become an international currency were irrelevant to American desires that the yen appreciate against the dollar. Japanese negotiators held their ground firmly, repeatedly emphasizing to their American counterparts what they saw as the key point: high US interest rates were *alone* responsible for the undervaluation of the yen against the dollar.

Japanese regulators feared that if the yen were allowed to be freely influenced by market forces the result could be catastrophic. They maintained that strong appreciation of the yen against the dollar would lead to higher interest rates, increased domestic inflation, and dramatically slower economic growth. Japan's controlled interest rates and tightly maintained monetary policy were perceived as essential to Japan's steady economic growth and low inflation.

American negotiators countered, of course, that rather than US interest rates being too high, Japanese interest rates were too low. They accused the Japanese government of keeping interest rates artificially low in order to assist domestic corporations and, increasingly, to help finance its budget deficit. American economists dismissed Japanese claims that a strong yen and higher interest rates would lead to inflation.

The Japanese perceived the issue differently. Ultimately, they believed, the Americans were cynically exploiting the issue of the US balance of trade deficit with Japan in order to prise open Japan's closed domestic financial market system. The US had become obsessed with the opening of Japan's markets to foreign institutions and was using heavy-handed threats to force dangerously rapid change. Privately, Japanese regulators noted that Secretary of the Treasury Regan had formerly been chairman of Merrill Lynch, the largest securities firm in the United States. Perhaps, they hinted, Regan had his own special interest in foreign participation in Japanese capital markets.

Japan's financial deregulation, which had been moving at a snail's pace (but moving nonetheless) for twenty years, entered a new phase in May 1984 when two reports were issued in Tokyo: 'The Current Status and Future Prospects for the Liberalization of Financial Markets and Internationalization of the Yen' by the Ministry of Finance and the 'Report by the Working Group of Joint Japan-US Ad Hoc Group on Yen/Dollar Exchange Rate, Financial and Capital Market Issues.' These dry and verbose bureaucratic titles concealed proposals for a complete overhaul of Japan's financial market structure.

In March 1984, when Regan pounded his fist on a Tokyo table, Washington was frantic to achieve a high profile agreement with Tokyo on the opening of Japan's capital markets. Such an agreement, it was believed, would assuage a host of domestic US trade pressures. At that time, Japanese exports were flooding US markets because, it was argued, the yen was simply too cheap in terms of the dollar.

The 66-page report released by the 'Ad Hoc Group' of the US-Japan Committee on the yen and the dollar, expressed Japan's agreement to liberalize its domestic capital markets, to ensure that foreign financial institutions be given the 'opportunity to participate fully in Japan's domestic financial system,' and to expand the Euroyen bond and banking markets. A key concession on Japan's part was an agreement to move steadily towards market-determined interest rates. No mention, however, was made of small deposit rates. The US Treasury Department reciprocated these promises by agreeing to continue efforts to reduce the budget dificit. Thus, while adopting the guise of a mutual exchange of promises, the yen–dollar accord was essentially a medium for documenting Japan's acquiescence to American pressure.

Japan fulfilled its promises. Not only did it deregulate its financial markets in 1985–87, as specified in the accord, it also permitted foreign institutions wider opportunities for participation. Foreign securities firms joined the Tokyo Stock Exchange and nine foreign banks were granted trust banking licences. The Ministry of Finance granted dozens of foreign securities firms the four licences necessary to qualify them as full securities companies in Japan. Foreign investment management companies were also granted licences to manage domestic funds.

As a result of the many changes implemented in the financial sector, Tokyo's status as a centre for international finance slowly began to match that of New York and London. Widening foreign participation in Japanese financial markets thus provides proof that foreign companies are welcome to compete with domestic firms in their quest for business. Yet, they continue to complain.

## THEY DON'T SPEAK OUR LANGUAGE: THE CASE OF THE KANSAI INTERNATIONAL AIRPORT

There is a Japanese proverb that says, 'When you come to a place, follow its customs.' In the West, the same sentiment is expressed by the maxim, 'When in Rome, do as the Romans do.' Yet foreign businesses have expected to walk into the Japanese marketplace and sell their products or services without regard for Japan's unique customs.

Foreign demands for participation in the construction of a planned new Kansai airport are a prime example of this insensitivity. The Kansai region is located in the centre of Honshu, Japan's main island; together with the Kanto region, it contains more than 50 percent of Japan's population and the lion's share of the nation's industry. Just as Tokyo is the capital of the Kanto region, so Osaka is the capital of the Kansai region.

When, in 1968, planners first proposed building the Kansai International airport (to replace the suburban Osaka International Airport) they never dreamed that two decades later the airport would become a symbol of the trade conflict between Japan and the United States. But it did.

The Kansai airport has propelled Japan's construction industry into the international limelight. The publicity has not been welcome. The Japanese construction industry is quite big, employing about 10 percent of Japan's work force and producing a substantial share of the nation's GNP. There are more than half a million contractors in Japan, ranging from massive construction companies to tiny sub-subcontractors.

The linkages between many construction companies and organized crime are known to be close and complex. According to the *Far Eastern Economic Review*, the Japanese police 'estimate that as many as 1,000 construction firms are under the control, or at least indirect influence, of gangster syndicates; and official police figures show that nearly 50 percent of all corruption cases ... implicating national and local government officials are tied to the construction industry.'* The Japanese construction industry practises a limited bid tendering system called *dango*. *Dango* is a form of bid-rigging in which projects are parcelled out in accordance with informal agreements. These agreements are an expression of the long-term relationships among construction firms, suppliers and government bureaucrats. Only 'authorized corporations' holding contractor's licences are eligible to participate in the *dango* system.

With a price tag of ¥1 trillion, the proposed Kansai International Airport, will be the most expensive airport ever built. About 75 percent of the cost will be consumed by the construction of an artificial island 511 hectares in area and located five kilometres out in Osaka Bay. Although the airport will be quite small (with a single runway 3500 metres long), it is designed to handle nearly double the number of passengers and five times the volume of cargo which currently passes through the Osaka International Airport. The airport, which is due to open in spring 1993, would be operational 24 hours per day and would generate a major expansion of business in the Kansai region.

Not surprisingly, foreign construction companies expressed a strong desire to bid for portions of the project. Their failure to procure major contracts† aroused anger and indignation in the United States and Europe. Incensed US construction corporations voiced four objections:

1   Between 1980 and 1985, the US was the world's leading exporter of construction services with contracts exceeding $225 billion. The comparable figure for Japan was less than $50 billion.
2   American construction corporations are more experienced than the Japanese at building big airports.
3   While Japanese construction firms enjoyed open access to the United States with $3 billion worth of contracts in 1986, no US firm had won a major construction contract in Japan since 1965.

---

* Bruce Roscoe, 'The tightest of closed shops still prospers ... ,' *Far Eastern Economic Review*, 11 June 1987, p. 71.
† The Bechtel Group Inc (the world's biggest construction/engineering firm) was given a small contract for the design and construction of an airport terminal.

4   The strong appreciation of the yen against the dollar enables US construction companies to underprice their Japanese counterparts.

Speaking on behalf of the United States construction industry, Senator Frank Murkowski suggested in 1986 that all federal airport and public works construction bids be closed to Japanese firms until American construction companies were allowed to participate in the construction of the new Kansai airport.

The president of the Kansai International Airport Company (KIAC) was perplexed by these foreign complaints. He questioned 'whether Americans are putting enough effort into entering the Japanese market'* and pointed out that although the initial civil engineering work had long since been contracted to Japanese construction companies, many opportunities were still available for foreign participation in other portions of the project.

In fact, a number of Japanese companies did extend offers of collaboration to American companies. It is also highly relevant that few (if any) American contractors had the land reclamation experience called for in a project of such exceptional magnitude. Furthermore, no foreign contractors held licences qualifying them to do civil engineering jobs in Japan.†

American companies are not willing to make the necessary efforts to conform to the Japanese environment. The staff of foreign construction companies do not speak Japanese and cannot communicate adequately with Japanese workers. As the president of the Kansai International Airport put it, 'Whether it's civil engineering or whatever, work cannot be done unless the workers understand.'‡

Foreign corporations seem to think that they can walk into Japan and conduct business on their own terms. Japan, however, is a sovereign nation with its own institutions and established traditions. Foreign construction firms can succeed in Japan only if they are willing to conform to Japanese expectations.

Japan is a unique country with traditions and characteristics which Westerners cannot appreciate. The issues are complex and misunderstood by special interest groups which quote trade statistics in support of their own limited concerns.

The long-term relationships which play such an important role in Japanese business are grounded in deeply embedded institutions

---

* Quoted in 'US criticized for "failures" in Japan deals,' *Financial Times*, 23 June 1987, p. 6.
† In September 1987, the Construction Ministry appointed the Bechtel Group Inc, as an authorized corporation eligible to receive a contractor's license.
‡ *Ibid.*

which cannot be dissolved. Japanese traditions, including reciprocity, embrace everyone from the poorest farmer to the most eminent politicians. Other countries hoping to do business in Japan would like to reap the benefits which belong to a long-term relationship.

Foreign participation in domestic business is welcome. However, foreign businesses must play by Japanese rules in Japan. It goes without saying that those foreign institutions which come to Japan and are sensitive to the Japanese way of doing business are likely to find success.

Abrasive and tactless foreign demands that Japan dissolve its established structures in order to allot foreign competitors a share of domestic markets are counterproductive. Japan will change at its own pace in its own way. Meanwhile, no good will come of foreigners making demands without taking full account of Japanese values. This is exemplified by the case of agriculture.

## JAPANESE AGRICULTURE: THE NEED TO BE SELF-SUFFICIENT

Japanese farmers, like masters of pottery or *bunraku*, are regarded as a national treasure. The farmer's methods, like those of the potter, may not be the most efficient and his products are admittedly quite expensive; nonetheless, farmers, like potters, need to be nurtured and preserved lest their art disappear. If there were no Japanese farmers, the Japanese people would be obliged to eat only imported food. This would not only involve an even greater dependence on foreign sources, but in some elusive way it would entail a dilution of the link (discussed in Chapter 3) between the Japanese and the land that gives them their sense of identity.

Japanese farms, with an average size of barely 1.2 hectares (2.47 acres), are the smallest to be found among the industrialized nations. The typical farm is too small to support a family and requires just one person to tend it. In the United States, by contrast, the average farmer tends an area of 45 hectares, or 37.5 times more land than his Japanese counterpart.

Japanese agriculture is far less productive *per capita* than manufacturing and most other forms of economic activity, and the agricultural sector produces less than 4 percent of Japan's total GNP. Nevertheless, Japanese farmers are by far the most powerful political lobby in Japan.

How could farmers, Japan's most inefficient producers, who are for the most part incapable of achieving self-sufficiency from their profession, have become and remained king-makers in a trillion dollar economy based on financial services and manufacturing? The answer to that question is the key to understanding many of the barriers blocking Japan's trade doors.

In Japan, agricultural products represent a specially protected enclave. Of Japan's 27 import quotas, 22 apply to agricultural commodities and one of the most rigorous systems of import controls in the free world insulates Japan's food from global competition. Import quotas on products ranging from peanuts to steak have resulted in domestic prices that are from three to ten times above market levels in the United States and other free world countries. At the same time, agricultural imports are subject to non-tariff barriers such as detailed customs evaluations stipulating stringent health standards. As a result, food prices absorb an estimated 30 percent of the average wage-earner's disposable income compared to 20 percent in Europe and 17 percent in the US.

In a country renowned for the efficiency of its production techniques, Japan's agriculturalists stand out as a curious anomaly. Using inefficient and costly methods, protected by import barriers and expensive price support mechanisms, Japanese farmers are an odd bunch. Only 13 percent of the farming families in Japan are able to support themselves from their harvests.* Without the largest agricultural subsidies in the free world, the percentage would be virtually zero.

Because the average Japanese farm is today too small to support a family, most Japanese farmers (and their family members) work in non-agricultural jobs to supplement their income.† Thus, weekend farming has become common in Japan. The small farm size has forced neighbouring farmers to pool their resources in order to buy automated equipment, farming their rice fields communally.

While non-tariff barriers keep out foreign agricultural produce, government subsidies insure that farmers profit. Eighty percent of Japan's agricultural products are subject to subsidies which will cost the government about $40 billion during fiscal year 1987. Moreover, government-mandated prices are estimated to cost the consumer an additional $20 billion. It has been estimated that if all protection were removed from the agricultural sector, permitting unrestricted imports, the cost of food for the average Japanese consumer would decrease by two-thirds.

---

* In 1980, Japan had 600,000 full-time farms and 4 million part-time farms. Thus, for the majority of Japan's farm population, farming is a subsidiary activity. See, Hillman, Jimmye S. and Rothenberg, Robert A, 'Wider Implications of Protecting Japan's Rice Farmers,' World Economy, vol. 8, March 1985, pp. 43–62.

† Hillman and Rothenberg point out that because part-time farmers who enter the work force receive lower wages than other industrial workers, they have 'helped to sustain the growth, profitability, and capital accumulation of secondary and tertiary industries in Japan.' (Ibid., p. 49.)

In terms of economic rationality, Japanese agriculture is a peculiar phenomenon. Indeed, if Adam Smith ruled Japan, there would not be a farmer in the archipelago.

How did this situation come about? How long will it last?

One of the most successful and durable of the reforms introduced by MacArthur during the early years of the Occupation was the Land Reform. The reform programme, which adopted the slogan 'land to the working farmer', reduced pure land tenancy (under which farmers owned less than 10 percent of the land which they cultivated) from more than 30 percent to 5 percent in two years. This redistribution was achieved by taking land from landlords* and giving small allotments to the tenants who farmed the land. In his inimitable style, MacArthur summarized the effect of the reform: 'Japan was transferred from a feudal economy of impoverished serfs and tenant farmers into a nation of free landholders. . . . Every farmer in the country was now a capitalist in his own right.'†

At the same time as they organized the land reform, the Occupation authorities mapped out electoral districts to which representatives were apportioned on the basis of population. Thus, the number of representatives in the *Diet* to which a district was entitled was determined entirely by the size of the district's population in relation to the population as a whole.

Throughout the subsequent years during which the Liberal Democratic Party (LDP) has ruled Japan, farming families have continued to wield the political clout which this system put into their hands. Their power has ensured the maintenance of the formidable barriers which have protected the farmers' produce from foreign encroachment and world market prices. As a result, the average household income for farming families (including income from non-agricultural sources) is more than 10 percent higher than that of urban 'salarymen'. Farmers pay less taxes, live in larger homes, and own more cars than urban workers.

As the effects of rural–urban migration became more pronounced during the 1970s, the population of Japan's rural farming areas declined drastically. Increasing numbers of farming children decided to move to the cities and abandon farming. Thus, the median age of farmers rose from 41 years in 1960 to 52 years in 1987.‡ But the representation of rural districts in the *Diet* was not modified to take

---

*Technically, the land was bought by the government. However, because pre-inflation prices were paid, the land was actually expropriated.

† Douglas MacArthur, *Reminiscences*. New York: McGraw-Hill, 1964, p. 359.

‡ After retiring from a full-time job, many part-time farmers become full-time farmers. Thus farming is a retirement activity in Japan, providing fulfilling work and a vital supplement to a pension or annuity.

account of demographic changes, and farmers continued to provide the LDP (Liberal Democratic Party) with its primary base of support. In 1987, farmers exercised an estimated 25 percent of Japan's voting power although they totalled only about 6 percent of the nation's population. With roughly 60 percent of its members representing rural or semi-rural districts, the *Diet* has been quick to respond to the farmers' demands.

The continuing decline in the size of the agricultural population during the 1980s caused a growing disparity between the number of votes required to elect a member to the *Diet* from a rural area and the far higher number required to elect a member from an urban area. As a result, the Japanese Supreme Court ruled that for the population of urban voting districts to exceed that of a rural district by a factor greater than three was a breach of the constitution. This decision led to small adjustments in the size of a few electoral districts. The Supreme Court is likely to make further decisions against gerrymandering which will alter the legal ratio to two in the near future, thus diminishing the political influence of farming districts and slightly increasing the power of urban districts.

But although changes in population distribution are shrinking the constituency of the farmers' union (*Nokyo*) and judicial decisions may reduce the farmers' voting power, it will be quite some time before Japan's farmers lose their crucial political influence. *Nokyo*, after all, contributes an estimated $110 million per year to its supporters in the *Diet*.

Nokyo's eight million members are politically conservative and, almost without exception, support the LDP. Thus, for the present, farmers remain a consolidated and well-organized voting bloc capable of determining the outcome of national elections. Every faction in the LDP depends upon the farm vote for the maintenance of its influence.

It is because urban voters believe that farmers reduce, by however slight a degree, the magnitude of Japan's dependence on the outside world that there has not been a popular outcry condemning the farmers' disproportionate political influence. However, the release of the Maekawa report (in April 1986) which urged increased consumption, imports and new housing, has helped to legitimate urban concerns about the LDP's preference for rural rather than urban development.

Rice is the centrepiece and staple of Japanese cuisine, having much the same connotations for the Japanese as bread, 'the staff of life', has for Westerners. Although the Japanese diet is rapidly changing, highly polished white rice still represents the mainstay of Japanese meals and the food eaten with rice is considered to be secondary in importance to the rice itself. The word for cooked rice in Japanese (*gohan*) also means 'meal'. *Sake*, an alcoholic beverage made from fermented rice, is consumed in a variety of symbolic rituals.

Rice for consumption, for storage, and for secondary purposes (for use in rice cakes, *sake*, and other products) is Japan's key cash crop. Nearly all irrigatable land in Japan has been devoted to wet rice agriculture, with other crops grown only in those fields that can not easily be made into flooded paddies. As a result, about half of all farmland is used to grow wet rice.

Much of this farmland, representing roughly one quarter of *all* non-mountainous habitable land in Japan, has soared in value. But although a good deal of the land is located in the Tokyo and Osaka metropolitan areas, where land prices are the highest in the world, it is rarely sold. Emotional attachments certainly contribute to the reluctance of farmers to sell their small parcels of land, but the key factor is taxation. For while farmland is virtually untaxed, a farmer who sold his land would transfer most of the profit to the government in the form of taxes, thus gaining little money and losing government subsidies as well as his family heritage.*

Despite the attention Japan devotes to rice agriculture, the country is by no means the world's biggest producer. With a harvest of about 11 million tons per year, Japan ranks eighth among the world's rice producers, supplying just 3.1 percent of total world production in 1983 compared to 37.7 percent for China and 16.5 percent for India.

The most costly of all the government's agricultural subsidies has been the support that has propped up Japan's rice farming. All rice imports are banned in Japan and, in order to ensure that Japan produce sufficient rice to satisfy its domestic consumption, the government purchases the bulk of the rice harvest at a fixed price determined each year (in 1987 it was roughly $2,000 per ton, or nearly ten times the average world price). This price is intended to counterbalance the extremely high cost of producing rice in Japan, which is about three times greater than in the US and six to eight times higher than in Indonesia or Thailand. The price support mechanism also ensures that Japanese farmers remain solvent.

Most of the other agricultural produce consumed in Japan is imported and the agricultural sector accounts for roughtly 14 percent

* The situation in Japan's cities is similar to that in the countryside. In Tokyo, for example, 6 percent of the land area consists of small plots of farmland scattered throughout the city. Because taxes on *urban* farmland are negligible, urban 'farmers' (who work in full-time city jobs and farm on weekends), like their rural counterparts, have little incentive to sell their tiny plots to developers. It has been estimated that Tokyo's residential area would increase by 10–15 percent if all the patches of farmland were converted to housing.

of Japanese imports. Because most of Japan's grain consumption is imported (68 percent in 1983 compared to 36 percent for Britain and 20 percent for West Germany) Japanese consumers have felt strongly that Japan should at least be self-sufficient in the production of rice. After all, Japan imports 95 percent of its wheat and 99.5 percent of its maize. The dramatic increase in the world price of wheat and maize that occurred in 1979 served to reinforce Japan's determination not to depend upon foreign suppliers for its rice.

In order to avoid a national rice surplus, many Japanese farmers are paid subsidies to cultivate crops other than rice. After buying the national rice crop, the government sells the rice to distributors at a big discount. Nevertheless, by the time the rice reaches the consumer, its price has risen substantially, and Japanese consumers pay more for their rice than their counterparts elsewhere in the world. Meanwhile, the Japanese have been eating less rice as their diets have become increasingly Westernized. Rice consumption has declined by 34 percent since 1960 and is likely to fall an additional 12 percent before 1990.

In 1986, the government reduced the price it paid to farmers for rice by 6.6 percent. Although subsequent 'negotiations' resulted in a halving of the reduction, Japan's influential *Zenchu* (the Central Union for Agricultural Cooperatives) and *Nokyo* (the farmers' union) were still dissatisfied with this compromise and systematically 'lobbied' LDP representatives, reminding them of their dependence on rural electoral support. Within a month, Prime Minister Nakasone announced that no reductions would be made in the price the government paid for rice. In 1987, however, mounting pressures led to a 5.95 percent reduction. Although the price cut will not affect consumers, it was the first such reduction in more than two decades and was an indication of a new government responsiveness to consumer dissatisfaction with high agricultural prices.

Japan's trading partners, led by the United States, have been clamouring for the demolition of the regulatory structure that protects Japanese farmers from foreign competition. It is argued that the abolition of the barriers that exclude agricultural imports could lead to a rapid reduction in Japan's trade surplus with the US and the EEC.

American rice farmers have demanded that Washington pressure Japan to open its rice market to US imports. The cost of American rice to Japanese consumers would be less than half that of Japan's domestic crop; nonetheless, Japanese government, farmers, and consumers want to maintain the *status quo*. The farmers enjoy their subsidized benefits, the LDP is dependent upon the farm vote, and

Japanese consumers believe that their country should be self-sufficient in rice.

Japanese farm trade negotiators have been pointing out for years that Japan is the biggest single export market for US agricultural products and that US farmers therefore have nothing to complain about. The Ministry of Agriculture maintains that the complete opening of Japan's agricultural markets would have a negligible effect on the US trade deficit with Japan.

In general, Japanese authorities have responded indignantly to foreign insistence that their agricultural markets be deregulated. They point out that all industrial countries subsidize and protect farming. US farming subsidies through the Commodity Credit Corporation, for example, totalled $16 billion in 1984 and the US imposes strict tariffs and import quotas on food products ranging from beef to sugar. Similarly, the EEC has established price supports which assure European farmers of high prices, regardless of the world market and, by virtue of protectionist policies, the prices of such commodities as milk and butter have been so artificially buoyed that the EEC has gained a disproportionate world market share.

Privately, Japanese bureaucrats express exasperation at demands by the US and other foreign countries that Japan relax all restrictions on agricultural imports. Japan, a nation with few natural resources, is obliged to import nearly all key staples, including 99.8 percent of its crude oil, 98 percent of its iron ore and all of its wool and raw cotton. A major industrial nation cannot afford to depend upon other nations for its food and thus render itself perpetually vulnerable to global commodity fluctuations and political risk.

The industrial nations which trade with Japan counter these defensive arguments with the observation that many non-tariff barriers in Japan are irrelevant to the emotive issues of food self-sufficiency. Take the case of wheat.

In fiscal year 1986, Japanese wheat consumption was about 4.7 million tons, of which 85 percent was imported from the United States, the EEC or Australia. The Japanese government, acting as the exclusive agent in all wheat purchases and sales, paid ¥43,686 per ton for imported wheat and ¥184,867 – 4.2 times as much – for domestic wheat. The government then sold the wheat to flour millers at a fixed price of ¥85,524, or double the price paid for the imported grain and less than half the price paid for the domestic grain. In this way, the domestic wheat market has been supported by subsidies and price manipulations at the expense of the Japanese consumers *and* foreign farmers.

Frustrated with Japan's regulations restricting agricultural trade, members of the EEC formally charged that, under the General Agreement on Tariffs and Trade (GATT), Japan's economic system was itself a trade barrier. From this perspective, the entire character and structure of the Japanese economy preclude open trade. The United States has concurred with this view and has sought more frequent GATT summits (every two years instead of every four) in order to pressure Japan to deregulate its agricultural sector.

In April 1987, US Agriculture Secretary Richard Lyng visited Japan in order to initiate comprehensive bilateral trade discussions. He demanded that Japan import rice (under a quota system), eliminate quotas on the importation of beef and oranges, relax restrictions on a dozen other agricultural products (including peanuts and processed cheese) and lower import tariffs on chocolate from 20 percent to 7 percent. Mutsuki Kato, Japan's minister of agriculture, forestry and fisheries, refused to let rice become an issue for bilateral trade negotiations and hedged the government's position on Lyng's other demands.

From the perspective of Japan's bureaucrats, farmers, and consumers, Japan has the right to determine what it will import and what it will produce at home. Japan, an island nation with few natural resources, depends upon imports for its survival. That Japan's food supplies, particularly rice, should be controlled by foreign producers is anathema to the Japanese people. They consider that it is the fate of Japan's consumers to bear the high cost of national self-sufficiency in food.

If all Japanese government farm subsidies and import barriers were demolished, then Japanese consumers would spend substantially less money on food. Some of the money thus saved, argue US trade representatives, would be spent on purchasing more imported products, thus relieving US and EEC trade deficits, and much of the rest would be spent on various services and domestic products, so stimulating an expansion of the Japanese economy.

It will, however, be a long time before Japan eliminates the densely woven web of subsidies and barriers that protect domestic agriculture from foreign competition. For Japan's trading partners, nothing could be more irrational, unfair, and opprobrious than the expensive shelter which the Japanese government has erected to protect farmers. Today, trade representatives from the US and Europe are determined to demolish that shelter and open Japan's agricultural market to the world.

## UNFAIR PLAY: THE CASE OF THE US SEMICONDUCTOR INDUSTRY

In Mid-April 1987, MITI responded pointedly to US acusations that Japan was ignoring the semiconductor agreement. In a thirteen-page paper, the Ministry criticized the US for failing to play fair in the negotiations, for concealing information and for using accounting methods that had created arbitrary discrepancies between US and Japanese statistics. Discounting American allegations to the contrary, MITI insisted that Japan had abided by the semiconductor agreement: the export prices of Japanese semiconductors had been raised, more US chips were being imported and the dumping of chips in third markets had been curtailed.

MITI argued that the US Commerce Department based its allegations of Japanese infringements on questionable data. The fact that the Commerce Department refused to reveal its statistics and analysis regarding Japanese chip-dumping served to reinforce MITI's belief that there was no basis to US accusations. 'Japan should not be charged with conduct which the US is unwilling to document . . . Japan has information of its own which demonstrates that the US allegations are incorrect,' the report stated.*

A major cause of the misunderstanding was the accounting method used to determine the cost of chip production. This is a vital factor in calculating the 'fair market value' of semiconductors, but while Japanese companies calculate the cost of chips at the date of shipment, US companies calculate the cost six months before shipment. In MITI's opinion, the US method of determining the 'fair market value' was 'not a universal principle' and was 'strictly an aberration.'†

MITI and Japan's semiconductor manufacturers expressed the view that the US was going too far in its attempt to impose tight controls on Japan's semiconductor prices; in effect, the US Commerce Department was attempting to impose its authority on other sovereign nations. Japan's leading financial newspaper‡ editorialized that determining whether a firm is dumping should be 'left to the government of the country where the product in question is sold – it is no business of the US government's.'

Accusations of chip-dumping incensed Japan's semiconductor manufacturers. They were persuaded that the dumping issue had been blown up out of all proportion in order to justify anti-Japanese trade measures. In March 1987, a group of leading Japanese executives responded to an EEC proposal to impose anti-dumping duties with a letter to EEC government leaders. The letter stated that if the proprosed anti-dumping measures were established then the flow of Japanese investment in Europe would be reduced, eliminating pros-

---

* Quoted by Carla Rapoport, 'Japan condemns "unfair play" of US in chip negotiations, *The Financial Times*, 13 April 1987.
 † *Ibid.*
 ‡ The *Nihon Keizai Shimbun* (Japan's equivalent of *The Wall Street Journal* and the largest circulation financial daily in the world). See 'More noise on chips' in *The Japan Economic Journal*, 14 March 1987.

pects of thousands of new jobs, and that existing Japanese-owned factories would be shut down, leading to increased unemployment.

Japanese bureaucrats and industrialists cogently argued that retaliatory measures discourage or directly penalize those in Japan who are determined to make efforts to improve Japan's trade practices. When the US threatened to impose punitive trade tariffs on Japan in March 1987, angry Japanese officials said that such action would 'pour cold water' on US-Japan trade relations and that the US would, in effect, pick a fight' with Japan.*

Many in Japan readily acknowledge that one major cause of trade friction is Japan's unique administrative system. Open-minded Japanese regulators recognize that this system is a complex and confusing labyrinth of bureaucratic regulations which are tacitly approved by most Japanese but totally incomprehensible to foreigners. Although enlightened Japanese industrialists and officials are striving to change this system, the process is necessarily a slow one. Foreign measures taken against Japan can only delay or negate internal efforts to alter Japan's trade practices and policies.

In Congressional testimony given in the spring of 1987, the late Malcolm Baldrige commented that he could 'only conclude that the common objective of the Japanese government and industry is to dominate the world electronics market. Given the importance of this market to United States industry in general and our defense base in particular, we cannot stand by idly.'†

Japanese government officials perceived Baldrige's comment, and others like it, as intentionally inflammatory. The Japanese government and Japanese industry do not necessarily share common objectives. The US was thus promulgating a 'Japan, Inc.' conspiracy in order to play upon American fears about Japanese trade strategies and goals.

In his discussions of the proposed acquisition of Fairchild by Fujitsu (see Chapter 1), Baldrige termed the deal a 'national security risk'. The Department of Commerce manufactured a 'domino theory' which declared that if Fairchild fell to the Japanese, then many other American manufacturers of vital technology would follow – the implication being that Japan, although a US ally, cannot be trusted.

Furthermore, the American government resorted to tactics of intimidation in order to suppress routine Japanese trade activities with the US. It was through such intimidation that Fujitsu was *forced* to drop

* Quoted by Stephen Kreider Yoder and Peter Waldman, *The Wall Street Journal*, 'Japanese Say Figures Show Compliance on Chip Pact, but US Data May Differ,' 19 March 1987.

† Quoted by Clyde H. Farnsworth, 'US Resentment Grows on Japan Trade Barriers,' *The New York Times*, 30 March 1987, p. 30.

its merger plans for Fairchild and Japanese semiconductor manufac-turers were *pressured* to alter their legitimate trading practices.

Yuzuru Hatakeyama, MITI's director general of trade, commented that 'if the fact that Japan is abiding by the [semiconductor] agree-ment is ignored, then the reaction of the Japanese people will be very anti-American.'* The Japanese government, seeking to minimize trade friction with the US, attempted to mollify heated American objections. However, rising Japanese unemployment combined with the devastating effects of the strong yen gave Japanese negotiators little room for maneouvre. At the same time, American insensitivity to how the Japanese political economy works and American blindness to Japan's short-term constraints encouraged the growth of anti-Amer-ican sentiment in Japan.

Japanese economists and bureaucrats recognize that Japan's current account surplus in general, and that with the United States in particular, is too high. Virtually no one in Japan disputes this. The ratio of current account surplus to gross national product was 3.8 percent in late nineteenth century Britain, when the British economy reached its zenith, and averaged 2.5 percent for the US during the period between the two world wars, when the US posted relatively large trade surpluses. By contrast, in fiscal 1986, the ratio for Japan was about 4.27 percent – far higher than the comparable figures for Britain and the United States during their heydays as exporters.

Japan's unprecedented trade surpluses, together with her signifi-cant dependence upon the US in other respects, are seen as the chief causes of the ominous trade friction between the two countries. Japan's dollar-based exports to the US (calculated on a customs clearance basis) accounted for 38.5 percent of total exports in 1986, a 15 percent increase over the figure for 1976. Japanese investments in the US have also increased sharply, as was shown by a JETRO (Japan External Trade Organization) survey indicating that the number of Japanese manufacturing plants in the US doubled between 1980 and 1985 (from 200 in 1980 to 404 in March 1985).

American and EEC responses to trade problems with Japan stress retaliation; such retaliatory strategies are perceived in Japan as gratuitous aggression, deriving from resentment of Japanese success. In an April 1987 poll conducted in Japan by the Tokyo Broadcasting System, a majority of the respondents described US-Japan relations as unfriendly. These results, when compared with the findings of a similar poll conducted a year earlier,† suggested there had been a

* Quoted by Ian Rodger, 'Tokyo digs in over chip dispute,' The *Financial Times*, 2 April 1987.
† See Clyde Haberman, 'Poll Reflects Trade Strife,' *The New York Times*, 5 June 1987.

major change in attitudes. In 1987, moreover, 77 percent of Japanese respondents indicated that the United States was blaming Japan for its own economic problems. Clearly, the Japanese would view the US tariffs imposed on Japan because of alleged infractions of the semiconductor agreement as one example of this phenomenon.

In early 1987, the United States Defense Department published a report stating that all memory chips in the department's supercomputers are produced by Japanese manufacturers. A key reason for Japanese dominance in the production of these memory chips is that Japan is virtually the exclusive supplier of the gallium arsenide transistors which are indispensable to the production of advanced guidance systems. The Defense Department's report expressed the concern that, with US military dependence on Japanese electronics ranging from 100 percent to 30 percent, America was becoming ever more vulnerable to any interruption in Japanese supplies.

Later in 1987, the House of Representatives Subcommittee on International Trade issued a report warning that Japan must not be allowed to usurp dominance of the semiconductor industry from the United States. Were that to happen, the report suggested, Japan would become the Saudi Arabia of chip production and, just as OPEC under Saudi Arabian leadership is now able to determine the price of a vital commodity and so pressure the United States, Japan too would be in a position to exert pressure on American foreign policy. Thus both the Department of Defense and the House subcommittee were using national security as an argument for maintaining and *protecting* an indigenous industry despite the availability of more economical foreign production. Why, then, do American trade representatives reject an identical Japanese argument when it is applied to agriculture?

Just as Americans fear that Japan could someday decide to suspend exports of semiconductors or gallium arsenide transistors to the United States, the Japanese fear that the US could halt exports of food to Japan. Indeed, in 1973, President Nixon temporarily halted the export of soyabeans to Japan. Because 98 percent of Japanese soya bean consumption is imported, the effects of this ban, although brief, have not been forgotten. Millions of Japanese housewives were forced to wait on long lines to buy their weekly supply of bean curd and bean paste (versatile ingredients in Japanese cuisine).

Several years later the United States used agricultural exports as a means of expressing anger over the Soviet Union's invasion of Afghanistan. President Carter's ban on the export of wheat to the USSR was regarded with considerable concern by the Japanese people. In the event that a war caused shortages, could Japan depend upon the

United States for its food? If the United States demands that Japan, its vital Pacific ally, should not worry about stable supplies of food, why does it in turn worry about stable supplies of semiconductors from Japan? This apparent contradiction suggests muddled reasoning or hypocrisy.

## 'WE DO NOT WANT A TRADE WAR'

Japan's markets are not closed. Certain so-called 'non-tariff barriers' have caused misunderstandings with trading partners. To avoid trade friction, Japan's labyrinthine system of domestic regulations is being transformed into a straight and simple path.

Japanese tariff rates are by far the lowest in the industrial world. At the end of 1986 they averaged just 2.1 percent compared with 4.2 percent in the United States and 4.8 percent in the EEC. All of Japan's import restrictions are compatible with the General Agreement on Tariffs and Trade (GATT).

Dozens of American and European companies have successfully set up operations in Japan whose products have achieved massive domestic sales. Indeed, the sales of US subsidiaries in Japan are quadruple the size of the US trade deficit with Japan. Kenichi Ohmae and others have even suggested that these sales are *responsible* for the trade deficit.* They contend that because the domestic sales and exports of US subsidiaries in Japan are not taken into account in the computation of US trade statistics, American perceptions of a trade deficit with Japan are false.

A short-term solution to Japan's apparent trade surplus can be achieved by expanding the domestic economy. In 1987, the *Diet* approved a number of economic measures intended to stimulate domestic demand and thus increase impo-ts. Japan is importing more foreign products than ever before and trade imbalances will gradually resolve themselves.

Japan wants to avoid a trade war. If, however, foreign governments introduce misconceived protectionist legislation, she may someday find it necessary to take counter-measures. Such action would only exacerbate the antagonism between Japan and its trading partners, particularly the United States.

Nonetheless, strong foreign opposition to now obsolete Japanese distribution and regulatory systems can be a positive force for change. Certain Japanese organizations (such as *Nokyo*) can go too far in

* Ohmae, Kenichi. *Beyond National Borders*, Dow Jones-Irwin, Similarly, a study (cited by *The Economist*, 11 April 1987, p. 68) written by Enzio von Pfeil, an economist with Smith New Court, concluded that Japan's surplus can be accounted for entirely by the production of overseas (particularly American) companies in Japan. On average, over the period of von Pfeil's study, 'the local sales of Japanese affiliates of American firms were four times larger than the two countries' trade balance.'

pursuit of their own narrow interests. In such cases, foreign trade representatives can play an important role as catalysts.

Japanese politicians and bureaucrats who want to modernize regulations but are prevented from doing so by the inertia of a ponderous system, can shift the responsibility for implementing change from their shoulders to the insistent demands of foreign forces. *Diplomatic* suggestions are always appreciated. Thank you.

# 3 THE WORLD OF JAPAN

Having, by virtue of the glories of Our Ancestors, ascended the Throne of a lineal succession unbroken for ages eternal. . . .

[*First words of the Meiji constitution*]

## MY FATHER'S HOUSE

When I worked in Tokyo my Japanese co-workers used to take me out to a wide variety of restaurants and bars so that I could experience the 'Japanese life.' They introduced me to friends as well as business associates over *sake* or Suntory whiskey. Sometimes I would be taken to private clubs that had no more than two tables and a tiny bar; here Japanese businessmen would relax in a convivial atmosphere in which drinking and singing songs were mandatory. It was a new experience for me to take a microphone and sing a duet with a bar hostess.

Perhaps because I was a foreigner, older drinking companions often delighted in ribbing me about 'my role' in World War II. After fending off the remarks of a particularly vehement general manager one evening, I jokingly expressed my feelings about the conversation to my friend. Instead of answering me with the laugh I expected, the Japanese friend took my arm and flagged down a taxi.

'I'll show you something which my father once showed me,' he said. Minutes later we were standing on a narrow street like many others in neighbourhoods throughout Tokyo.

'There,' my friend said pointing upward. 'That was my family house for generations.'

My eyes scanned the six-storey glass and concrete office structure in front of us. 'Nice house,' I said conversationally. 'I didn't realize your family was so rich.'

My friend shook his head. 'This building (or its predecessor, to be precise) was built on the rubble left by your bombers. My great-great-grandfather built the house which was levelled in 1944. My family lost everything. Of course, I wasn't born until 1948 so I had no direct personal involvement in the events. But my cousin still has weak bones because of the milk shortage during the immediate postwar period. He broke his back in a minor accident in 1965 and was hospitalized for two years as a direct result of a systemic calcium deficiency. He remembers the war clearly although he was an infant at the time. I'll introduce you soon.'

'No hurry,' I said, feeling uncomfortable.

This was not to be my last social blunder in Japan. One morning while I was walking down the street, I saw a new Lincoln Continental double-parked in front of an office building. Large American cars are a rarity in Japan where their size and gasoline consumption make them impractical. This one caught my attention because it was carelessly blocking traffic and its tinted glass windows added an aura of mystery. I wondered whether the car perhaps belonged to a visiting dignitary, or to a movie star.

As I pondered the anomaly, three men wearing similar blue polyester pin-striped suits walked out of the building and entered the car. All of them wore sunglasses, despite the overcast day, and as they passed me I made a mental note of their identical company pins. I memorized the pin design so that I could later ask my friend the identity of their company. I wondered which Japanese firm extravagantly used American limousines as corporate vehicles.

Later, in the office, I quickly sketched the pattern of the company pin I had seen earlier and asked what prestigious Japanese firm it represented.

'Yes, very prestigious,' said my friend while he laughed uproariously at my question. In fact, while he was still laughing he began to show my sketch around the office and soon at least a dozen people were giggling.

Somewhat nonplussed, I waited for the laughter to die down. 'Well,' I asked expectantly. 'What's the joke?'

'The name of the company,' my friend replied soberly, 'is the *Yamaguchigumi.*'

'It's not listed on the first section of the Tokyo Stock Exchange,' I replied authoritatively, proud of my familiarity with the listed firms.

'No,' said my friend, 'it's not.'

'What do they produce?' I asked.

'Nothing,' he answered with a poker face.

'Oh, it's a service company,' I said, becoming impatient with the guessing game.

My friend laughed again. 'Yes, it provides a range of special services, from extortion to prostitution,' he answered. 'It is also the primary source of amphetamines and heroin in Japan, and it imports illegal firearms.'

'They wear company pins to announce all of this to the world?' I asked incredulously.

'It keeps people out of their way,' my friend explained, 'Unlike your American gangsters,' he continued, 'who are uncontrollable and violent, our *yakuza* are organized and generally cooperate with the police. The *yakuza* consist of various factions, some of them quite large, and each faction has its own company pins and business cards.'

'Business cards?'. I was perplexed. 'Each gangster has a card with his name on it, his position, and the gangster group he belongs to?' 'What does it say?' I asked facetiously. ' "K. Watanabe, pimp, member of the *Yamaguchigumi*" or "Yamada, senior dealer in illegal substances?" '

'That's right, although as far as I know, the position of the gangster is not included on the card.'

At this point during my stay in Japan, nothing the Japanese might do would have amazed me.

The longer I worked in the Japanese financial sector the more aware I became of how greatly Japanese finance differed from that of the United States or Europe. This did not surprise me, because everything about Japan differed greatly from the West.

But the differences, which at first seemed insignificant to me, gained in importance and began to loom over me. For instance, wherever I went in Japan there seemed to be an excessive number of employees; people milling about offices, with apparently little to do, ready to wait on me in restaurants, bowing to me at department store elevators, and ever-present wherever services were provided. 'Sunshine boys,' so-called because they had no assigned duties other than to sit in the sunlight in corporate offices reading newspapers, pretended to busy themselves in the office where I worked. The over-staffing which seemed extravagant, inefficient, and irrational to me at first, gradually became intelligible as I grasped the Japanese orientation. But, when I first asked my friend about over-employment, I was mystified by his explanation.

'There is no welfare in Japan. Japanese corporations exist so that they can employ people,' he said.

'What about profitability?' I inquired with a trace of sarcasm.

'Whereas Western companies exist for the bottom line, profits are a by-product and not an end,' he replied.

At first I thought that he was being evasive or humorous. Gradually, however, I came to appreciate the truth inherent in his glib observation. Contrary to Western views of labour utilization, the deployment of workers in Japan is not necessarily based on the assumption that good employees are those who contribute the maximum of which they are capable at any given point in time. Instead, the white collar employees of major Japanese corporations resemble, in certain respects, recruits in the armed forces in the US and elsewhere.

Like the armed forces, Japanese companies accumulate the best recruits they can locate and attempt to keep them as long as possible in the knowledge that their services, although perhaps unnecessary at present, could become vital in the future.

For example, every year each Japanese company hires a new crop of fresh college graduates. The graduates are hired, without the companies having any fixed idea of how or where they will be employed within the corporate structure. This minor detail will be determined much later, after they have worked for a number of years in a variety of low-level tasks. These unchallenging responsibilities are designed not only to train them but also to reveal strengths and weaknesses to their superiors and, perhaps most important, to give them a sense of corporate identity.

These early, tedious years of an employee's career resemble boot camp. The counterpart of the private's stripe which the soldier receives on leaving boot camp, is the company pin, which the Japanese recruit is given after about two years of employment. Thereafter he will wear the pin on the lapel of his suit every day of his working life. Although fascinated by my new perception of the system, I did not understand its significance at that time. My goal was to get a company pin. Although I was not planning to spend the rest of my life working for a Tokyo securities firm, I thought that a company pin would be a unique souvenir of my stay in Japan.

Imagine my surprise when I was told by a senior officer of the company that I would never be qualified to receive a company pin. Up until that point, everyone in the office had acceded to all of my requests with remarkable courtesy and the unyielding simplicity of his denial seemed incongruous. That afternoon, while sipping bean curd soup in the company cafeteria, I asked my friend for an explanation.

'Why did the director refuse to give me a company pin?' I inquired as I tossed some seaweed into my mouth.

'Why do you want a company pin?' my friend countered.

I could immediately sense that one of our baffling discussions was about to begin.

'For a souvenir?' I suggested tentatively.

'Company pins are not souvenirs,' my friend replied matter-of-factly.

'What are they then?' I asked pointedly.

'They are like *hachimaki*,' he explained.

I shook my head to indicate that I had no knowledge of *hachimaki*.

'*Hachimaki*,' he explained patiently, 'are headbands.'

'Oh,' I replied uncertainly.

'We Japanese, unlike you Americans, like to do things in groups. We know that the group is more powerful than the individual. When a group is facing a very difficult task, extra strength is needed. So, all of the group members wear identical *hachimaki*. The *hachimaki* focuses the power of their concentration and dedication to the group goal. By wearing a *hachimaki*, a person abandons his selfish interests and insecurities. He devotes himself entirely to a single objective. *Hachimaki* can be worn by all kinds of people. Next time we go to a *sushi* restaurant, I'll point one out to you. *Sushi* makers wear them. Students at *juku*, special schools for exam preparation, also wear them. During the Pacific war, *kamikaze* pilots tied them on each other's foreheads before entering their planes.'

'Well,' I began firmly, returning to the subject of the pin, 'I'm part of the company, so why can't I wear a company pin? Perhaps it would improve my work.'

My friend shook his head, indicating pity. 'You haven't understood anything I've said.'

My perplexity increased because I thought that I had followed his argument quite well.

'Although you are an employee, you are not part of the company. You cannot wear a company pin.'

'I'm not part of the company?' I repeated. 'Who is paying my salary?'

'The situation is very simple. This is a Japanese company and you are not Japanese. Therefore, although you are an employee of the company, you are not a part of the company. For example, we rent a mainframe computer. It is very expensive and is a valuable component of our corporate operations. The computer, of course, is not a part of the company. We use its services and pay for its availability accordingly. You are like the computer. Your abilities are valued and we all appreciate having you with us.'

'It sounds as though you are suggesting that I'm not human.'

'No,' he said. 'I'm saying that you are a foreigner. You are human, but you aren't Japanese. Your heritage derives from the United States, so your goals belong to the United States. Your goals will never be Japanese. So how can you truly be a part of a Japanese company?'

We sipped our green tea in silence as I pondered my origins. I wondered whether Kipling was right after all when he suggested that 'East is East and West is West and ne'er the twain shall meet.'

## THE RISING SUN

The rising sun is the symbol of Japan. The Japanese national flag has a white background upon which the red orb of the sun is suspended as though it were floating in its own light. The sun is one of Japan's most ancient symbols. The Imperial family claims descent from the sun and during World War II, when the emperor was considered to be a divinity, the rising sun symbolized Japan's emerging military power.

Archaeologists can trace the origins of the Japanese people to successive waves of migration from the Asian continent (and possibly Southeast Asia). But folklore indicates a different origin. During Japan's earliest history, the country was divided into clan groupings, termed *uji*. Each *uji* controlled a particular geographic area and worshipped its own god who was defined as a founding ancestor. The *uji* battled each other for control of arable land until members of the Yamato *uji*, descendants of the sun-line, consolidated power during the fifth century.

Today, the imperial family traces its descent directly to the Yamato and from the Yamato to the sun. In the absence of genealogical information, it is assumed that all Japanese can claim ancestry from the gods of the *uji*. Thus, all Japanese people are descended from gods.

## WE THE JAPANESE

The human heart is made up of cells. When separated and suspended in a sterile medium the individual cells beat independently. If two cells are pushed together so that they are in contact, they eventually conform to the same rhythm, beating synchronously. In fact, if cells from different hearts of the same species are put together they invariably beat together.*

The Japanese, like individual heart cells, combine into a unified entity which they term, 'We the Japanese.'

'We the Japanese' is a category which conveys the shared culture, language, history, and location of one national group. The Japanese regard themselves as racially and linguistically homogeneous, despite some evidence to the contrary. The roots of 'we the Japanese' are partially explained and justified by Shinto and its myths.†

Shinto, a tradition rather than a religion, combines Chinese and

* This is a necessarily simplified description. For more detal see N. Sperelakis, 'Electrical Properties of Embryonic Heart Cells.' In DeMello, W. C. (ed.), *Electrical Phenomena in the Heart*. New York: Academic Press, 1972.

† In addition to Shinto, Zen Buddhism subtly permeates Japanese culture. Zen, because of its complexity and elusiveness, will not be discussed here. However, the critical influence of Zen will be explored in my forthcoming book.

Buddhist influences with ancient animistic beliefs. In this tradition the worship of natural forces and parts of nature itself, such as trees and rocks, is linked with ancestor worship. After death, ancestors become *kami*, which may be loosely translated as gods. These *kami* dwell within the land, giving the land a soul, the soul of Japan. The soul of Japan, the souls of the ancestors, and the souls of the living Japanese people are believed to be interlinked.

Thus, according to the Shinto beliefs that still permeate many aspects of Japanese culture, the Japanese people ('we the Japanese') cannot be separated from the land of Japan. A Japanese person not resident in Japan is not fully Japanese. Thus, in terms of Shinto tradition, the Tokugawa ban on travel outside Japan was entirely understandable.

Today, Japanese businessmen who return to Japan after long assignments abroad are not at first regarded as full members of their companies. A period of adjustment must mediate between the residence abroad (a period of enforced 'non-Japaneseness') and residence in Japan. During this adjustment period, the Japanese businessmen gradually lose the 'smell of the foreigners' which figuratively clings to their skins and their thoughts. Similarly, Japanese schoolchildren who return to Japan after a period of foreign residence are usually harassed by their peers because of actual or putative foreign influences. To be separated from the land for more than a brief period is to lose a component of Japanese identity.

## IN-GROUPS AND OUT-GROUPS

From earliest childhood, each Japanese learns that he belongs to a group of peers. Incalculable importance is attached to a primary loyalty to this immediate group. In both folklore and contemporary society betrayal of the group is seen as the most heinous of acts. Children have beaten, almost to the point of death, other children who were perceived as abandoning their group. An individual Japanese, like a single heart cell, is useless without the support of a group.

There are many types of groups in Japan. Even within a single corporation one person may belong to a number of different, but overlapping, groups. Dedication to the group can be as strong in a school or a sports club as in the workplace. The primary group, of course, is 'we the Japanese' – the entire nation.

Foreigners accustomed to cultural heterogeneity have difficulty in comprehending Japan's homogeneous society. Nearly all the residents of the archipelago share a common history and what is reputed to be a common racial heritage. Within this homogeneous society considerable value is attached to conformity. Prime Minister Nakasone's much published comment in 1986 that the average level of intelligence in

America is reduced by the presence of 'quite a few black people, Puerto Ricans and Mexicans' is indicative of the Japanese attitude toward racial mixing.

There are, however, certain segments of Japan's population which are excluded from 'we the Japanese'. Japan is one of the few countries in the world where place of birth does not assure citizenship. Second- and third-generation 'residents' of Japan, including 700,000 Koreans, are not entitled to citizenship. This distinction is emphasized by the fact that they must submit to periodic fingerprinting as aliens and such treatment is a small inconvenience when compared to established discriminatory practices which exclude such groups from many opportunities.

Unlike the Koreans, another out-group, the *burakumin*,* are Japanese citizens, free to live as ordinary Japanese. Indeed the *burakumin* have not existed as an official category since the Emperor Meiji declared them 'new citizens' in 1871.

The *burakumin*, who are believed to be descendants of an ancient caste of leather workers, were originally shunned as polluted people dealing with carcasses. They were termed *eta* (meaning 'much filth') because, in a Buddhist society which prohibited the slaughter of animals, contact with the dead was defiling. The *burakumin* of pre-Meiji Japan were forced to live in specified sections of the cities or settlements (*buraku* means 'community' and *min* simply means 'people') and were prohibited from wearing shoes. They were required to use straw to tie their hair and a patch of leather sewn to their clothes identified them as a separate polluted caste of non-humans.

Today's officially non-existent *burakumin* number between one and three million and continue to live as a distinct group. They can rarely hope to marry ordinary Japanese and their educational and employment opportunities are severely constrained. As in pre-Meiji Japan, they live in slum areas in Japan's cities. They are still an out-group.

Heart cells from different hearts beat together. Cells from other organs have no compatibility with heart cells.

In Japan there once existed the belief that the *burakumin* carried an inherited physical stigma – a blue mark under each arm.† Although such a stigma was mythical, it resembled the alleged smell of butter which is believed to cling to the skin of Europeans.

---

* For further discussions of the burakumin see Sueo Murakoshi (ed.) *Discrimination Against Buraku, Today*, Osaka: Burakumin Liberation Research Institute, 1987. Hiroshi Wagatsuma, 'Socialization, Self-Perception, and Burakumin Status,' in De Vos, George A., *Socialization for Achievement, Essays on the Cultural Psychology of the Japanese*, Berkeley: University of California Press, 1975, pp. 391–419.

† Wagatsuma, *op cit.*, p. 413.

## OFFICE FURNITURE

Of all the changes and reforms introduced in Japan during the twentieth century, none could be more apparently irrelevant to understanding Japan than office furniture. Yet the interior décor and use of space found in Japanese offices provides a compelling example of the role of the individual in Japan's post-industrial society.

The standard narrow, steel-gray desks and uncomfortable gray swivel chairs used by the staff of the Supreme Commander for the Allied Powers (SCAP) quickly found their way into the rebuilt and reorganized offices of Japan's various ministries – and from the ministries to Japanese postwar corporations.

Today, undersized gray metal office furniture is still *de rigueur* in Japanese corporate and government offices. The ranks of bureaucrats, managers, administrators and other personnel who are the body and soul of every institution in Japan, work in offices packed with serried rows of gray desks.

Each desk supports a number of gray bins overflowing with stacks of paper. As in the military, most desks do not hold personal mementos such as photographs of family. And, as in the army offices of the late 1940s, the desks rest on linoleum floors which are seldom maintained. Cigarettes smoke fills the air while uniformed women (who never smoke in the office) fulfil low-level secretarial and administrative tasks.

Long after the computer revolution transformed American offices, technology to facilitate the rapid use of the Japanese written language (which uses ideographs as well as several syllabic systems) had not been developed. By the mid-1980s, however, new software permitted a wide use of the Japanese language on computer screens and spreadsheets had advanced to remarkably high levels of refinement. Nonetheless, the ratio of Japanese office workers to desk-top computers in 1987 was 25:1, compared to a ratio of 7:1 in the United States. While accountants continued to do their work with an abacus or handheld calculator, robots constructed automobiles. In contrast to the crowded and antiquated working conditions of Japan's offices, the manufacturing environments staffed by blue-collar workers were immaculately neat and production utilized the most advanced technological methods.

Why have Japanese offices lagged behind the modernization of all other areas of Japanese business and industry? The answer to this question has more to do with the concept of 'we the Japanese' than with the cost of office improvements or technological ignorance.

In Japanese corporate organizations fewer than six of the highest ranking executive officers (including the chairman, the president, and the executive vice-president) have private offices. Indeed at certain institutions (e.g. the headquarters of Osaka-based Sanwa Bank, Japan's fifth largest) only the president and chairman are entitled to private offices. In Japan, accomplishments are regarded as the direct product of group effort. An individual alone, it is believed, can accomplish little. To isolate the individual in a private office is to negate his value as a contributor to the development of the business.

Remove one cell from a human heart and the heart will be unaffected. However, continue removing the heart cells and eventually the organism will cease to function. The life of an organization depends upon the harmonious combination of its employees. The contribution of one employee, like a single heart cell, is incidental.

It follows, therefore, that individual employees do not require the luxurious indulgence characteristic of American offices where a philosophy of individualism prevails. Carpeting, large wooden desks, or separate work units (offices or cubicles) are all inappropriate to the design of a Japanese environment. A Japanese executive, regardless of his contribution to corporate progress, is not entitled to a personal computer or a personal secretary. Just as ideas are shared and developed through group participation, so tools are shared.

The Japanese office, derogatorily termed a 'bull-pen' by foreign visitors, is filled with dozens of desks and still looks much like the US army headquarters in the Tokyo of 1948. However, unlike a US army office, the desks are not separated from each other. Desks are pushed together so that each row of three to fifteen desks is in contact with adjacent desks and often the desk fronts are pushed against a facing row of desks. The actual contact of the desks symbolizes the social contact of the employees, who not only spend much of their working lives seated at them but also a portion of their leisure time interacting with the workers seated at neighbouring desks.

Japanese offices have been slow to modernize because, in a real sense, the individuals who would directly benefit from small changes (ranging from carpeting to desktop computers) are unimportant. While individuals are unimportant, however, the group is all-important.

Technology tends to separate people from each other. If each employee in a Japanese office had his own desktop computer, then his concentration would be devoted too exclusively to the screen and his data. In this way, American developments in office technology would disrupt the group.

## SWORDS, SAMURAI AND RONIN

In Japan an unusual parallel exists between the *samurai*, the swords that symbolized their power and the *ronin* of the past, on the one hand, and today's businessmen, the money which facilitates their business and the contemporary gangsters (the *yakuza*), on the other.

*Swords : Samurai : Ronin :: Money : Businessmen : Yakuza*

Like the swords, which were the tools of the *samurai* and embodied their accomplishments, money is now the tool of Japanese businessmen, its accumulation facilitating their continued success. Of course, swords were not collected and deposited in banks or invested in fungible instruments, nor is money made by master craftsmen. However, each – the sword of the *samurai* and the money of modern Japanese businessmen – has been the quintessential implement of power in its own time.

The image of businessmen as contemporary versions of the *samurai* is a popular one in Japanese culture, and Japanese businessmen enjoy seeing themselves as a modern-day version of courageous *samurai*, going out to battle in the business world. The accuracy of this comparison is less important than its widespread appeal.

Just as contemporary Japanese businessmen identify themselves with the samurai, so Japan's gangsters, the *yakuza*, enjoy comparing themselves to another historical group, the *ronin*. They believe that they are the direct descendants (through tradition) of *ronin* from villages who fought bandits during the Tokugawa period. The *ronin*, a group of outcasts, were pursued and eventually destroyed by government authorities. Today's *yakuza* factions, like *ronin* groups, consist primarily of outcasts. The *burakumin* make up an estimated 70 percent of the *Yamaguchigumi* (the largest *yakuza* faction),* and the majority of *yakuza* members who are not *burakumin* are of Korean descent and are also outcasts in Japanese society, deprived of citizenship and treated as aliens.

The link between today's businessmen and the *samurai* of the past is even stronger in the case of particular individuals who can document their lineage and have inherited a great-grandfather's sword. Although Japan does not have a recognized class system based upon the relationships that obtained during its feudal history, the descendants of leading Tokugawa era *samurai* are not working in factory assembly lines or as waiters.

## Swords

The great fourteenth century swordsmith Muramasu, spent weeks hammering a single sword. The sword would be heated in the forge, pounded with a hammer, reheated and then pounded again – a procedure that was repeated thousands of times. The process continued

---

* According to unofficial statistics cited by Kaplan and Dubro, *Yakuza, The Explosive Account of Japan's Criminal Underworld*, p. 145.

until the edge of the sword contained an estimated four million layers of perfectly forged steel. Although the edge of the sword was extraordinarily strong, the remainder of the blade was pounded far less so that it would be softer. If an entire sword blade contained millions of layers it would be hard but brittle. Such a blade would break on impact.

Thus Japanese master swordsmiths perfected a method of varying the hardness of a single piece of forged steel. This technique was never developed in Europe and as a result, the steel of the finest Japanese swords was far stronger than any steel which could be produced in Europe. With a single blow, a *samurai's* sword could slice through an inch of European steel as though it were butter.

The long and short swords which the *samurai* carried became their emblems. The craftsmanship of the finest swords transformed them into works of art which were displayed with great pride by their owners. Today, burnished sword blades glisten inside the glass cases of museums and are admired more for the graceful harmony of their lines than for their potential as weapons.

Today, unlike matchlocks and other antique implements of war, *samurai* swords have not been relegated to a nostalgic corner of obsolete technology, of interest only to collectors. On the contrary, the *samurai* sword still remains a special symbol that embodies the combination of Japanese manufacturing skill with traditional Japanese values.

Indeed, no object expresses traditional Japan better than the *samurai* sword. Those swords which have been kept as heirlooms by the descendants of *samurai* are still removed from their velvet lined boxes on special occasions to be unwrapped and admired.

Although there are many other links with the past, a family sword exudes the vitality and confidence of the departed *samurai* who once carried it. Perhaps no other symbol expresses the potency and power of traditional Japan better than a *samurai's* sword. And just as the sword rests quietly in its protective box, so the spirit of the *samurai* rests in the hearts of all Japanese – quietly radiating strength.

## Samurai

A thousand years ago, during Japan's Fujiwara Period (857–1160), the authority of the central government was weakened to such an extent that the ruling family had little control over the provinces. Armed struggles between rival factions were common place throughout the islands and piracy became the scourge of many coastal areas. In order to exercise some control, provincial bureaucrats were given the power to maintain armed militia and eventually acquired military titles. In addition, the proprietors of rural estates assembled armed groups to protect *their* local interests. Throughout this period, amalgamation of local military groupings resulted in the development of fiefdoms bearing a strong resemblance to medieval kingdoms.

By the tenth century, the Fujiwara family and the imperial house had grown to be too large to delegate power effectively to all qualified male members. As a result, excess family members were thrown out of the lineages and were given new names (Minamoto and Taira). This prevented the dilution of the political control exercised by more direct descendants.

Excluded from the imperial court, the expelled men left Kyoto, the capital, and travelled to the provinces where they became the managers of lands officially owned by the emperor. Although these men were no longer formally connected to the ruling or imperial families, their outstanding pedigree enabled them to create a rural aristocracy. Using their wealth as a tool for the accumulation of power, these disinherited aristocrats became the leaders of small, rurally-based armies.

Gradually, a warrior class termed *bushi* (warrior) or *samurai* (retainer) emerged. From the middle of the Fujiwara period (about 950) until the beginning of Tokugawa rule (1603), the *samurai*, by virtue of their military activities, played a key role in Japan's political economy, and the sporadic wars and skirmishes in which they engaged resulted in rearrangements in the deployment of political power.

Like the knights of Europe, the *samurai* were mounted and armoured, fighting other *samurai* in individual encounters. Their weapons included the long bow as well as the sword.

The men who ruled the feudal domains were termed *daimyo*. Each *daimyo* employed an army of *samurai* who were totally dependent upon him ffor financial support. Wars waged between rival *daimyo* for the control of land were fought by the *samurai*. Military defeat was considered a disgrace and *samurai* were expected to die in battle rather than suffer the humiliation of failure. Often, however, the *samurai* of a defeated *daimyo* abandoned the battlefield and wandered, homeless and usually poor, through the countryside. Such leaderless *samurai*, called *ronin*, functioned as mercenaries and were often hired by *daimyo* planning a military undertaking. Some of the *ronin* became bandits and terrorized villages. Others banded together and fought the outlaws. Thus, in Japanese folklore, the countryside was peopled by two types of *ronin*, one bad and one good.

## Ronin

In 1603 Ieyasu Tokugawa unified Japan, ending centuries of civil war and inaugurating two centuries of peace. As a result, more than 500,000 *samurai* were rendered superfluous. Some became merchants, and the ones of highest rank entered the civil bureaucracy. Many poor *samurai*, however, having no capital to begin business and no avenue for bureaucratic success, drifted through the countryside.

These unemployed *samurai* resembled the *ronin* of earlier periods. Having no special skills other than martial training, many became wandering bandits and plundered farming villages for a living. Termed *kabuki-mono*, these masterless *samurai* were wanderers who had renounced normal Japanese morality. Stories of *kabuki-mono* randomly killing farmers in order to test a new sword abound.

One of the oldest and most popular Japanese stories is the tale of the 47 *ronin*. The *daimyo* Asano Naganori was insulted by a high official of the *shogun*. Because he drew his sword, a forbidden act in the *shogun*'s palace, he was ordered to commit ritual suicide. The *daimyo*'s loyal *samurai*, Oishi, rendered a *ronin* by his master's death, vowed revenge. For seven years Oishi and 46 other former *samurai* of Asano Naganori feigned abandonment of their military lives and led drunken and dissolute existences in Edo (the capital city).

When the moment was right, during a blizzard, the 47 *ronin* seized the house of the offending official and after killing his armed guard beheaded him. The official's head, placed in a temple beside their master's ashes, symbolized the revenge of the *daimyo*'s loyal retainers. While the action of these *ronin* was considered to be exemplary, they were ordered by the *shogun* to commit suicide.

Modern Japanese regard the story of the 47 *ronin* as a parable expressing the irreconcilable conflict between loyalty to the master (the *group*) and loyalty to the shogun (the *state*). The 47 *ronin* committed the ultimate act of honour by choosing loyalty to their master above the rule of law and subsequently submitting to the rule of law and paying the price of their act. In this way, the 47 *ronin* honoured both systems without compromising their own integrity.

Although the contemporary Japanese is never forced to choose between his loyalty to the group and his loyalty to the state, the potential conflict remains implicit. Ideally, loyalty to the group always takes precedence, but it does not justify neglect of the larger institution (the corporation, the school, the state).

The tale of the 47 *ronin* adds respectability to the wanderer who finds that fate has deprived him of his group affiliation. Thus high school students who fail their university entrance examinations and spend years working in odd jobs while studying to take the examinations again, are today termed *ronin*. The fate of these modern day *ronin* is pitied and respected. Those who succeed and pass their exams become successful people and their former status as *ronin* is forgotten. However, those who fail in their final attempt at redemption are relegated to a lifetime of employment in obscure, poorly-paid jobs. There is no pity for the failed *ronin*.

## MONEY, BUSINESSMEN, AND YAKUZA

Japan's position in world business and finance is the direct outcome of unique historical forces and conditions. Japan possesses a martial history spanning more than a millennium and ending with the Occupation in 1945. Martial traditions, exemplified by *bushido* (the *credo* of the *samurai*), are an intrinsic part of Japan's cultural inheritance. Officially, all aspects of Japanese militarism, together with the glorification of martial activities, were abolished in the new Japanese constitution drafted under the auspices of the supreme commander for the allied powers. But traditions deeply embedded in literate cultures cannot be obliterated by decree. If the attempt is made, the traditions will simply be expressed in other ways; thus Japan's contemporary business entities have replaced the military groupings of the past, providing in certain respects an outlet through which national pride can be expressed.

### Money

Every day the Japanese people save $1 billion while Japan's corporations accumulate $500 million. Japan has the highest savings rate in the world, about 350 percent more than the American savings rate. Japan's vast accumulation of savings has made Japanese banks the biggest in the world and Japanese securities companies have waxed rich on the commissions generated by stock purchases.

Like the four million layers of the *samurai* sword, which made it the strongest implement of its time, the layers of money which fill banks, securities companies, insurance companies, and corporations have made Japan's financial institutions the strongest in the world. Just as the brittleness of the sword's edge was balanced by the soft steel in its centre, the hollowing out of Japanese industry caused by the high yen is being counterbalanced by growing Japanese investments in factories and securities abroad. Such overseas investments will gradually help to prevent trade friction and will protect the Japanese currency from becoming too strong.

The *samurai* sword was able to effortlessly slice European steel. Will Japanese money be able to cut through foreign corporate ownership of assets in the same way? Will the power of Japanese money be wielded with the same unshakeable confidence as the *samurai* wielded his sword?

## Businessmen

Japan's modern businessmen date back to the early Meiji period (late nineteenth century). While the *samurai* were commanded by law to put away their swords, a new class of corporate leaders began to emerge. Dressed in Western suits and often living in Western-style homes, by the twentieth century Japanese businessmen had become as distinctive a group as the *samurai*. Their uniform consisted of dark suits, Western ties, and black shoes. Easily recognizable, they staffed trading companies and filled the offices of Japan's developing industrial corporations and emerging financial institutions.

The *samurai* never contributed directly to the prosperity of Japan, but they assured prosperity by protecting their *daimyo* from invasion. Similarly, by devoting their lives to the development of their corporations, modern businessmen have enhanced Japan's autonomy and increased its export capability and wealth. The *samurai* were military defenders of Japan; businessmen are its economic defenders.

## Yakuza

Japan has an enviably low crime rate. For example, more homicides occur in the city of Detroit every year than in all of Japan. Until recently, many Japanese city dwellers did not even lock their houses. Cases of murder, burglary, and mugging in Japan are more often the result of intrafamily disputes than of random crime. The *yakuza* take credit for Japan's peaceful streets.

At least 200 years old, the word *yakuza* is derived from the lowest losing combination in a card game and originally connoted uselessness. Today, the term refers to a collection of independent criminal factions or gangs.

The leaders of *yakuza* factions, unlike the leaders of organized crime elsewhere in the world, are popular figures. When the boss of Japan's largest *yakuza* faction, the *Yamaguchigumi*, died, famous Japanese politicians, businessmen, and movie stars attended his funeral. The ceremony in which the new boss was initiated was broadcast live on national television. Subsequently, NHK, the national broadcasting company, interviewed the top leaders of the *Yamaguchigumi* in a programme that was viewed by tens of millions of Japanese.

The *yakuza* perceive themselves as the honourable *ronin* of twentieth century Japan. Like the good *ronin* of the eighteenth century who suppressed the banditry of the bad *ronin*, today's *yakuza* claim to control crime by ruling the streets. Petty criminals who are not affiliated with a *yakuza* gang cannot survive. The *yakuza* insist that Japan's low crime rate is the direct result of their vigilance. Over the years, consultations and collaborations with the police have developed into a close working relationship between law enforcement officials and gangster leaders. Traditionally, the *yakuza* leaders have opposed the importation of heroin and have prohibited violence against ordinary Japanese citizens.

Politically aligned with the far right, all of Japan's *yakuza* factions are ultranationalist. They support virtually all of the extremist and militarist movements that call for rearmament and a strong Japan. Like the 47 *ronin* who sacrificed their lives to avenge the wrongful death of their leader, today's *yakuza* perceive themselves as devoted to avenging the wrongful death of Japan's military supremacy. The connections linking the *yakuza* political extremists, certain industries (such as the construction industry) and Japan's political machine (leading factions of the Liberal Democratic Party) have been well-documented.*

## JAPAN THE INVINCIBLE

The myth of the *kamikaze* is one of the best-known myths of Japan. It derives from the thirteenth-century Japanese victory over Kubilai Khan.

By the year 1259, Kubilai Khan had already conquered much of Asia and parts of Europe and would complete his conquest of China by 1278. In 1266 he sent emissaries from Peking, the capital of the eastern section of the Mongol empire, ordering Japan to submit to his rule. Although the royal court in Kyoto was ready to yield, the ruling Hojo family refused to become a tributary vassal of a foreign power. In 1274, Kubilai sent an amphibious force consisting of about 30,000 troops to Hakata Bay in Kyushu, the southernmost of Japan's major islands.

The Mongols, utilizing the massed cavalry tactics that had enabled them to overrun much of the civilized world and equipped with superior weaponry, seemed assured of a quick victory against the Japanese defenders. However a severe storm forced the invaders to return to port with considerable losses before decisive battles could be fought. Kubilai subsequently sent envoys to Japan demanding submission. The envoys were beheaded.

In anticipation of a new invasion the Japanese built a wall around Hakata Bay. They lacked weaponry that could match the Mongols' catapults and gunpowder, but they did train troops in the use of Mongol mass cavalry tactics in order to combat the invaders with their own devices.

In 1281 Kubilai Khan sent 140,000 troops back to Hakata Bay in

---

* It is beyond the scope of this book to explore these interconnections. For English language readers, Kaplan and Dubro, in their study of the *yakuza*, provide clear documentation. There are hundreds of books in the Japanese language which discuss various facets of these linkages.

Kyushu. For two months the Japanese kept the invaders confined to a small beachhead below the defensive wall. It was only a matter of time, however, before the invading army, which had already smashed through the Great Wall of China, would penetrate the Japanese defences. The moment never arrived. A typhoon struck the coast of Kyushu, sinking more than half of the Mongol fleet. Some of the invaders were able to retreat; the rest were killed or enslaved. This was by far the biggest defeat ever suffered by the Mongols under Kubilai Khan.

The Japanese referred to the typhoon as the *kamikaze*, the 'divine wind,' the wind sent by the protective *kami* (the Shinto divinities). With encouragement from the Shinto priests, the *kamikaze* quickly became a mythic symbol in Japanese folklore and tradition. Over the centuries, the *kamikaze* came to exemplify the divine singularity of Japan and of the Japanese people who were inseparable from its islands.

## FROM IMPERIAL LIGHT TO THE DARKNESS OF WAR

The earliest Japanese word for government (*matsurigoto*) means religious observances or worship.* The leader of the ancient Yamato clan was above all else a religious functionary.†

Traditional Shinto beleifs did not establish a sharp distinction between nature and society. After death, society became nature and the souls of people were united with the land. This link between the ancestors and the land of Japan was simply the inversion of the evolution of society from the gods of nature. Furthermore, the distinction between the individual person and society, like the demarcations separating particular souls within the land, was hazy.

In the world of Shinto, the divine and the human, nature and society, are a totality. Not surprisingly, Japanese folklore is filled with entities that are part human and part god. It is a small step from this (necessarily oversimplified) cosmic model to the belief that the emperor is himself a divinity.

Throughout most of Japanese history, the emperor (a religious and sovereign symbol) has been sharply separated from the shogun (a political leader). In the Shinto tradition, the emperor symbolized absolute religious authority but had no *de facto* political power. Even after the Meiji Restoration, when political power was officially 'restored' to the imperial family, the emperor remained a symbol of national unity rather than an active participant in political decision-making.

Japan's first constitution, drafted under the auspices of the Meiji

* Bellah, Robert N. *Tokugawa Religion*. Boston: Beacon Press, 1970, p. 87.
† *Op cit.*, p. 86.

regime, was promulgated in 1889. It established a bicameral parliament under the moral jurisdiction of the emperor. Although this constitution was based on a German model, the *kokutai* (the national entity – a harmonious totality), which radiated from the imperial family like beams of light radiate from a rising sun, was central to it. The *kokutai* consisted of the emperor (and his lineage, which linked him with the sun goddess) and the unique Japanese people.

Long after the death of the Emperor Meiji, during the 1920s and 1930s, the concept of the *kokutai* was subtly reinterpreted. According to a vague socio-political ideology prevalent during the two decades that preceded the Pacific war, the *kokutai* could no longer be perceived as having two components: the emperor and the Japanese people. Instead, the *kokutai* was an absolute unity corresponding to the Japanese state which was itself 'a single great family' whose 'main house' was the imperial family.*

Japanese textbooks during the 1930s communicated this Shinto political and social cosmology. Not coincidentally, this view of history and Japanese society, which prevailed during the 1930s and early 1940s, was not incompatible with the ultranationalism which the military used as a force to seduce Japan into war.

As is well known, Germany's own brand of nationalism used a peculiar blend of philosophies to justify the superiority of the Germanic (Aryan) race. Many of these philosophies, from the Volkism of Fichte to the works of Nietzsche and Heidegger, were adopted by Japanese intellectuals.

More importantly, however, the fact that Germany had provided Japan with a model for its constitution meant that the subversion of the German constitution (and all democratic principles) under Hitler had no little impact on Japan. The growth of fascism in Japan, the emergence of wartime orthodoxy during the late 1930s, and the tragedy of the Pacific war are well known.

## DEFEAT

For 664 years following the 'divine wind' no invader violated Japanese soil. In 1944 and 1945, facing inevitable defeat in the Pacific war, young Japanese pilots used their planes as missiles in massed attacks against US task groups. Named *kamikaze*, these suicide planes were a final desperate attempt to destroy an implacable amphibious force about to invade Japanese territory. They failed.

Japan's defeat and occupation (1945–52) involved a great loss of pride for 'we the Japanese'. Not only was Japanese sovereignty held

* Of course, Japanese political philosophy between 1910 and 1945 was far more complex, consisting of different (and often opposing) views. However, this simplified summary conveys the attitude predominant during the period.

prisoner, but the sacred and mystical bond linking the people with the land was sullied by the presence of foreign authorities. Institutions were altered or liquidated and traditional networks were destroyed or rechannelled. For those who lived through the war and its aftermath, indelible scars were left, serving as life-long reminders of the humiliation wrought by foreign power. The fundamental cause of the catastrophe – the fact that a war had been initiated and lost – was irrelevant to the emotive response to it.

Most of Japan's senior financial bureaucrats in the 1980s were children during the intense fire-bombing of Japanese cities during 1944–45. They witnessed, at first hand and at an impressionable age, the national loss of face. These men (they are nearly all men) are sophisticated specialists. Some of them are among the most urbane and refined diplomats in the world. Although they may harbour little or no bitterness toward the West, they remember the humiliation of defeat. In their speeches the doyens of Japan's financial sector rarely fail to make some reference, however obliquely, to the war years. For most Americans or Europeans currently engaged in international finance, World War II is a remote memory or an irrelevant piece of history. But for their Japanese counterparts, regardless of age, it is one part, however small, of the definition of a Westerner.

Forty years after the Pacific war, Japanese financial institutions competed for underwriting business in the Euromarkets with the biggest universal banks and investment banks of the West. Predatory pricing, an activity far more respectable in underwriting than in manufacturing, was used by Japanese securities houses. As a means of seizing market share, Japanese underwriters sold bonds at a loss. These bonds were referred to as *kamikaze* issues.

The use of the term *kamikaze* to characterize a type of bond can easily be disregarded as a trivial linguistic means of emphasizing the 'suicidal' aspect of selling at a loss. Nevertheless, the reappearance of this term in the international financial world of the 1980s was not coincidental. The Japanese promoters of these bonds, not surprisingly, heatedly denied that they were loss-leaders and would have ridiculed any suggestion of an intended allusion to divine winds and suicide. Yet, the use of the term had a purpose and it was illustrative of a collective world view.

## MONSTER MOVIES

Monster movies were once a Japanese product. Although the genre was not invented in Japan, such films were produced in quantity in Japan's movie studios during the 1950s and 1960s, both for domestic consumption and for export. We have all seen them.

Typically, a bizarre monster, of gigantic proportions and impervious to weapons, begins to destroy the metropolis: buildings topple, trains are derailed, people flee in terror; soon the nation itself is threatened with destruction. Heroes, usually fearlessly dedicated scientists, work tirelessly against impossible odds to find some way of destroying the monster. In the end, they succeed and peace returns. As the film concludes, the viewer knows that, although the damage will be repaired, the memory of the monster and the destruction it has caused will last forever. Often the film concludes with hints that the monster could return.

*Mysterians*, directed in 1958 by Inoshiro Honda, the creator of Godzilla, is one of the most famous examples of the Japanese monster movie genre. It tells the tale of alien superbeings who attempt to conquer the Earth by first taking over Japan. The aliens' arrival is first indicated by a range of localized phenomena, similar to those which occurred in the vicinity of Hiroshima and Nagasaki after the atomic bomb explosions. The ground becomes hot and dead fish float in the rivers. A metallic monster, exuding radioactivity, ravages the countryside. Subsequently, the aliens announce their presence by annexing a small circle of land (one kilometre in radius) outside Tokyo. Later in the film, the aliens demand the right to intermarry with Japanese women. Eventually, Japanese ingenuity, technology, and a hero's self-sacrifice (*kamikaze*-style) defeat the aliens, enabling life to return to normal.

That dozens of monster films were made in Japan, and experienced a period of great popularity among Japanese, during the era of post-Occupation recovery is significant. The wanton and mindless destruction wrought by the monster bears more than a coincidental resemblance to the wartime destruction of Japan's urban centres. Indeed, not only did each monster movie provide a symbolic re-enactment of wartime devastation but, more significantly, it also portrayed the victimization of the Japanese people by irrational forces beyond their control. In the face of the terrifying threat of total annihilation, the populace unites in order to combat the danger. The destructive forces always die and life returns to normal.

Honda's 'mysterians', like the allied occupation forces, were preceded by the devastation of radioactivity and later sometimes took (intermarried with) Japanese women. For the Japanese, whose country had never been occupied and who valued the myth of racial purity, the lost war and the subsequent occupation were very much like an invasion of monsters.

Monster movies were not made for children and they provided the adults who viewed them with a means of unconsciously coming to terms with the effects of the war. Because the monster was unique, and therefore unclassifiable, it could symbolize both the attacks of a foreign military and the awesome danger of the regime that held Japan hostage during the war years.

During the 1960s, as the postwar industrialization and Japan's economic miracle rendered the Japan of 1945 more remote, monster movies faded from popularity. By 1985, Japan had become the world's preeminent manufacturer and trader, achieving a degree of success which stunned the West.

## PEACE AND ARROGANCE

The American Occupation lasted seven years.* In those seven years Japanese history was re-directed along a course it would never otherwise have taken.

In September 1945 Japan resembled a newborn child whose brain is waiting for environmental programming. The country consisted of institutions without superstructure inhabited by people without leadership. Japanese cities were piles of rubble, few factories were left standing, railroads were in disarray, and the people were malnourished. When the emperor's surrender speech was broadcast to the nation, the entire population lost its direction. Instead of a final and devastating 'battle for Japan' civilians and military were faced with unexpected peace.

The American Occupation authorities filled this void in a manner that took the Japanese people by surprise. Expecting a vindictive and merciless rule, the Japanese encountered something quite different. Foreseeing the need for a strong US ally in the Pacific and aware of Japan's strategic location between the United States and the Soviet Union, the American government was determined to transform Japan the totalitarian enemy, into Japan, the democratic ally.

In 1945 the Japanese political system contained both democratic and totalitarian characteristics. Wartime mobilization had entailed a controlled and highly centralized economy. These features were reinforced by institutions for national planning and a close integration between industrial combines (the *zaibatsu*) and government bodies. Such institutions as secret police and severe censorship resulted in a system resembling that of the Soviet Union. Indeed, if Japan had been occupied by the Soviet Union instead of the United States there can be little doubt that Japan would now be a communist nation.

In order to establish Japan as a durable democratic state, comprehensive reforms were instituted. One of the guiding principles of these

* Officially, the occupation of Japan was international, consisting of a thirteen-nation Far Eastern Commission based in Washington as well as an Allied Council based in Tokyo. In reality, however, the Occupation was entirely American, directed by General Douglas MacArthur who had the title of Supreme Commander for the Allied Powers.

reforms was the concept of decentralization. Like Alexis de Tocqueville, the nineteenth century French philosopher, American Occupation experts were persuaded that centralized institutions provide totalitarian rulers with a key to power. Occupation reforms therefore were directed towards the decentralization of every sector of Japan's institutional structure, from the police to the universities.

Eighty-three so-called 'merchants of death' (*zaibatsu* holding companies) were dismantled and anti-monopoly laws were drafted to prevent their reestablishment. Corporate leaders were purged and *zaibatsu* families were stripped of their wealth. Corporate stock was transferred from the hands of the *zaibatsu* into individual ownership. Many government financial institutions were transformed into private institutions. Overall, a comprehensive programme for economic deconcentration was designed and implemented by the Occupation authorities.

The Japanese empire was formally dissolved. *All* ultranationalist organizations were disbanded and made illegal. *All* Japanese soldiers and civilians scattered throughout East and Southeast Asia were sent back to Japan. The entire Japanese armament industry was abolished.

Meanwhile, a new constitution, drafted by Occupation specialists in 1947, renounced war and permitted the maintenance of only a small 'self-defence force'. Japan's martial traditions were officially banished forever.

After the Occupation ended, some reforms were reversed. The *zaibatsu*, for example, regrouped around banks, forming the contemporary *keiretsu*. Thus the anti-monopoly legislation imposed by the Occupation was circumvented. Private ownership of stock fell from 69.1 percent in 1949 to 46.3 percent in 1960 (today it stands at 23 percent).

Although certain sectors reverted back to former patterns during the post-Occupation years, Japan had as a whole been decentralized, deconcentrated, and demilitarized. However, as a result of the massive and enduring changes established by MacArthur and his entourage, the people's national pride was also rechannelled into new outlets. The military and all symbols of military strength were gone. In their place were new postwar industries. Japan's postwar generals were industrialists whose activities were guided by the long-term plans of MITI.

Yet, could the changes established by the Occupation have truly succeeded in destroying a deeply embedded martial tradition? Even more to the point, did Japan's parochial nationalism simply evaporate in 1945? Did the abolishment of ultranationalist organizations mean that ultranationalism disappeared? The answers to these questions, although obvious, are also complex.

During the late 1960s and 1970s, Japan became the free world's second largest economy. At the same time, ultranationalist organizations, banned under the Occupation, reappeared. Concurrently with the development of Japan's strong economy there occurred a resurgence of the same arrogance which had led the Japanese military of the 1940s to believe that its invasion forces would be welcomed by the nations of Southeast Asia.

During the postwar era, Japanese industries exported their products and expanded their market share in Asia and Europe. The riots which greeted Prime Minister Tanaka's visit to Thailand in 1974 were an early symptom of the powerful resentment of Japanese exports which was to be expressed globally a decade later. Many Japanese industrialists and bureaucrats (exemplified by MITI's Kuroda – discussed in Chapter 1) responded aggressively to foreign complaints.

In 1987, with the fires produced by trade friction approaching a flash point, the annual policy statement published by Japan's Ministry of Foreign Affairs contained an unprecedented *critique* of Japanese attitudes. The ministry urged Japanese industry to gain humility in order to accept other cultures. The report warned that nationalism could only result in Japan's isolation from the world community.*

The criticisms presented by the foreign ministry indirectly recognized that Japan had become a major economic power very largely by exporting to the US and Europe. Japan could not afford to neglect the welfare of its trading partners. 'It is imperative in today's increasingly interdependent international community that we share in both the pain and the gain, and it is unacceptable that any one country should selfishly seek to profit at others' expense,' the report lectured Japanese industry.†

Although approved by the cabinet, the report did not necessarily reflect the views of Japanese industry and government, nor was its reprimand likely to be taken to heart by all of Japan's trade negotiators. Japanese bureaucrats who are too young to remember World War II are now approaching senior levels within their ministries. A new generation of corporate executives who know little about the war will soon qualify for senior positions. By the end of the century, Japanese politics and industry will be directed by people who have known only a strong Japan.

Perhaps with this knowledge in mind, the Foreign Ministry pointed out that

there have been some people who say that the Japanese have recently become more arrogant in their perceptions and behaviour.

* Foreign Ministry, 'Blue Book,' Tokyo 1987.
† *Ibid.*

It is impossible either to improve ourselves or to win the trust of other nations unless we have the humility needed to accept other cultures and values and to respect diversity. Should parochial nationalism take hold, Japan could well find itself isolated in the international community.*

The *samurai* placed no value on humility, nor have Japan's ultra-nationalists of the past and present. Will Japan's industrial, financial, and bureaucratic community abandon its arrogance and adopt 'the humility needed to accept other cultures and values?'

* *Ibid.*

# 4 THE WORLD OF INTERNATIONAL FINANCE

**THE YELLOW RIVER**

Despite its imposing title, this brief chapter makes no attempt to provide a detailed atlas of the exotic and arcane world of international finance. Those who seek to map the colourful jargon and abstruse formulas, the deals, the rumours, and the other paraphernalia which are as alien to the average layman as a remote planet must look elsewhere. Instead, the chapter will focus, like a telescope, on just a few selected points in order to reveal their significance; nonetheless, although the distant world cannot be seen in its entirety, these points may reveal something of its nature.

Many financial markets have been international for a long time – at least since sovereign European territorial states began their official existence following the Peace of Westphalia in 1648. Nevertheless, during the past 25 years, and particularly during the past three, a new pattern of global investment in the world's major financial markets has been altering the character of international finance.

There is nothing subtle about these changes. Just as the Yellow River periodically shifts its course by hundreds of miles, altering the topography of China, so today the world's capital flows are changing their course. As in China, the floodwaters will recede, leaving many casualties and a permanently changed environment.

**GLASS-STEAGALL AND OTHER AMERICAN ANTIQUES**

Over the past two decades finance has become totally dependant upon electronic and telecommunications technologies previously undreamed of and, at the same time, the Euromarkets (discussed below) have taken on a life of their own while new and complex financial instruments sired by investment bankers have been born in New York and London. In this new world, American financial institutions are still governed by regulations written in 1927 and 1933.

American commercial banks and securities firms conduct their domestic business under the guidance of archaic laws which could not have anticipated the creation of the high-speed computers and satellite communications that have facilitated the awesomely competitive global finance of the late twentieth century.

The Banking Act of 1933, best known as the Glass-Steagall Act, was a child of the New Deal. It was based upon the assumption that it was the dominant position of the banks in the securities industry during the 1920s, leading to widespread conflicts of interest, which had precipitated the Great Depression. The Act, which was intended to eliminate corrupt self-dealing by the banking industry, created a so-called Chinese Wall between commercial banking (the business of taking deposits and lending money) and investment banking (the business of underwriting and dealing in non-government securities). Thus, most American banks cannot be affiliated with securities companies and banks are prohibited from owning or being owned by an entity that is not part of the banking industry.

The most important consequence of Glass-Steagall is that American commercial banks are prohibited from issuing, underwriting, selling, or distributing new corporate securities offerings as well as most municipal revenue bonds. By the same token securities companies cannot take deposits or extend loans. The effect of separating the issuance of new securities from investment in those securities in fiduciary accounts, was to deny commercial banks virtually all access to the securities industry. One consequence is that today American banks – unlike Japanese banks which are simultaneously primary shareholders (limited to 5 percent) and creditors of domestic corporations – do not buy corporate stock for their own accounts. US banks do not own a piece of corporate America.

The decline of the Glass-Steagall Act is already underway, as was demonstrated by a number of regulatory and judicial decisions in 1986 and 1987. For example, a federal court of appeals ruled in 1986 that Bankers Trust was entitled to sell commercial paper (uncollateralized short-term corporate debt). A 1987 decision permitted the subsidiaries of bankholding companies to provide investment advice. Later in 1987 the Federal Reserve Bank authorized seven bankholding companies to underwite consumer-related receivables.

At about the same time, several major American banks bought stakes in Canadian securities dealers (for example, Security Pacific's acquisition of Burns and Fry). Although a few US banks already owned British stockbrokers (Security Pacific bought London-based Hoare Govett in 1982), a move into the securities industry so close to home indicated a growing conviction that Glass-Steagall would eventually be abrogated.

In the autumn of 1987, the Chairman of the Senate Banking Committee, William Proxmire, announced plans to introduce legislation that would repeal Glass-Steagall. At the same time a report from a House committee recommended a restructuring of US financial services laws that would permit an amalgamation of commercial and investment banking as well as ownership of banks by non-banking companies. Nevertheless, although the letter of the law will be liberally interpreted, the *total* elimination of Glass-Steagall – which would pave the way for the establishment of large multi-service US bank-holding companies – is not likely to occur soon.

Meanwhile, US stockbrokers have long offered domestic customers 'cash management accounts' (pioneered by Merrill Lynch) which bear a striking resemblance to savings accounts. Brokers also provide other services which are paving the way for the union of broking and banking. For example, the Advest Group Inc (a diversified financial services holding company based in Hartford, Connecticut) has since 1985 offered clients a service that connects banks and brokerage firms by computer. The system enables money deposited in a brokerage account to be transferred to the client's bank account.

While Glass-Steagall remains a topic of debate, the McFadden Act of 1927, which (along with the Douglas Amendment of 1956) bans interstate banking, is disintegrating. As big regional banks merge with banks in other states, America's embedded banking tradition of geographical segmentation is fading away. This trend was exemplified by the 1987 merger of First Fidelity of New Jersey and Fidelcor of Pennsylvania, which created the seventeenth largest bank (in terms of assets) in the United States.

As a result of the development of inter-regional banking, commercial bank deposits in particular states will increasingly be owned by out-of-state institutions. Already, the five largest commercial banks in Maine are owned by banks located in other New England states.

Of course, not all of America's more than 14,000 regional banks and the hordes of 'thrifts' (savings and loan companies and credit unions) will evaporate in a new torrid financial climate, nor will monster 'superbanks' (or 'megabanks') emerge to dominate the financial jungle.

Nonetheless, major bankholding companies in the United States will significantly expand the range and scale of their national and international business. Mergers of large commercial banks, and even hostile takeovers within the banking sector (a trend initiated by the Bank of New York in September 1987), will become commonplace.

Such mergers will produce larger and better-capitalized 'super-regional' banks. Facing declining profitability, the regionals and thrifts will be forced to experiment with new financial products.

Another development that will occur in parallel with the emergence of interstate banking, will be the entry of American banks into areas that have previously been the exclusive preserve of the securities industry. Sectors of securities underwriting such as commercial paper, mortgage-backed securities, mutual funds and municipal revenue bonds will eventually fall firmly into banking territory. In the process, Glass-Steagall, like a piece of old furniture, will be relegated to an attic corner. But it will not be destroyed and, in the event of a banking crisis, it could be restored and modernized. Today's cast-outs become tomorrow's antiques.

## ARTICLE 65, JAPAN'S FINANCIAL CONSTITUTION

Japanese securities companies were born the unique world of late nineteenth- and early twentieth-century Japan. During the Meiji Restoration (1868–1912) Japanese finance was transformed from unregulated medieval transactions to a modern system. Giant banks blossomed at the centres of the *zaibatsu* holding companies; mutual loan companies (termed *mujin*) provided funding to small businesses and brokers traded securities (primarily bonds) in Japan's small but proliferating stock exchanges. During the half century from the establishment of the Bank of Japan (1882) to the maturing of Japan's economy in the 1930s, Japan's securities companies plied their trade as small financial institutions devoted primarily to the sale of bonds.

In their efforts to 'democratize' Japan, the Occupation authorities attempted to create a modified Japanese financial system based on the American model. Just as one group of American experts wrote a democratic constitution for Japan, another drafted legislation for the financial sector. Article 65 of the Securities and Exchange Act of 1948 was designed as a Japanese version of the Glass-Steagall Banking Act. Those who formulated it believed that Japan's big banks would be prevented from consolidating new power if a separate securities industry were permitted to develop.

Article 65 separates the Japanese banking and securities industries. It prohibits banks from selling equity or underwriting primary securities issues and under its terms Japanese securities companies, like their American counterparts, are not allowed to accept deposits or extend loans in their domestic market.

By assuring that the major banks – with their national networks of branches and established corporate relationships – could not compete with securities firms, Article 65 enabled the Big Four securities companies (Nomura, Daiwa, Nikko and Yamaichi) to grow rapidly and to become Asia's biggest investment bankers and brokers.

Just as Glass-Steagall has been eroded by the financial deregulation and liberalization of the 1980s, so holes have begun to appear in the edifice of Article 65. The substantial budget deficits resulting from the two oil 'shocks' led the Ministry of Finance to allow Japanese banks to sell government bonds in the secondary market and, beginning in 1980, the Big Four began to sell government bond funds that functioned as virtual savings accounts.

Article 65, like Glass-Steagall, was enacted with domestic issues in mind and was not intended to regulate the foreign financial activities of Japanese institutions. Banking operations were established by Japanese securities firms, first in Luxembourg and Amsterdam, and subsequently in London. Simultaneously, overseas branches of Japanese banks engaged in the underwriting of foreign corporate securities and their financial subsidiaries participated in a wide range of activities denied to their parents in the home market. London and other foreign financial centres became the testing grounds for financial activities that could not be attempted in Japan.

At home, while Japanese banks have been completely excluded from stock market business, foreign banks have been allowed to set up securities branches in Tokyo. Beginning with the universal banks of Germany and Switzerland in 1985–86 and continuing with American banks in June 1987, more than two dozen foreign banking institutions now conduct brokerage business in Japan. As a result, foreign banks are now able to underwrite corporate securities in Japan while Japanese banks are still denied that opportunity by Article 65.

The Ministry of Finance, however, does not customarily favour foreign institutions at the expense of the domestic firms that it is designed to protect and regulate. It is only a matter of time (a few years at most) before Japanese banks receive authorization to establish partially-owned securities branches in Japan. When that happens, Article 65 will have become an amalgam of regulatory tension and deregulatory relaxation.

## MERGING, ACQUIRING AND DIVERSIFYING

Carlo de Benedetti (the chief executive officer of Olivetti and a leading European entrepreneur) has commented that, 'The traditional multinational approach [to business] is dépassé. Corporations with international ambitions must turn to a new strategy of agreements, alliances, and mergers with other companies.'* This trend is becoming ever more apparent in the financial world.

*Quoted by *Business Week*, 24 August 1987, p. 42.

Manufacturers, for example, have been joining the financial services industry through acquisition and structural change. American Can Company, which owns the investment bank Smith Barney, transformed itself into Primerica, a financial services conglomerate. Volvo has an in-house bank and a stockbroking subsidiary.

Similarly, the old-line retailer Sears Roebuck has used more than the stars to plot its special route to the securities industry and banking. The largest retailer of financial services in the United States, Sears provides brokerage (through its Dean Witter subsidiary), property and life insurance (though its Allstate subsidiary), savings (through the Sears Savings Bank and other facilities) and real estate services (through Coldwell Banker). In 1986, Xerox Corporation derived 47 percent of its operating profits from financial services sold by leading financial boutiques that it had acquired.

In Japan, the Ministry of Finance has not permitted non-financial corporations to merge with banks or other financial institutions, whether Japanese or foreign-owned. But, Japanese corporations have been free to set up financial subsidiaries overseas. During the 1980s, more than fifty major Japanese corporations, from Nippon Steel to Sony, have created new financial businesses in Europe and the United States. In 1986, for example, the Sumitomo Corporation, one of Japan's leading trading companies, created three foreign subsidiaries: Sumitomo Corporation Overseas Capital, Ltd, incorporated in the Cayman Islands, Sumitomo Finance International SA, incorporated in Panama, and Sumicorp Finance, Ltd, incorporated in London. These financial subsidiaries are designed to increase corporate profits by participating in international financial arbitrage, termed *zaitek* in Japan (*zaitek* is discussed further in Chapter 5).

## STOCKMARKET GROWTH AND TURMOIL

At the end of 1986, total global stockmarket capitalization reached $5.616 trillion. The fastest-growing stockmarkets have been in Japan. From 1975 to 1986, while the US share of global equity capitalization fell from 61.2 percent to 39.2 percent, Japan's share grew from 12.3 percent to 31.8 percent.

Many of the world's major equity markets doubled in value between mid–1985 and mid–1987. During one eighteen-month period (31 December 1985 to 31 July 1987), the world's major stockmarkets performed outstandingly. Curiously, the most growth occurred in the countries famous for bullfighting: Mexico led the world's equity markets with an index gain of 1,722 percent (in pesos) – a gain of 544 percent in US dollar terms – and Spain, the runner-up, gained 133 percent.

While the New York Stock Exchange reached record highs in the summer of 1987, the leading Pacific Basin markets (Tokyo, Hong Kong, Singapore and Australia) gave investors local currency return of roughly 100 percent. Because of these opportunities to reap handsome profits, combined with the promise of foreign exchange gains, American investors increased foreign investments in 1986 to $1.068 trillion (up 13 percent from 1985).

This period of outstanding global stockmarket performance was attributable to many causes. In addition to factors such as low interest rates and stable oil supplies, there were other, less familiar, influences at work. *Financial innovation* combined with positive *supply-demand factors* was instrumental in spurring the world's equity markets to heights that would have been considered beyond reason several years ago. The continuing *deregulation* of most of the world's financial markets and the concurrent *privatization of government assets* also played their part in stimulating equity market growth.

On 'Black Monday,' 19 October 1987, the 'crash of '87' wiped out a sizeable portion of world stockmarket growth. On that day, the Dow Jones Industrial Average fell 508 points, a decline of 22.6 percent. European stock prices plummeted and Asian equity markets followed. The Hong Kong Stock Exchange was closed and, when it reopened the following week, the Hang Seng Index lost one third of its value.

Portfolio insurance (a hedging technique that involves the sale of stock index futures to protect an equity portfolio from the effects of a declining market) was a primary cause of the US crash. Another potent catalyst was a growing fear of a sharp rise in US interest rates. By the early autumn of 1987, substantial central bank intervention to support the dollar was believed to be the inevitable precursor of tightening US monetary policy.

At the year end, by which point the dust had begun to settle, the British equity market had grown a modest 3.6 percent in 1987 while the US stockmarket had lost virtually all of its 1987 growth (down 30 percent from its peak). At the same time, France and Switzerland had each lost 30 percent, Italy 33 percent, and West Germany 40 percent. Alone among the world's major stockmarkets, Japan had risen significantly over the year – up 8.2 percent in yen terms.

While foreign investors in the Japanese stockmarket frenetically liquidated their holdings during the week of Black Monday, Japanese investors were net buyers of stock. As a result, although price volatility increased, the Japanese stockmarket remained remarkably stable. Good economic growth, growing domestic demand, and expanding domestic liquidity, promise to sustain the Japanese stockmarket for some time to come.

Throughout the free world, from Tokyo to Turkey, shares in government-owned companies have been sold to the public. Pension

funds, mutual funds, and individuals hungry for a high return fever-
ishly purchased these shares in 1985–87. Significantly, a sizeable
portion of these purchases were made by foreign investors. International US mutual funds, for example, tripled in size in three years,
rising from $5 billion in 1984 to nearly $16 billion in 1986. Because
international investment improves overall risk-adjusted returns, institutional investors often sought to diversify their portfolios by
purchasing issues from the world's major markets.

The most international of these markets is the Euromarket, where
traders study screens to learn the latest prices and use telephones or
telexes to execute their buy or sell orders. In the Euromarket, the
model for the markets of the future, exchange floors peopled by traders
excitedly buying or selling shares are as obsolete as slide rules.

## STATELESS (BUT NOT HOMELESS) MARKETS

In the summer of 1944, although much of Europe already lay in ruins;
the decisive Battle of the Bulge had not yet been fought and Japan
was not to surrender for another year. The meetings of the Western
allies that occurred at the time mostly involved military men and
were primarily concerned with the war effort. An exception was the
meeting of allied representatives in Bretton Woods, New Hampshire
in July 1944. In this quiet place economists from the United States,
Great Britain (John Maynard Keynes was there) and other allied
nations met in order to reach an agreement regarding the structure
of the postwar international monetary system.

The Bretton Woods Agreement had one goal: the establishment of
stable, mutually convertible currencies. The outcome of the meeting
is well-known. The International Monetary Fund (IMF) was created
as an international agency, designed to facilitate cooperation among
nations within the postwar international monetary system. This would
be achieved, it was hoped, through the stabilization of exchange rates
and the establishment of a multilateral payments system among
member countries. The Agreement also resulted in the creation of the
World Bank (officially known as the International Bank for Reconstruction and Development) which was intended to ensure capital
adjustments among member countries in order to promote postwar
reconstruction and the development of remote areas.

By means of the IMF, member nations submitted a par value of
their currencies expressed in terms of gold (or of the US dollar).
Subsequently, all exchange transactions were conducted at a rate
permitted to diverge by no more than 1 percent from this par value.
Overall, the Bretton Woods Agreement laid the foundations of the
postwar international monetary system.

During the 1950s virtually all of the nations in the free world maintained (directly or indirectly) a stable relationship between the dollar and their own currencies. Officially, within this system, the US dollar was the only currency that was directly convertible into gold. As a result, the reserves of most central banks came to consist predominantly of dollars (rather than gold).

During the late 1950s and 1960s, the growth of the US balance of payments deficit gradually threatened to destabilize the system based on the Bretton Woods Agreement. In order to prevent, or at least forestall, the inevitable demise of the agreement, the US government took a number of actions which were to have unforeseen and profound effects on the world of international finance.

In 1963, in an attempt to prevent the outflow of private capital from the United States, the Kennedy Administration imposed an Interest Equalization Tax (IET) on the value of all foreign securities purchased by US residents. The 18.75 percent tax* forced foreign borrowers to raise funds outside the United States and compelled most American investors to abandon the purchase of foreign securities.

Although the tax reduced the outflow of funds for foreign investment, the desired result was not achieved because American banks increased their lending to foreign borrowers while US corporations increased their foreign direct investments. Consequently, in 1965, the Johnson Administration applied the IET to bank loans to foreigners and encouraged US banks to voluntarily curb overseas lending. Three years later, this 'voluntary restraint program' was replaced by 'mandatory investment controls' which required that the overseas subsidiaries of American corporations raise their funds outside the United States.

The IET and the introduction of investment controls stimulated the swift growth of Eurocurrencies, particularly Eurodollars. A Eurocurrency is simply a bank deposit in a European bank located outside the country which issued the currency. Thus, for example, a dollar deposit in a London bank creates Eurodollars. Eurocurrencies were made possible by the Bretton Woods Agreement which assured the free convertibility of currencies.

Financial markets based on Eurocurrencies grew rapidly during the 1960s as the overseas operations of American corporations, prevented from raising money in the US, fulfilled their borrowing needs by issuing dollar debt in Europe. Eurocurrency banking developed during this period as a wholesale banking sector serving corporations, governments, and supranational organizations such as the World Bank. Because the Euromarket was free from government regulation, it provided an avenue for the rapid mobilization and allocation of funds.

*Later reduced to 11.25 percent and finally abolished in 1974.

A corporation wishing to raise capital in a hurry could go to the Euromarkets and issue debt without waiting for government approval.

During this same period the US government's balance of payments deficit continued to increase while, simultaneously, international confidence in the dollar plummeted. Finally, on 15 August 1971, the Bretton Woods Agreement collapsed when President Nixon halted the gold convertibility of the dollar, permitting the currency to float in the foreign exchange markets. This action, which was termed the 'Nixon shock' in Japan (see Chapter 2), caused the yen to appreciate by nearly 17 percent in less than a year.

The Eurodollar bond market continued to thrive during this period of currency crisis, growing from $17.4 billion in 1966 to $65 billion in 1971, a growth rate of about 28 percent per year. It continued to grow throughout the 1970s, reaching $575 billion in 1980 and doubling in size again by 1985. At the same time, securities markets and money markets in a whole range of Eurocurrencies (e.g. yen, deutsche marks, Swiss francs) slowly blossomed.

In 1979, major European countries eliminated foreign exchange controls. A year later, under international pressure, Japan enacted a new free-in-principle foreign exchange law. During the 1980s, most of the major economies in the non-communist world established liberal foreign exchange laws. An exception to this trend was Taiwan, one of the newly industrialized countries of East Asia, which maintained strict foreign exchange laws and, as a result, had by June 1987, amassed $60 billion in foreign exchange reserves, the second largest reserves in the world after West Germany.

Throughout the 1980s US corporations continued to borrow funds in the Eurodollar market in order to take advantage of interest rates below those available at home, while the United States was forced to pay out more in dollars for imported goods than it received for US exports. As a result, expanding US balance of payment deficits caused Eurodollars to become the largest short-term pool of funds in the world, exceeding $2 trillion in 1986.

During the 1980s the world's financial institutions were able to move funds freely among most countries and currencies. This new freedom encouraged the creation of new products designed to protect investors from currency and interest rate volatility. While bonds with fixed interest rates did not become extinct, new vehicles providing interest rates which floated with the market were introduced.

In 1979, before the removal of foreign exchange controls, about 5 percent of British pension funds were invested in foreign stock; by 1986 the figure was more than 16 percent. Similarly, US investors increased their holdings of foreign equity from $19 billion in 1982 to $41 billion at the end of 1985.

New technologies facilitated the invention of novel and complex market instruments which thrived in the unregulated Euromarkets. During the 1980s, developments in electronics and telecommunications made it possible to trade vast blocks of securities with unprecedented ease, via video screens and on exchange trading floors.

Although the first Eurobond issued in yen was floated in 1977, it was not until December 1984 that the Japanese Ministry of Finance authorized foreign corporations to float yen denominated debt in the Euromarkets. In 1986, Euroyen issues totaled $18.66 billion, making the yen the most popular currency of issue in the Euromarkets after the dollar.

By 1987, the Eurobond market had become the third largest securities market in the world (after New York and Tokyo) in terms of total debt and the second largest market in terms of volume traded. Thus, in just fifteen years, the Euromarket became an intrinsic part of the global financial system, representing a vital source of financing for international trade and investment.

Yet no sooner had the Euromarket achieved this remarkable size and liquidity, than it began to show signs of old age and incipient decrepitude. At the end of 1986, the market in perpetual floating rate notes collapsed, leaving bankers and investors with an estimated $18 billion worth of useless paper. Perpetual debt, a Euromarket 'innovation', is undated which means that its holder is never paid back. (Semi-annual interest, indexed to a money market rate, is paid out but the debt can only be traded not redeemed.) The demise of this new Euromarket sector damaged the market's reputation, bringing into question its capacity to maintain long-term liquidity.


Dollar and yen deposits in Singapore and Hong Kong led to the emergence of 'Asia dollar' and 'Asia yen' markets which constituted a smaller scale parallel of the Eurocurrency markets. During the 1980s, Asia dollar bonds and Asia yen bonds were underwritten by Japanese securities firms for East and Southeast Asian borrowers. At the same time, markets in Asian certificates of deposit emerged in Tokyo, Hong Kong, and Singapore. Most of these 'Asian CDs' were denominated in dollars or yen. In Japan, foreign currency denominated bonds ('shogun issues') were floated on the domestic market; but, due to regulatory constraints, the 'shogun bond' market was not able to compete with the Euromarket. Offshore banking in Singapore, Hong Kong and, most recently, Tokyo, will assure the continuance of markets in Asia currencies.

In 1985, the Swiss food company, Nestlé, raised the equivalent of $425 million from three equity issues. For each of the three issues, Credit Suisse First Boston assembled a syndicate of US and European banks which underwrote and sold the Nestlé shares directly to investors, so bypassing the stock exchanges. Thus, like the Euroband market, the emerging market in primary Euroequity issues is international and has no trading floor, employing Eurobond syndication techniques. The international Euroequity market enables corporations to raise more capital more quickly than would be possible by means of individual domestic equity markets. In 1986, Euroequity issues of all types reached roughly $12 billion compared to $1 billion in 1983.

As deregulation makes global capital markets increasingly interdependent and prone to move together, instruments and prices will become ever more uniform. As a result, the Euromarket will lose its central role as the international market *par excellence*. Investors intending to buy bonds denominated in a range of currencies will find it easy and economical to do so in their home markets. Thus, one measure of the deregulation among the world's major economies and the parallel globalization of securities markets will be the decline in importance of the Euromarket.

## THE ROLE OF TECHNOLOGY
The Euromarket, a product of financial pressures in the world of the 1960s, became the outstanding example of the application of high technology to finance during the 1980s. The sumultaneous distribution of information and the virtually instantaneous processing of orders resulted in the creation of a remarkably efficient marketplace.

Because all borrowers and lenders in the market had access to virtually identical information, intermediaries found it necessary to offer new instruments in order to increase their market share. Of course, financial instruments can be swiftly copied by competitors. There is, therefore, a constant need to innovate and financial institutions were forced to devise new products – or products which seemed to be new – and a host of novel investment instruments, some with exotic acronyms such as LYONS, COLTS, TIGRS, and CATS, appeared.

Computer programs designed to hedge complex chains of risk were devised and new financial instruments proliferated like rabbits. Products such as Nomura Security Company's 'Heaven and Hell' bond (which involved three interest rate swaps as well as five currency swaps) appeared on the scene. Hybrid creatures such as 'stock performance exchange linked bonds' enabled investors to obtain unique exposure to equity and fixed income components in a single product.

In their efforts to differentiate between virtually identical products, underwriters contrived ever more imaginative special features intended to enhance appeal without necessarily improving yields.

At the same time, new financial technology improved the ability of commercial banks to 'securitize' their loans by repackaging them as debt instruments (issuing negotiable securities backed by them). The securitization of mortgages, bank loans, auto loans, and credit card receivables became standard procedures. In the United States, public issues of securities collateralized by mortgages and other assets surpassed $60 billion in 1986, a three-fold increase over the preceding year. Meanwhile, bonds were routinely 'stripped' in order to enable buyers to invest in either principal or interest coupons.

Technological developments thus began to transform long-term credit risks into market risks and this, in turn, is gradually changing the character of commercial banking. When Glass-Steagall has been transformed from a hulking, fearsome guardian of the border between banking and securities to an emaciated and ineffectual symbol, American banks will be experts in the art of creating and marketing securities instruments.

Not only has technology given birth to new markets and market instruments, it has also enabled existing markets to grow to extraordinary size. Daily transactions on the foreign exchange markets, for instance, ordinarily surpass $200 billion per day. By 1987 international capital flows had expanded in volume to the point at which they were fifty times as great as the total volume of world trade.

Some technical innovations were particularly successful. For example, the development of collateralized mortgage obligations (CMO) by Shearson Lehman created a vast market. (A CMO is simply a floating rate debt security collateralized by a portfolio of mortgages, such as GNMAs, and carrying lower rates than long-term fixed rate securities.) The US market in these and other mortgage-backed securities exceeded $300 billion in 1985 while secondary market trading reached $1.6 trillion. (In 1987 a single investment bank, Merrill Lynch, lost more than $300 million in the mortgage-backed security market.) Trading volumes such as these would have been impossible without modern developments in computer hardware and software. Thus, as new technological developments occur in the future new financial instruments are likely to follow.

In late 1987 US bond rating agencies, led by Moody's Investors Service Inc, decided to give triple-A ratings to securities backed by junk bonds. The $150 billion US junk bond market consists of bonds with ratings of double-B-plus (S&P) or Ba1 (Moody's) or lower. Offering yields from 2 to 5 percent above those on triple-A securities, junk bonds will provide a basis for a vast pool of new collateralized securities.

## SILENT COMPUTERS IN THE OFFICE REPLACE THE OUTCRY IN THE PITS

It has long been known that 'pit trading' with the 'open outcry' produces the most efficient and liquid markets. It is this knowledge which underlies the method of floor trading found in the world's stock markets and futures exchanges. Despite its benefits, however, the open outcry may be slowly replaced by automation.

So far, it must be said, automation has not been readily accepted in the world's stock and futures exchanges. The first fully automated financial futures market was Bermuda's International Financial Futures Exchange (Intex). But although the automated system enables trades to be executed accurately in less than three seconds from anywhere in the world, Intex has been struggling to survive since it opened in October 1984. Citicorp and McGraw-Hill were forced to abandon an electronic oil and petrochemical trading venture after only six months of operation because of insufficient trading volume. The largely automated Tokyo Stock Exchange's bond futures market, which has no trading floor, has however been thriving.

Most of the world's futures exchanges have recognized the need for globalization but are at the same time reluctant to encourage automation. Instead, futures exchanges in the United States, Europe and Asia have been establishing linkages which permit identical contracts to be traded on exchanges on different continents.

The American Stock Exchange established linked trading in stock index options with the European Options Exchange in Amsterdam. In a modestly successful venture, the Chicago Mercantile Exchange (Merc) has tied-up with the Singapore Monetary Exchange for linked Eurodollar futures trading. The Sydney Futures Exchange has attempted tie-ups with the London International Financial Futures Exchange (Liffe) and the New York Commodity Exchange (Comex) for linked trading in US Treasury bond futures and gold futures, respectively. The tie-up has been a dismal failure with negligible trading. The problem with these, and nearly all other exchange linkages, is that major and minor exchanges are tied together. Invariably, the smaller exchange does not have sufficient liquidity to attract the major traders of the big exchange.

A number of futures exchanges have established night trading hours. The Chicago Board of Trade introduced a three-hour weekday evening trading session in April 1987 and, later in the year, inaugurated a Sunday night session to coincide with the opening of Monday morning business in Tokyo. The Philadelphia Stock Exchange added a four-hour session to its regular trading hours for foreign currency options. However, these attempts to establish around the clock trading opportunities in particular contracts will inevitably be outmoded by total automation which will render trading floors functionally superfluous.

In the United States the National Association of Securities Dealers Automated Quotations (NASDAQ), in which stocks are traded on video screens, has become the world's third largest equity market. Among US stock exchanges, only the New York Stock Exchange requires that members transact all business on the floor. In 1987, California-based Security Pacific National Bank received authorization from the Federal Reserve Board to create an automated marketplace for domestic government security options.

In Canada, the Toronto Stock Exchange (through its Computer Assisted Trading system) provides fully automated trading and execution of orders. In 1985, Toronto became the first of the world's stock exchanges to establish a trading link with a foreign stock exchange (Amex – the American Stock Exchange).

The Paris Bourse abandoned its traditonal trading system (involving 45 licensed stockbrokers) and adopted an automated system developed and operated by the Toronto Stock Exchange. Similarly, the seven Swiss stock exchanges used NASDAQ as a consultant in order to adapt the NASDAQ system.

The first section of the Tokyo Stock Exchange has been computerized since 1986 and on-line connections provide access via computer terminals at all of the securities companies. Through the Computer Assisted Orders Routing and Execution System (based on the Toronto system) trading of shares is fully automated (with the exception of 250 heavily traded issues which are still traded on the floor). Thus, orders can be immediately executed during trading hours by using the Cores system at any securities company office.

Instinet, a Canadian subsidiary of Reuters (the UK-based information group) offers an equity trading system which automatically matches buy and sell orders. Used extensively by block traders in the United States, Instinet handles billions of dollars of trading business per month. Although currently opposed by British regulatory authorities, Instinet will eventually be used in the UK (probably within five years) for the execution of small orders.

An event which shocked futures traders in September 1987 has foreshadowed the eventual demise of open outcry trading. Reuters successfully concluded negotiations with the Chicago Mercantile Exchange (Merc) and, under a new agreement which will take effect in 1989, Reuter's 130,000 screens will be used for the automated trading of financial futures and options contracts when the Chicago market is closed. During off-trading hours the Reuter Dealer Trading System will instantly execute trades, including preprogrammed instructions.

In order to compete with Merc, other exchanges will institute similar arrangements. The Matif financial futures exchange in Paris (which made its debut in 1986) is planning electronic trading before and after its regular session. The New York Mercantile Exchange has discussed the electronic trading of oil futures through a tie-up with Reuters. If these developments materialize and flourish they will signify a big leap in the direction of 24-hour dealing in financial instruments *and* a major weakening of the importance of the open outcry method.

Automation is now rendering the world's stock exchanges accessible to every trader in the free world, regardless of nationality or location. Consequently, competition will become ever more intense and will result in cheaper prices and greater product uniformity.

A small number of securities will always be traded on the floors of the world's major stock and futures exchanges; but the day is not far distant when trading in the pits by open outcry will be seen as a quaint anachronism, like the Dixie Land Jazz of New Orleans.

## GNOMES NEVER SLEEP

Currencies are uniform and can be traded in vast volumes. It is therefore scarcely surprising that foreign exchange trading led to the development of the first truly global 24-hour financial market. As early as the 1960s, major international banks were using their excess liquidity to exploit significant arbitrage opportunities in the foreign exchange markets. When President Nixon effectively demolished the Bretton Woods Agreement in 1971, he blamed international bankers, exemplified by the 'gnomes of Zurich,' suggesting that they were scheming to undermine the US monetary system.

Today, the automated trading of major currencies occurs around the clock in the world's commercial banks, investment banks, and merchant banks. In Tokyo, for example, trading houses (*sogo shosha*) have established their own foreign exchange trading rooms while the international offices of Japan's city banks 'pass the book' from Tokyo to London to New York to Los Angeles. Foreign exchange trading follows the sun.

The second global market, which is now emerging, is trading in government bonds. Government bonds resemble currencies – like money, they are backed by the government that issues them and they can be traded in large amounts.

Government bond yields have been adjusting with increasing rapidity to underlying currency pressures. As a result, the effort on the part of the central banks of the industrial nations to stabilize currency exchange rates and interest rates has begun to look like a zero-sum game. For if foreign exchange rates stabilize then interest rates become increasingly volatile. This may be inevitable, because foreign exchange and interest rates are the expressions of changing economic forces in the world of nations. Like drainage canals alleviating pressure in a riverine system, exchange and interest rates provide the outlet for the forces that underlie changing global economic factors.

Offshore bond trading (that is, the trading of yen bonds in London or dollar bonds in Tokyo) has grown steadily during the 1980s and will continue to expand as the world's securities markets are deregulated. The development of markets in bond futures in Chicago, New York, London, Singapore, and Sydney has provided investors with a vital means to hedge their positions.

A key event in the development of a 24-hour bond market has been the dramatic increase in the net purchases of American Treasury issues by Japanese investors. In 1985, Japanese purchases of Treasuries totaled $19.2 billion, a threefold increase over the preceding year; and the volume almost tripled again in 1986, reaching about $50 billion. This enormous net investment in US bonds encouraged the trading of Treasuries in Tokyo while New York slept.

In London, the biggest market in the world for the trading of foreign exchange and Eurobonds, global 24-hour trading in Eurobonds has become routine. Eventually, deregulation of the Japan Offshore Banking Market will lead to the relocation of the Euroyen bond market to Tokyo.

If Tokyo, London and New York are regarded as three corners of a market triangle, then the structure for a unified (and unlinked) global stockmarket already exists – thanks to differentials between the time zones. A company listed on all three markets can be traded 17.5 hours per day, and the hearty trader determined to doggedly follow the three markets need only adhere to the schedule in the table below.

Already, at the end of each trading day in New York, major American and Japanese brokers pass on unexecuted orders to Tokyo, and when trading in Tokyo closes, brokers send new or unexecuted orders to London.

In addition to these three major markets, the Amsterdam Stock Exchange (which lists more foreign than local issues) offers 24-hour trading in a selected number of stocks listed on the New York and Tokyo stock exchanges. Not surprisingly, all the big Japanese securities companies (except Nikko) are members of the exchange. The Zurich Stock Exchange also offers trading in some major foreign shares.

The 49 market-makers on the London Stock Exchange provide prices for more than 200 international stocks. More than half of the dealing in these foreign issues involves investors based outside Britain. Before long, options on some foreign stocks will also be traded on the London Stock Exchange.

Today, New York and London stand alone as the world's two truly international financial markets. But Tokyo is gradually developing the market depth and diversity necessary to compete in 24-hour global trading. During the course of the next five years, Tokyo will join London and New York as an international financial market, providing the same opportunities to international investors. Eventually, the New York, Tokyo, and London stock markets will be connected by a single computer system so that orders unfilled in one market can automatically be transmitted to the next. Gradually, fixed trading hours will become superfluous and will be abandoned in favour of perpetual, computer executed, trading.

### ONE DAY IN THE LIFE OF A TRIPARTITE STOCK MARKET

|  | New York | London | Tokyo |
| --- | --- | --- | --- |
| New York Stock Exchange opens | 09:30 | 14:30 | 23:30 |
| London Stock Exchange closes | 10:30 | 15:30 | 00:30 |
| New York Stock Exchange closes | 16:00 | 21:00 | 06:00 |
| [Sleep 4 hours] |  |  |  |
| Tokyo Stock Exchange opens | 20:00 | 01:00 | 10:00 |
| Tokyo Stock Exchange closes | 01:30 | 06:30 | 15:30 |
| [Sleep 2½ hours] |  |  |  |
| London Stock Exchange opens | 04:00 | 09:00 | 18:00 |

## GLOBALIZATION OF THE WORLD'S STOCKMARKETS

A market can be simply defined as a system in which buyers and sellers of a product are in communication with one another. But an efficient market is also a system which brings into focus all of the forces which determine prices. In the strict sense of the term, world markets for most commodities have existed for a long time.

The gold prospector in the remote Brazilian jungle sells his nuggets at the trading post in accordance with prices determined in London and Chicago. Similarly, a particular US treasury bond costs the same in New York or Brasilia. If it were possible to buy US treasury bonds for less gold in Brasilia than in New York, New Yorkers would fill their suitcases with gold and take a Brazilian holiday. Market prices would swiftly adjust.

Of course, there will always be arbitrage opportunities between bonds or bills of exchange with different maturity dates when the interest rates diverge. Foreign exchange trading will always flourish.

But overall, so long as free competition is unconstrained, efficiency will guide market prices. Keep your eye on the invisible hand.

Today, bonds are traded in dollars, yen or deutsche marks and the links between the yields on these securities and currency movements create a chain which encircles the globe. The world's stockmarkets will eventually follow the bond markets.

Unlike the bond markets, however, most of the world's stockmarkets are still domestic markets of stocks where locals peruse the inventory and buy in accordance with expectations and fashions. Nowhere is this more pronounced than in Japan. Japanese investors buy stocks as short-term speculative investments on the basis of trends, fads, and rumours.

If an obscure Tokyo stock sheet hints that a certain pharmaceutical company may have discovered a cancer-curing drug, the prices of *all* pharmaceutical stocks in Japan may suddenly rise. During the great bull market of 1986–87, Japan's stock prices rose so high that the ratio of price to earnings (the PER) soared to quadruple the comparable multiple prevalent in the United States or Britain.

In the US and the UK, where institutional investors are guided by modern portfolio theory and securities analysis is a high-tech art, corporate earnings have acquired cabalistic significance. If a famous stock analyst forecasts that a particular corporation will have poorer than expected earnings, institutions will sell their positions and the stock price will decline well in advance of official earnings announcements.

The forces which contribute to the determination of stock prices in different national markets are influenced by market regulations, by taxation of income from equities and capital gains and by a nation's accounting practices, as well as being subject to a host of socio-cultural factors which underlie the investors' psychology.

Among the world's stockmarkets, liquidity and the speed with which an investor can sell local equity vary enormously. Although these factors will never disappear, their significance as forces in price determination will slowly fade as global stock trading grows. Financial regulators in Japan, France, and Australia have already eased restrictions on equity purchases by foreigners at home and by locals abroad.

In 1986, British net purchases of US stocks exceeded $4.7 billion, a rise of 275 percent over the preceding year. Japanese purchases of US stocks were roughly eight times as high in 1986 as in 1985, and they quintupled again in 1987. Meanwhile, traders and brokers in the United States buy and sell shares listed on all of the world's major stockmarkets.

Dealers in Britain are now trading American Depository Receipts (ADRs represent stock, priced in dollars, of foreign companies whose shares are held abroad). Every business day, London ADR traders scrutinize their screens, searching for arbitrage opportunities among currencies and between the price of the ADR and the price of the underlying stock.

In the case of certain Japanese ADRs, an excess of demand over supply has caused the ADRs to be converted back into common shares and sold to investors in Tokyo. As a result, the supply of ADRs in such popular issues as Sony, Matsushita, and NEC have severely contracted since 1985. Declining liquidity in the market for Japanese ADRs will increasingly send investors directly to the Tokyo stock echange to buy common shares.

Led by the world's multinational corporations, the number of foreign stocks listed on the London and Tokyo stock exchanges has been steadily growing. Swedish companies are listing their shares on the Helsinki Stock Exchange and in 1987 Nixdorf Computer became the first foreign company to obtain a listing on the Madrid Stock Exchange.

As increasing numbers of multinational corporations regard the world as a single marketplace, a coherent global equity market will gradually emerge. The development of such a marketplace will in turn lead to the routine trading of securities around the clock in the world's major markets. This will lead to price convergence. The day of the global equity market is not so distant. The world of international finance is a small world indeed.

# 5 JAPAN VERSUS WORLD FINANCE

## SUMO

'Japan,' my Japanese friend once said to me, 'is an island.' We were sitting in a coffee shop at midday and I was busy reading a newspaper article on *sumo* wrestling.

The comment seemed rather obvious and I grunted noncommittally.

'Actually, Japan is many islands,' he continued, apparently intent on gaining my attention.

'Yes, many islands,' I agreed without diverting my eyes from the article.

'But for us Japanese,' he continued relentlessly, 'Japan is just one island like the circle that surrounds the sumo wrestlers.'

At the mention of *sumo*, I looked up from my newspaper.

'*Sumo*,' he continued, 'expresses the essence of Japan. It is unique. It *is* Japan.'

'Are you suggesting that Japan is a wrestling match?' I asked.

'Sumo is more than a thousand years old,' he continued, ignoring my question. 'As with other Japanese rituals and arts, *form, ceremony*, and *appearance* are as important as the activity itself.

'Before a match, each sumo wrestler carefully stamps his feet, claps his hands, throws salt, and, finally, stares with intensity at his opponent. Only the soles of the wrestlers' feet can be in contact with the area of floor enclosed by the circle. Finally, only one wrestler can remain within the circle. The typical match lasts less than half a minute.

'The match represents the collision of power. When the match is over, one sumo wrestler stands within the circle as the solitary victor.

Through a uniquely Japanese combination of *size, skill* and *harmony* he occupies the inner circle and in a sense becomes the circle.'

'Is that how Japan views competition in business?' I asked. 'Does one manufacturer or one bank use its size and skill to dominate the inner circle?'

'No,' my friend replied. 'There are always at least four to six leaders. If there was only one sumo wrestler there would be no match; if there were only two then competition would be too limited.

'But, remember, while all of the sumo champion's skills and qualities are indispensable to his victory, size is vital. A sumo wrestler weighing a mere 250 pounds doesn't stand a chance.'

## CAPITALIZATION

Compared with their Japanese counterparts, American financial institutions are under-capitalized. In 1986 only two American commercial banks were among the world's top 25 in terms of capitalization (Morgan Guaranty and Citicorp ranked 19th and 21st, respectively). The twelve largest banks are Japanese, followed by the great universal banks of Switzerland and Germany. The biggest Japanese bank, in terms of capitalization, (Sumitomo) today has roughly eight times the capitalization of America's best-capitalized bank (Morgan).

Much the same situation holds true for non-bank financial institutions. The best-capitalized American firm, American Express Company, for example, has only about 20 percent of the capitalization of Japan's Nomura Securities Company. In terms of capitalization, the Big Four Japanese securities companies are among the biggest brokers in the world.

Capital is as vital to financial industries as food is to the *sumo* wrestler. Without enough of it, investment banks and commercial banks become too thin to compete. A big capital deficiency can cause a financial institution to wither and die. In the investment banking world, big capitalization means big profits.

It was the need for increased capital that forced privately held firms (such as E. F. Hutton and PaineWebber) to go public in the early 1980s, or to merge with large diversified conglomerates (e.g. Salomon Brothers with the commodities group, Philbro, and Lehman Brothers with American Express). In 1986, privately-held Goldman Sachs (the fourth largest firm on Wall Street) traded a 12.5 percent share of its profits for a $500 million cash infusion provided by Sumitomo Bank and not long afterward Shearson Lehman Brothers Holdings, Inc did much the same.

In Japan, all major securities companies, like banks, have been publicly traded for decades. Until recently, however, bank shares and other financial stocks were only thinly traded and maintained stable prices. But in 1983 bank shares began to rise rapidly, and today shares in Japan's major banking institutions are trading at 6–10 times the prices which ruled five years ago. Price to earnings multiples in the banking sector now range from 60 to more than 150 times.

The share prices of leading securities companies have also rocketed. Shares in Nomura Securities Company, for example, which traded at ¥250 in 1983 were valued by the market at ¥4550 five years later. This was an eighteen-fold increase which gave Nomura a price to earnings ratio of 55 (compared to 9 for Merrill Lynch).

By mid–1987, Japan's financial sector had come to represent about 40 percent of the total value of all issues listed on the first section of the Tokyo Stock Exchange. This rise in the total stock market capitalization of Japan's financial institutions has ramifications which extend far beyond Japan's national borders.

Suddenly, Japanese financial institutions have acquired the financial clout to expand from their domestic habitat to far away places with strange sounding names – such as New York and London. Eventually, the biggest Japanese financial institutions will set up semi-autonomous headquarters in these cities and will fiercely compete with local firms for local business.

Within a period of just a few years (between say, 1982 and 1992), Japanese banks and securities firms will have been transformed from highly regulated domestic institutions to multinational organizations with extraordinary flexibility and incomparable assets.

## THE GIANTS' ETERNAL OBSESSION: MARKET SHARE
Although rice is Japan's traditional staple food, bakeries have been thriving in Japan. Market research undertaken by Matsushita Electric Industrial Co (the world's largest consumer electrical appliance maker), revealed that 46 percent of Japanese families eat bread for breakfast rather than rice. Identifying a potential new market, Matsushita invented a new home electrical appliance.

Priced at ¥36,000 ($250), the new machine makes dough, controls fermentation and bakes a loaf of bread. The housewife (Japanese men never cook) need only pour a mixture of flour, salt, butter and dry yeast into the machine, add water, and set a timer. In the morning fresh baked bread will be waiting for the family.

The automatic baking machine was introduced by Matsushita in February 1987. Certain of success, Matsushita set initial monthly production at 50,000 units. In less than four months, Toshiba, Hitachi, Sanyo, and Funai Electric were all selling virtually identical machines at prices ranging from ¥33,000 to ¥40,000.

Matsushita's optimism was justified and in 1987 total sales of automatic baking machines in Japan were estimated to be about one million units. However, Matsushita will be obliged to share the market with its competitors.

All five producers of automatic baking machines increased production capacity and began competing intensely by establishing differences in design and price. Although Matsushita invented the device, it probably did not resent the sudden surge of competition. In Japan, inter-industry competion is viewed as a means of increasing product variety and of improving public recognition.

Not all the producers of the baking machines will necessarily profit immediately from the new product line. But *all* will struggle to secure and hold a particular segment of market share; and all will continue to increase production in accordance with their long-term sales projections.

In Japan, market share is pursued regardless of immediate costs and short-term losses. Long-term strategy invariably takes precedence over the need to secure an adequate return on investment. In both the manufacturing and the service sector, market share is the ultimate measure of performance. Once market share is secured, profits will eventually follow. Market share is the laurel of victory, the symbol of corporate success.

The six massive *keiretsu* (mentioned in Chapter 2) represent a hefty segment of Japan's industrial and financial sectors. The six groupings compete in virtually every area and member firms in each sector usually produce similar products.

Each of the six banks which constitutes the core of one of the major *keiretsu*, belongs to an exclusive club (the 'Six Bank Club'). Representatives from each bank (Dai-Ichi Kangyo, Sumitomo, Fuji, Mitsubishi, Sanwa and Mitsui) meet regularly and discuss collective strategies.

If one company creates a new product, the appropriate company in each *keiretsu* rushes to produce an idential product in order to lock up a portion of the domestic market. This strategy is pursued in order to realize long-term objectives rather than to meet short-term sale or profit targets.

Because six or more companies are usually deploying identical techniques to produce almost identical products, competition in Japan is fierce. This encourages a perpetual drive to refine and improve products (while reducing cost) in order to hold market share. It is this dynamic which is responsible for the widespread use and success of quality circles and other devices for which Japanese management has become well known.

In many areas, it is expected that capital investment will precede profits by a decade or more. Competition with other producers and an expanding market may often require frequent expansion of production facilities which in turn postpones the return on investment. Indeed, in order to keep pace with expanding markets, producers must expand production in advance of demand, and this nearly always results in excess capacity. Among manufacturing industries, the creation of excess capacity invariably leads to excess production. This, in turn, forces producers to seek new markets for their surpluses. Surplus production, which must be disposed of, can be sold in markets throughout Asia, North America, and Europe at less than production costs.

In this way, Japanese products – by offering cut-prices combined with outstandingly high quality – can successfully compete with local equivalents. As a result, a domestic problem (*unavoidable surplus production*) is resolved by means of an international solution (*the procurement of overseas market share through predatory pricing*) which leads back to the source of the problem: over capacity. As foreign demand increases, domestic capacity will increase further and a corporation's concern with market share (a domestic issue) is transformed into the relentless drive for export markets (a global issue).

Concern with market share is not limited to the manufacture of specific products. When a major Japanese company establishes a new subsidiary in order to provide a new type of service, all of its competitors soon set up identical subsidiaries. In the mid–1980s, for example, the major city banks, the trading companies, and some corporations all set up, almost simultaneously, finance subsidiaries in Luxembourg and London. A primary function of the subsidiaries was to engage in *zaitek*.

## ZAITEK

*Zaitek* is to Japan's corporate accountants what free love was to the hippies of the 1960s: it eliminates the need for competition while providing momentary fulfillment. In its most fundamental sense, *zaitek* is financial arbitrage. It involves the use of moderately sophisticated financing techniques to derive short-term profits from the securities and foreign exchange markets. For 'zaitekeurs' the world is a playground and the object of the game is to increase annual corporate pre-tax profits.

Like so many things in Japan, the word *zaitek* is an amalgm of Japanese and foreign elements. *Zai*, which means money, is the root of the Japanese term for finance, *zaimu;* -tek is derived from the English word technology. The term gives expression to a special

Japanese activity which has been growing since the spring of 1984 (when the Ministry of Finance allowed non-financial institutions to participate in many financial activities in overseas markets).

In 1986 and 1987, while the Tokyo stockmarket was booming, Japanese corporations raised money in the Euromarkets. They floated straight Eurodollar bonds, convertibles, and bonds with warrants attached. In 1987, the coupon prices (the interest rate paid on a bond) on Japanese warrant bonds dropped as low as 1–2 percent. When the proceeds were swapped from Eurodollars into yen, the issuing corporations achieved negative interest rates. That is to say, some Japanese corporations succeeded in being paid to raise money in the Euromarket.

Funds raised in this way were then invested in the Tokyo stockmarket, in the domestic and international bond markets, and in the volatile domestic bond futures market. Successful corporate investors made big profits, the losers remained mum.

It quickly became common practice for manufacturing companies to derive a hefty segment of pre-tax profits from financial activities. According to a *Nihon Keizai Shimbun* survey, roughly one-third of all publicly listed firms which are *not* in the financial services industry profited from *zaitek* in 1986.* The biggest winners were Toyota Motor Corporation with a cash surplus of ¥123.6 billion (about $850 million) followed by Hitachi Ltd (¥39.6 billion).

During the period 1985–87, when the yen appreciated against the dollar by 85 percent, most of Japan's manufacturing industries suffered. *Zaitek*, however, enabled some companies to accomplish the impossible: while their operating profits declined drastically, total profits remained roughly constant, or even grew. In 1986 and 1987, many Japanese companies thrived and their corporate surpluses ballooned.

Take the case of Renown. Renown, Inc is Japan's largest wholesaler of secondary textile products. In 1986, business was not good and operating profits declined by 60 percent. But, the firm's *zaitek* activities saved the year. *Zaitek* adventures, including $130 million in warrant bonds, gave the company a cash surplus which neutralized most of its decline in profits. As a result, 56 percent of Renown's pretax recurring profits for the year ending December 1986 were derived from *zaitek*.†

---

*Japan Economic Journal*, September 5, 1987.
†Statistics regarding Renown Inc. derived from the *Japan Economic Journal*, September 5, 1987.

Not all Japanese companies have been as consistently successful as Renown. In September 1987 Tateho Chemical Industries Co (*Tateho Kagaku Kogyo*) suffered losses in the Tokyo bond futures market which exceeded its net worth. Tateho, established in 1966, is a small rural firm (about 300 employees) with a virtual monopoly on the production of electrofused magnesia (used in the steel refining industry). In order to counterbalance severely declining profits resulting from poor sales (the decaying Japanese steel industry and the strong yen were the culprits) Tateho's accountant invested heavily in Japanese government bonds.

Tateho's operating profits, like those of Renown, were in a tailspin, but the company's balance sheet, again like Renown's, looked wonderful. For while Tateho's operating profits for the year ending March 1987 were 63 percent lower than those for the preceding year, ordinary profits climbed 47 percent. *Zaitek*, take a bow.

In late May 1987, however, when the bond market proved to be a bad bet, Tateho's 40-year-old accountant attempted to counterbalance trading losses by buying contracts on the bond futures market. With an investment position of about ¥400 billion (or about 23 times the company's net worth!), Tateho announced losses of ¥28 billion against net assets of ¥16.9 billion. Thus, *zaitek* produced its first disaster. Or, more accurately, a small corporation devoid of financial savvy, failed to establish controls on its corporate investments.

World markets quivered for a moment. Traders and portfolio managers imagined other Japanese companies on the brink of similar calamities. What monsters could be lurking in the deep, opaque waters of Japanese corporate accounting and cash management? But, like all nightmares, this one was soon forgotten.

Japanese corporations do not have finance departments. Instead, corporate finance is subsumed by the accounting division which has not traditionally played a major role in corporate management. In Japan, accountants never become company presidents and rarely rise to the level of director.

The purpose of finance in the majority of Japanese firms is to maintain banking relationships and to assure the smooth transmission of capital to each segment of corporate operations. The finance section of a corporation may, rarely, voice its disapproval of a management decision but can never countermand it.

*Zaitek* could alter this traditional arrangement. Gradually the personnel structure of Japanese corporations may change as corporate finance becomes a vital part of corporate profits. If *zaitek* continues to stuff company coffers, financial decision-making will play an ever greater role in management.

Just as starving drug addicts use heroin highs as a substitute for food, Japanese companies have been compensating for declining export earnings by shooting cash into the domestic capital markets. Often speculating with borrowed money, Japanese businesses have been attempting to counterbalance eroding profit figures by speculating on the stock and futures markets. Partly as a result, the broadly defined money supply (in mid–1987) has been increasing by 9–11 percent, while inflation has been almost flat.

Windfall profits from the stockmarket and real estate markets have been keeping troubled companies solvent. However, just as the drug addict cannot survive indefinitely without protein, *zaitek* cannot be a perpetual subsitute for production.

There can be little doubt that a serious market correction could lead to a plethora of Tateho-style incidents. But Japanese industry's carefully constructed sandcastle will not be washed away by the waves of a financial crisis. The Big Four securities companies with their vast retail sales networks, enormous capital and considerable funds under management will support the domestic markets because it is in *their* best interest to avert widely publicized crises. In retrospect, it may be that *zaitek* will be seen to have served as a bridge that allowed Japanese industry to walk across a temporary gulf in profitability created by the strong yen.

## THE FUTURE OF FUTURES

In October 1985, a single bond futures contract was introduced on the Tokyo Stock Exchange. Based on price indices for fictitious issues of ten-year government bonds, it was the first financial futures contract traded in Japan during the postwar period. Thus, for the first time in 40 years, investors were given a means to hedge positions or sell short.

After an initial setback, the market thrived. Domestic firms from Toyota Motors to Tateho Chemical participated in the market. In less than one year, the new futures instrument became the most actively traded coupon futures contract in the world. Today, only the Euro-dollar futures market is bigger.

On 13 July 1987, trading in the contract began on the London International Financial Futures Exchange (Liffe). For Japan's 'zaite-keurs', however, the London contract was a superfluous invention. Trading during business hours in Tokyo has been more than enough to keep corporate accountants happily busy. In June 1987, trading in a stock exchange average futures contract (consisting of a package of 50 stocks) began on the Osaka Stock Exchange. As with the bond futures contract in London, participation in the Osaka stock average futures was no more than middling.

Trading in stock index futures (based on the Nikkei Stock Average of 225 issues or the Tokyo Stock Exchange Average of all issues listed on the first section) is likely to begin on the Tokyo and Osaka Stock Exchanges in 1988. It is likely that the Ministry of Finance will authorize the establishment of an integrated market that includes trading in additional financial futures as well as interest rates and currency. This development will add a new dimension to *zaitek* speculation.

Stock index futures based on Japan's Nikkei 225 were first traded on the Singapore International Monetary Exchange (Simex) in late 1986. Trading was thin, largely because Japanese law prohibited Japanese investors from trading in the instrument. Subsequently, the May 1987 decision by the Japanese Ministry of Finance to allow domestic institutions to participate in foreign futures and options markets enhanced the prospects for Simex's Nikkei contract, as well as those for futures trading throughout the world's exchanges. Soon after the decision, 307 domestic financial institutions quickly became active players in the world's major futures exchanges. Other limits placed on overseas futures trading by Japanese financial institutions will gradually be raised or eliminated.

Japanese institutions, which are among the world's biggest investors in the securities markets, have the potential to become major players in financial futures and options markets throughout the world. In 1987, the Big Four securities companies bought seats on the Chicago Mercantile Exchange (the Merc) and the Chicago Board of Trade (CBT). Initially Japanese trading interest focused on the CBT's Treasury bond contracts and the Merc's S&P 500 stock index contract. But, as Japanese investments in overseas securities grow ever larger, Japan's investors will turn to the diversity of the world's futures markets as a means to hedge their investments. Futures contracts will be used as a technique for allocating assets among the world's major markets.

Before long, Japanese institutional investors will swiftly move in and out of market sectors by trading enormous volumes of futures contracts. In far less than a decade, Japanese investors are likely to account for at least half of all global futures trading. This prospect – together with the sheer size of Japan's domestic stock and bond markets – has encouraged the world's futures exchanges to try to arrange tie-ups with Japan's stock exchanges.

Japanese authorities, however, have been largely uninterested in such tie-ups. They perceive that automated trading is the way of the future. The Tokyo Stock Exchange is developing technology which would fully automate futures trading. Thus, Intex, Bermuda's tiny futures exchange (mentioned in Chapter 4), will someday be seen to have been the model for futures and options trading in Japan.

## MIXED BLOOD

According to the 'Aspirin Count Theory', a leading US stockmarket indicator, the market can be expected to slump approximately one year after American aspirin production increases and to rise about one year after it decreases. There are other, similar, indicators that relate the state of the market to ice cream sales, the performance of particular football leagues, and the length of women's skirts. Equally frivolous, but more concrete, is the relationship that obtains between migration policies and financial market regulation.

In those countries that exercise an absolute ban on the emigration of residents (e.g. the Soviet bloc nations) there are virtually no financial markets. Countries that severely curtail the emigration of residents (e.g. China or Taiwan) have only marginally developed capital market structures. In countries that permit free emigration, the degree to which immigrants are admitted and rendered eligible for citizenship correlates with the degree of capital market regulation.

Thus, at one end of the continuum are Britain and the United States, with highly developed securities industries and an open willingness to admit quotas of immigrants and grant citizenship to them in accordance with longstanding regulations. At the other end of the continuum is Japan.

In Japan it is difficult, almost to the point of impossibility, for an immigrant to become a citizen. Japan is, moreover, one of the few countries in the world in which a native-born resident has no right to citizenship. The children born in Japan of Japanese mothers and non-resident fathers, for example, have not, until recently, been Japanese nationals. Japanese citizenship has been traditionally determined on the basis of the newborn's patrilineage as set out in the *koseki*, a document detailing the patrilineal descent (and affinal links) of each Japanese. No other country has insisted upon such strict requirements for citizenship. And no other country in the free world has maintained such highly regulated and restricted financial markets.

It is unwise to draw conclusions from whimsical indicators. Nevertheless, Japan has a long history of maintaining harsh rules that distinguish 'in groups' and 'out groups'. Indeed, throughout most of the Tokugawa era (1603–1886), Japanese who ventured outside the archipelago were executed if they dared to return. The regulations that have dictated who is Japanese are the product of the same socio-political traditions that have given rise to financial market regulations.

In 1985, the government liberalized citizenship requirements, allowing children born in Japan of Japanese mothers and foreign fathers to be made citizens – upon the completion of necessary paperwork at the local government ('ward') office. The government firmly gave its directives to the local bureaucrats who were expected to implement them.

Few were surprised, however, when the directives had no immediate effect. The bureaucrats did not refuse to implement them, nor were any public objections voiced. Instead, they wore down the applicants by an apparently endless series of demands for documentation. Those applying for citizenship on their children's behalf were required to provide materials determined by the bureaucrats. Some local offices requested letters from the child's father's employer. Others insisted upon scrutinizing the birth certificates of the child's paternal grandparents. The requests for supporting materials were varied and almost wholly irrelevant, and the delays were innumerable.

Some applicants, weary of the process and hoping for an easier time in the future, abandoned their applications. Others complied with all requests, persisted relentlessly, and eventually procured Japanese citizenship for their Japanese-born children. Meanwhile, the application procedure is gradually becoming more standardized and the number of approved applications is increasing.

Japan's financial markets resemble the nation's half-native children. Sired by foreign forces, yet born in nineteenth or early twentieth century Japan, the structure of the capital markets and money markets was largely based on US and European models. Just as the half-natives combined foreign and Japanese facial features while speaking Japanese with native fluency, so also the financial markets bore the imprints of foreign structures *and* indigenous practices, while operating exclusively in a Japanese mode.

Though inspired by Western capital structures, Japanese financial markets had no room for foreign participants. While the monetary system was influenced by – was indeed a component of – the international financial nexus, Japan denied its capital markets a role in global finance. Prior to the 1970s, foreign securities firms were excluded from the brokerage industry. Prior to 1986, foreigners could neither join the Tokyo Stock Exchange nor participate in pension fund management. Today, while several Japanese securities firms have become primary dealers in the US Treasury market, foreign institutions are still precluded from full underwriting participation in the bellwether ten-year Japanese government bonds.

The opening of Japan's financial markets has proceeded in much the same way as the naturalization of her half-native children. Once completely closed to all foreign institutions, Japanese financial markets initiated the process of compromise with foreign elements during the 1960s. At first, some developments which were allowed by law were not implemented in practice. The law regulating foreign securities companies, for example, positively sanctioned the opening of securities branches which were 50 percent owned by banks; until recently, however, regulators ignored the provisions and denied access. In the 1980s, in a process orchestrated by the Ministry of Finance*, the markets began to open with increased rapidity and will continue to do so.

In 1988, more foreign securities firms will join the Japanese stock exchanges. Stock index futures will be traded in Tokyo. Shelf registration, floating rate notes and domestic commercial paper, as well as other new instruments and procedures, will be introduced while this book is in press.

At the same time, Japan's domestic institutions are being granted unexpected (and sometimes unwanted) freedoms. Interest rates on large bank deposits, money market instruments, and a broad range of financial transactions have been deregulated. By 1990 interest rates on small deposits will be determined by market forces. Previously prohibited financial instruments (CD repurchase arrangements, banker's acceptances, treasury bills, stock futures) have been officially recognized. Foreign currency swaps and Euroyen borrowing are now routine.

Beginning in 1988, Japanese corporations will be authorized, for the first time since 1933, to issue straight bonds on the domestic market with only a bank guarantee. As a result, small, expanding companies will be able to issue unsecured bonds. This move may revive the desultory domestic bond market which was forced into obsolescence by the more modern Eurobond market.

Today, Japanese banks are permitted to deal in government bonds while securities companies are gaining increasing freedom to deal in money market instruments. Indeed, during the mid–1980s Japan's

---

*The Ministry of Finance regulates all financial institutions in Japan, as well as the budgets of all government ministries. It also establishes and administers the national tax structure. This comprehensive authority has made it the most powerful and prestigious arm of the Japanese government. The minister of finance is appointed by the prime minister and is a possible future candidate for the nation's top political position.

The Ministry of Finance contains seven distinct bureaux, each of which oversees its own precisely defined area of responsibility; Finance, International Finance, Banking, Securities, Budget, Tax, Customs Tariff. The Bureaux are in turn segmented into between six and thirteen divisions, each division consisting of a number of sections.

Collectively, the seven bureaux control the Japanese economy. Fiscal policies are implemented by the various bureaux through taxation debt, expenditures, loans and investments. The ministry's policies, determined through consultation with the prime minister, are communicated overtly through legislation (introduced by the ministry, and approved by the *Diet*) and, more discretely, through 'administrative guidance'. Adminstrative guidance is usually communicated verbally by the appropriate bureau to the institutions which it regulates. Although guidance is not supported or enforced by the rule of law, delayed negative sanctions are imposed on institutions which flout it.

'open-market', once a tiny portion of the money market, far outgrew the interbank market.

Japan's financial deregulation can be viewed as one instance of the global deregulatory trend mentioned in Chapter 4. It is, however, much more than that. Not only are Japan's half-native children becoming citizens but their foreign past has become irrelevant. They have been naturalized and are now as 'native' as automobiles.

Japan's domestic financial deregulation will facilitate the growth and internationalization of the biggest Japanese banks and securities companies; already a handful of these institutions are taking their places among the world's most successful bankers and brokers. At the same time, as mentioned in Chapter 4, Japan's insurance companies and trading companies have been setting up financial subsidiaries in Europe to participate in the Euromarkets and to generate profits from *zaitek*.

## THE BIGGEST OVERSEAS ASSETS IN THE WORLD
Several centuries ago, a tiny European country famous for its tulips seized control (through the organizational skills of its official agent) of the largest archipelago in the world. The Dutch East Indies was 46 times the size of Holland and gave the Dutch a global monopoly on the production and sale of a number of rare spices. This is just one example of the way in which, throughout history, nation states have dramatically expanded their national wealth and global political power.

Although (sadly) the annexation of sovereign territory is not an obsolete practice, it is not conventionally viewed as a component of macroeconomics. At least among the world's 'civilized' industrial nations (those who belong to that respectable club, the Organization for Economic Cooperation and Development – OECD), overseas assets consist of foreign securities, bank deposits, real estate, and plant and equipment which a nation's government, corporations, banks, and individuals purchase in accordance with the law of the lands in which they are situated.

In 1986 Japan engaged in an overseas buying spree that resulted in a major expansion of the net size of the nation's overseas assets. According to a May 1987 report, submitted by the Minister of Finance to Japan's cabinet, overseas assets held by the Japanese government, corporations, and individuals totalled $727.31 billion at the end of 1986. After subtracting debts, this gave Japan net overseas assets of $180.35 billion, the largest in the world. This represented an increase of 39 percent over the level of the preceding year.

Investment in foreign bonds was responsible for a large part of the increase and represented 35 percent of the country's total overseas assets. In 1986, Japan's investments in foreign securities rose 129 percent over the 1985 level and almost one half of the total investment of $257.93 billion were accounted for by US Treasuries. Of the balance, the investments in foreign stock, foreign real estate, and corporate acquisitions, although not of staggering proportions, were also substantial.

Japan cannot afford to buy the world. Perhaps if it could, it would. However, Japan's overseas investments will continue to grow at a rapid rate and while net assets may not continue to grow at the same rate as in 1986, the proportional values of major sectors will change.

Direct investment will grow rapidly during the course of the next five years as Japanese manufacturers attempt to rationalize their industries by moving production to countries with low labour costs. This growth will also be stimulated by the fact that direct investment enables certain Japanese industries to avoid restrictions on expansion within Japan. Already, constraints in the domestic market and the severity of competition at home are forcing many smaller Japanese firms to expand into overseas markets. Even the largest Japanese companies have found that their growth (and ability to achieve economies of scale) depends upon overseas expansion.

Efforts will be made to reduce trade friction by increasing the role of foreign-produced goods in foreign trade. At the same time, investment in foreign services will mushroom during the next several years. Soon, Japan's aggregate investments in services and real estate will surpass direct Japanese overseas investments.

Japan's purchases of foreign bonds will rise to a net level of about $200 billion per year (more than double the current level) before reaching a plateau, and investment in foreign stocks will expand exponentially for some time to come. As a result, Japanese investors will become increasingly vital market movers in New York and, eventually, in London.

The yen will inevitably strengthen further against the dollar, and this will result in an increase of Japanese purchases of real estate in the United States and Hong Kong (the Hong Kong dollar is tied to the US dollar) – a bargain which few Japanese investors will be able to ignore. In the United States, Japanese buyers will soon begin to look beyond the familiar cities (Honolulu, Los Angeles, New York, Boston) to other vital real estate opportunities. Concurrently, they will buy and build more factories in order to lower production costs and reduce trade friction.

The following sections will briefly discuss eight instances of Japanese overseas investment:

1. Competitive collaboration
2. Venture capital
3. Direct investment in overseas production facilities
4. Mergers and acquisitions
5. Investment in US real estate
6. Investment in foreign securities
7. The Big Four securities companies
8. The city banks

These discussions are not intended to be exhaustive, but rather to provide an indication of Japan's expanding role in overseas markets.

## COMPETITIVE COLLABORATION

Collaboration among competitors in Japan is at least as old as the *zaibatsu* holding companies. Top executive officers from competing companies traditionally meet on a regular basis in order to discuss industry-wide developments and political strategies. Umbrella organizations (such as *Keidanren*, the Federation of Economic Organizations) and industry-wide organizations (such as the Japan Industrial Technology Organization, or *Zenshinren*, and the National Federation of Credit Associations) are popular in Japan and have acquired considerable political clout.

In Japan, 'cooperative competition' often takes the form of 'research associations' created by members of particular associations or a smaller number of competing industries. Intended to pool funding and personnel in an effort to pioneer a new sector or solve a vital problem, such joint undertakings are a valuable means of accelerating research and development.

Discoveries or new products resulting from joint research ventures are, of course, shared among the participating companies. Often these cooperative ventures have been fallaciously construed by Japan's trading partners as unequivocal evidence of the existence of 'Japan, Inc'. The fact that discoveries are shared does not, however, diminish the competition among members of a research association. Moreover, individual companies continue to conduct their own in-house R&D in addition to collaborative ventures.

Joint research ventures have also become increasingly common among members of the European Economic Community (EEC) and some have been instituted in the United States (see, for example, the discussion of Sematech in Chapter 1). During the 1960s, many individual Japanese companies sought opportunities to enter into joint marketing or production ventures with foreign partners. These ventures were pragmatically conceived as a tactic to learn about new practices, procedures, and products. Once a Japanese firm learned everything about its partner's business, the venture was usually terminated.

As a result of the proliferation of such joint production ventures in North America and Europe, the term 'competitive collaboration' acquired a perjorative meaning in the West, where it was used to identify an unbalanced situation in which a Japanese corporation would take advantage of its partners and pursue its own 'hidden agenda'. Japanese companies were, for example, accused of using business connections resulting from collaborative arrangements as a means of ferretting information from a partner's customers, or of conducting more general market research which would subsequently be used to gain a competitive edge over their former collaborators.

Despite its negative connotations, however, competitive collaboration between Japanese and foreign companies has become increasingly common. Many European and American companies welcome the opportunity to utilize leading-edge Japanese technology in developing new products.

Such joint ventures have become particularly popular in the auto industry. General Motors, for instance, has collaborated with Toyota Motors and Suzuki Motors in order to produce vehicles in factories in North America and has become a junior partner in a joint venture with Isuzu to produce vans in Bedford, England. Similarly, Volkswagen A.G. and Toyota Motors will jointly produce pickup trucks (designed by Toyota) in West Germany beginning in 1989. In 1987 Daimler-Benz AG, one of the largest manufacturers of vehicles in Europe, entered into a joint venture with Mitsubishi Motors. Daimler and Mitsubishi will jointly develop and produce vans in Europe. Both sides should benefit. Daimler will gain access to distribution channels in Japan while Mitsubishi will gain similar access to networks in Europe.

Joint ventures between Japanese and foreign competitors have not been limited to the manufacturing sector. In the capital management industry, for example, many Japanese banks and capital management firms have entered into joint ventures with their British and American counterparts. In some instances, the Japanese partner has managed funds which are marketed by its Western partner; in other cases, a new foreign based company has been created (e.g. Yamaichi-Murray Johnstone in Glasgow).

Despite hostility in the United States and the European Community, competitive collaboration is likely to gain in importance during the course of the next decade. The technological know-how and the substantial capital available to Japan's corporations will offer North American and European companies appealing opportunities to gain new knowledge, new products, vital funding, and access to Japanese contracts.

## VENTURE CAPITAL

Declining Japanese industries (from steel to trading companies) have found it vitally necessary to diversify into new growth sectors. This is particularly difficult to achieve in Japan, where opportunities for mergers and acquisitions are severely constrained (see the discussion below).

Members of a single *keiretsu* often band together in order to share the cost and risk of creating a new undertaking. In order to move into the communications sector, for example, five Mitsubishi group chemical companies created a jointly owned telecommunications firm (Newcom Five Ltd) in 1987. The new firm will provide a network of high-speed digital telecommunications lines linking major Japanese cities. In 1987 again, another Mitsubishi group member (the Mitsubishi Corporation – the largest trading company in Japan) established an advertising firm (Media Five).

An alternative to the creation of new companies or the strategic collaboration of a joint venture is the venture capital enterprise. Venture capital enterprises involve investment in new, unproven undertakings. By participating in the risk of new ventures (the total sum of an investment is unsecured – hence the term *risk capital*), investors receive a significant portion of the equity in the business. Thus, if a venture succeeds, investors can reap substantial gains.

In the United States, specialized venture capital firms – which perpetually search for a diversity of new companies in which to invest – have developed into a $25 billion industry, and many old-line corporations have also backed one or two venture capital projects in order to expand into a new field or to derive beneficial information and new products.

In the 1980s, following this example, the Big Four Japanese securities firms set up venture capital subsidiaries (such as Yamaichi's, Uni Ven Co Ltd) designed to derive long-term capital gains from venture capital investments. Although these subsidiaries have focussed primarily on domestic venture businesses, they have also engaged increasingly in overseas investments.

In addition to establishing specialized venture capital subsidiaries, many Japanese companies have actively pursued opportunities to invest in 'start-up' overseas enterprises, particularly in the United States. One substantial investor has been Mitsui USA, the American subsidiary of Mitsui Bussan (Japan's second largest trading company), which poured ¥1.5 billion into nine new US companies between

1984–87. Mitsui's investment represents about 2 percent of the Japanese funds directed into US venture capital projects since 1984.

Venture capital investments enable Japan's mature industries to enter new businesses and offer high-technology companies the chance of procuring new products at a fraction of in-house development costs. Discoveries in foreign high-technology areas can be purchased in advance by channeling funds into a promising overseas start-up. In this way, Japanese companies can gain access to the newest American or European technology.

Foreign firms also benefit significantly from the presence of Japanese partners. Cash investments from Japan assure adequate funding for research, and Japanese investors, because of their long-term view, tend to be more willing than Western investors to engage in undertakings with considerable start-up time. A Japanese investor may also be able to provide the venture company with engineering assistance. Once a product line has been developed, a Japanese partner can provide a manufacturing plant or a bridge to Japanese distribution.

Start-up companies in a variety of high-technology fields will proliferate throughout the industrial world during the next several years. Japanese investors, motivated as much by the opportunity to procure new technology as by windfall profits from equity appreciation, will quickly emerge as a vital source of funding. This, in turn, will give Japanese corporations increasing access to their trading partners' leading-edge research and development.

## DIRECT INVESTMENT IN OVERSEAS PRODUCTION FACILITIES

Overseas direct investment offers Japanese manufacturers a number of benefits which justify the often unpleasant task of sending senior and middle managers abroad and hiring large numbers of foreign employees. Improved market access, lower labour costs, access to superior market information and the opportunity to reduce Japan's surpluses (and thus trade friction) are the most obvious reasons for shifting production abroad.

In addition, overseas production units enable corporations to establish foreign currency microcosms in which all of a firm's subsidiaries in a particular country can form a self-contained economy. Thus, production costs can be paid, revenue earned and profits invested – all in one foreign currency.

During the past several years, there have been repeated complaints, particularly from the European Community, that Japanese overseas factories are 'screwdriver operations', devoted primarily to the assembly of imported components. European trade representatives allege that Japan has deliberately planned its overseas production to maximize the use of unskilled workers and minimize the integration of its production into local economies. Japanese representatives have dismissed these allegations as 'Japan bashing' and maintain that 'screwdriver operations' are the necessary precursors to full production facilities. Both the European and the Japanese contentions are well founded.

On the one hand, Japanese manufacturers, particularly the motor manufacturers, *are* developing their overseas factories in the mirror-images of their domestic plant and equipment. On the other hand, however, Japanese companies prefer to avoid training foreign personnel. 'Job hopping' is a Western trait, and, from the Japanese perspective, money spent on training foreign staff is money eventually lost. Furthermore, the structural approach of Japanese manufacturers differs from that of Western companies. A focus on product in preference to national integration is a vital component of Japan's international operations. This will be discussed further in Chapter 6.

Japan's overseas direct investment climbed $14.01 billion in 1986, an increase of more than 30 percent over the level of the preceding year. In the United States, for example, Japanese direct investment rose from $16 billion in 1984 to $24.4 billion in 1986 (the latter figure represented about 11.5 percent of total foreign direct investment in the United States).

Japanese corporations have been enthusiastically building and buying factories in the United States and the European Economic community. The industries which have triggered the most trade friction (such as auto and electrical machinery) are likely to increase their overseas direct investments the most quickly.

The bulk of Japan's direct investment in manufacturing facilities has been channelled into new factories rather than towards the purchase of existing plants (or of entire companies owning needed factories.) In the United States, for example, Japanese manufacturers often build their own plants and subsequently hire non-union employees who are receptive to the practices of traditional Japanese management. It is estimated that more than 200,000 Americans are currently employed in such factories. However, as mentioned above, Japanese acquisitions of American and other foreign companies will become increasingly common during the next decade.

The Japanese auto industry (which accounted for roughly half of Japan's trade surplus with the United States in 1986) has spent, or plans to spend, a total of about $4.5 billion on US-based plant and equipment during the 1980s. By 1990, Japanese factories in the United States will have the capacity to produce about two million cars per year – more than Japan's total auto exports in 1986, and about 25 percent of total American production.

Japanese auto production facilities have in fact been among the most visible direct investments throughout the world. In the United States alone, more than 350 Japanese companies that manufacture auto parts have established factories in order to supply Japanese *and* American manufacturers.

Honda Motor Company, Japan's fourth largest auto maker, expects to export 70,000 American-made cars each year – 50,000 of which will go to Japan – when its new car assembly plant in central Ohio becomes operational in 1989. Similarly, Nissan plans to produce 100,000 cars a year in the United Kingdom by 1991, of which one third will be exported to members of the European Community. Meanwhile, Honda Motor is investing $41 million in a motorcycle factory in Mexico and Nissan Motor has plans to export 90,000 engines from Mexico to its factory in Tennessee.*

### JAPANESE AUTO FACTORIES SPROUT IN THE US

| Company | Investment Cost ($millions) | Annual Capacity (units) | First Year of Production |
|---|---|---|---|
| Honda Motor | 530 | 360,000 | 1982 |
| Nissan Motor | 745 | 240,000 | 1983 |
| Toyota Motor (with General Motors) | 400–500 | 250,000 | 1984 |
| Mazda Motor | 450 | 300,000 | 1987 |
| Toyota Motor | 800 | 200,000 | 1988 |
| Mitsubishi Motor (with Chrysler) | 600 | 240,000 | 1988 |
| Fuji Heavy (with Isuzu Motor) | 500 | 240,000 | 1989 |
| Honda Motor | 380 | 150,000 | 1989 |

Source: *Japan Economic Journal*

In 1986, West Germany had a trade deficit with Japan of 15 billion marks ($8.15 billion), about one-third of the total European Community deficit with Japan. Roughly 10,000 Germans are employed by 650 subsidiaries of Japanese companies. Although direct Japanese investment in West Germany so far amounts to only a small fraction of that in the United States and Britain, it has been expanding dramatically, reaching 1.3 billion marks ($706 million) in 1986 (five times the 1983 level).

In Hong Kong, Japan is the second largest foreign investor (after

*According to *Business Week*, 'Mexico Looks Better and Better to Japan,' 8 June 1987, p. 58.

the United States). Nine Japanese department store chains account for nearly one-third of Hong Kong's department store sales. In 1986, Japan invested $502 million in Hong Kong, $493 million in Singapore, and $436 million in South Korea. Direct investments in all of the newly-industrialized nations will increase considerably during the next five years as a variety of Japanese businesses open subsidiaries in order to exploit cheap labour and large market bases.

Japanese companies are discovering that *zaitek* is not the only way to convert losses to profits. In 1986, Aiwa Company (a producer and exporter of audio equipment which is 54.7 percent owned by Sony Corp) suffered a 25 percent decline in sales, resulting in an after-tax loss of ¥5.7 billion (about $38 million). The appreciation of the yen had rendered Aiwa's products non-competitive in world markets.

Working on the assumption that sales would continue to decline, Aiwa decided immediately to move a large portion of its total domestic production to Singapore, where the cost of labour was far lower than in Tokyo. Within eight months of the decision, 1200 jobs at Aiwa's Tokyo facility had been terminated (primarily through early retirement and offers of unusually large severance). By the end of 1987 it is estimated that Singapore production will amount to half of Aiwa's total output.

The Aiwa strategy is likely to be adopted increasingly by those Japanese industries which are squeezed by the strong yen. In 1987, such leading Japanese electronic firms as Sony, NEC, and Matsushita Electric Industrial all announced plans to invest in Singapore.

As more and more Japanese firms expand overseas production for a variety of reasons, growing numbers of local nationals will become dependent upon them. The more jobs Japanese employers control in particular countries, the greater will become the influence of Japanese companies on local economies. Just what this may imply was indicated by the case of the Toshiba Corporation. When faced with trade sanctions in 1987 (see Chapter 1), the company's immediate reaction was to point to the 4,500 Americans whom it employs.

## MERGERS AND ACQUISITIONS

Mergers are not unusual in Japan. During the decade 1976–85, according to the Japan Fair Trade Commission, mergers averaged about 1,000 per year. This compares with a comparable figure of nearly 3,000 in the United States.

Mergers most commonly occur when, under the guidance of MITI or the Ministry of Finance, companies facing immediate or likely bankruptcy are merged with other firms in the same industry. In 1986, for example, Heiwa Sogo, Japan's sixth largest mutual savings bank, was faced with insolvency and merged with Sumitomo Bank.

Most mergers or acquisitions that have taken place in Japan since the war have involved businesses within the same industry and the deals are usually initiated by an appropriate ministry or by the selling firm. The majority have entailed acquisitions of subsidiaries by parent companies or mergers among subsidiaries at the parent's initiative. In some cases the acquisition of a small distributor by a major corporation is accomplished through the discreet transfer of a block of shares. In others, companies needing land will buy real estate companies in order to acquire their holdings.

While acquisitions in Japan are far more unusual than mergers, hostile takeovers are as rare as white elephants. Frowned upon by both industrialists and the bureaucracy, they have been firmly opposed by the government. In 1973, for instance, MITI overtly prevented Sanko Steamship from taking over Japan Line and Minebea Company's hostile bid for Sankyo Seiki Manufacturing Company in 1985 (still under negotiation in late 1987) is a rare example of a practice that is generally considered underhanded and immoral. As for a *hostile* takeover of a Japanese company by a foreign company, this is something that has yet to occur. Even friendly acquisitions of Japanese companies by foreigners, though feasible, are very infrequent.

Between 1978–84 only 20 Japanese companies were acquired by foreign organizations, all after prolonged and friendly negotiations. Between 1984 and 1987, a handful of foreign (primarily US) firms purchased small, beleaguered Japanese companies. Kodak Japan, for example, bought three units of Kusuda Business Machines Company as well as a small share in a local camera manufacturer (Chinon Industries Inc). With few exceptions, those Japanese companies acquired by foreign interests have been small and financially troubled. Foreign buyers are perceived, at best, as occasionally acceptable agents in minor domestic mergers.

One of the many comparative strengths of Japanese corporate structure has been the system's aversion to hostile takeovers. Japanese corporations can conduct business without building defences which could preclude the accumulation of valuable assets or inhibit long-term research and development strategies. Because the Japanese shareholder is *not* a shareholder in the American sense (that is, the minority shareholder is not truly an owner, but rather a corporate supporter, an agent expressing goodwill), the shareholder's interests are irrelevant to corporate strategy.

A Japanese corporation is viewed as an organic whole that consists of relationships – among employees, between employees and suppliers and between customers and employees. Traditionally, employees stay with a single company throughout their working lives. 'Job hopping' between blue-chip corporations is still rare and those people who are not hired directly out of a university (late-comers) can seldom hope to advance to the highest levels of management. The corporation's relationships with its customers are carefully nurtured and, depending upon the business, individual employees often cultivate professional friendships with their customers.

Ideally, in Japan, long-term relationships transcend immediate financial constraints. This means that the established networks among companies and between a company and its employees are believed to be more durable and important than the short-term problems which may threaten to interrupt them. The relationships which link people within a company are considered to be as vital and inviolable as Japanese culture itself. Declining industries, therefore, make every possible effort to retrain unneeded employees rather than dismiss them. In the banking and securities industry, employees are fired only in the event of a major act of wrong-doing.

The primary reason for a corporation's existence is to enable people to work and prosper. In this sense, a company belongs to its employees rather than to its shareholders. Whatever the letter of the law may say, it is of secondary importance when set against the pragmatic fact that the management and staff who run and maintain a corporation are more than its heart and blood – they are its soul.

Because corporate vitality and identity are inseparably linked with employees, the personnel department of a Japanese corporation embodies a significance and wields a degree of power not found in non-Japanese corporations. By simply refusing to amalgamate, the personnel departments of two corporations considering a merger can subvert merger plans.

Of course, this ideal model is not always realized. However, the myth that relationships are never severed and that the corporation *is* a tightly knit family is paramount. Since the sale of a company is tantamount to the sale of family members, such a step carries 'implications of immorality and social irresponsibility.'* The word *nottori*, a term which is applied to airline hijackers, is also used in the context of corporate takeovers.

To prevent a reemergence of the dismantled *zaibatsu*, the Occupation authorities revised Japan's Commercial Code to make holding companies illegal and to give considerable power to a shareholder with as little as one-third ownership. In the absence of holding companies,

---

*James C. Abegglen and George Stalk, Jr, *Kaisha, The Japanese Corporation*, New York: Basic Books, 1985, p. 202.

expansion through the acquisition of companies in nonrelated businesses is difficult. The vital power associated with one-third ownership makes it virtually impossible to gain control of a company through a tender offer for shares. Since World War II, there have been only two tender offers in Japan (both friendly).

It is sometimes possible for a block of investors (termed a *kaishime*, or 'corner group') to buy one-third or even one-half of a corporation's shares, thus gaining a major voice in its decision-making. Because of beneficial cross-shareholding, however, there are few, if any, publicly listed companies in Japan with a float equivalent to more than two-thirds of outstanding shares.

Finally, the Commercial Code prohibits corporate mergers without the *unanimous* consent of the directors of the corporations to be merged. But even after such consent has been achieved (usually following years of negotiations), redundancy is still a major stumbling block. Workers are not ordinarily fired in Japan's 'lifetime employment system', while new positions can be difficult to create. Employees identify primarily with the entity for which they worked prior to the merger. As a result, factions based on premerger corporate definitions become firmly established.

In 1971, for example, the Kangyo Bank merged with the Dai-Ichi Bank to form a sprawling new entity, the Dai-Ichi Kangyo Bank. The merger created a bank with more branches and employees and a larger asset base than any other commercial bank in Japan. In Japan, where bigger is always better, the new bank thrived. But there were problems.

For more than a decade following the merger, employees considered themselves as 'Dai-Ichi men' or 'Kangyo men' and the Dai-Ichi group tended to look down upon the Kangyo group. Only those employees hired after the merger were indifferent to the distinction. Although all the directors of both banks had approved the merger, some directors of the merged bank actively discouraged the smooth integration of the separate work forces. The result was inefficiency. Fifteen years after the merger, the Dai-Ichi Kangyo bank was still plagued by redundancies and ranked below many other city banks in terms of profitability (return on assets).

Because of the problems and barriers associated with mergers or acquisitions, Japanese corporations have traditionally diversified through the introduction of new product lines and the establishment, when necessary, of new subsidiaries to develop, manufacture, and market leading-edge products.

Today, the maturing of many Japanese industries, the gradual internationalization of Japan's corporate sector, and the need rapidly to establish new products, are leading to a recognition of the need for diversification through acquisition. Invariably, Japanese domestic acquisitions entail the purchase of a small company by a large one.

In 1986, for example, Tokyo-based Orient Leasing Company (in terms of capital, the fourth largest financial services company in the world) acquired Akane Securities (a third-tier securities company). At about the same time, Kanematsu Semiconductor Corporation acquired Pacific Electronic Trade Corporation. Megamergers in the American or European style, such as Chevron's $13.2 billion acquisition of Gulf Oil or General Motors' $5 billion acquisition of Hughes Aircraft, have not yet occurred in Japan. Leveraged buyouts on the scale of the Kohlberg Kravis acquisition of Beatrice Foods are currently inconceivable in Japan. Indeed, no Japanese-owned company has ever been acquired in a leveraged buyout.

Takami Takahashi, the President of Minebea Co, one of the world's leading manufacturers of miniature ball bearings, is one of Japan's few corporate raiders.* In addition to making fifteen domestic acquisitions, Minebea paid $139.2 million to acquire a US firm, New Hampshire Ball Bearings, a supplier to the Pentagon, in 1985. At that time, US sentiment had not yet turned against Japanese acquisitions of strategically important US firms. Minebea's purchase of New Hampshire Ball Bearings stands in sharp contrast to Fujitsu's failed attempt to acquire Fairchild (discussed in Chapter 1).

Today, most Japanese industrialists still openly condemn 'the trend of trading Japanese corporations as if they were merchandise.'† Privately, however, some Japanese bankers and industrialists admit that profit margins can be increased by buying existing businesses rather than developing new sectors from scratch.

In the retailing industry, it is often more profitable to buy an existing chain of stores with established market share than to open new stores. In Japan, where legislation inhibits the opening of new supermarkets, for example, acquisition is the only means for domestic expansion. As Japanese companies become accustomed to the acquisition of foreign businesses, domestic acquisitions are likely to become more frequent.

In the United States, cash-rich Japanese companies have begun actively to seek acquisition targets. The strong yen has made many US companies seem cheap by comparison with their Japanese counterparts. According to the Sanwa Bank, publicly disclosed Japanese

---

*See the discussion of Minebea in Aron Viner, *Inside Japanese Financial Markets*, Homewood, Illinois: Dow Jones – Irwin, 1987 pp. 89–90.
†See 'Mergers & Acquisitions, cash-rich companies go on overseas shopping spree,' *The Japan Economic Journal*, 29 November 1986.

takeovers (including joint venture investments) of foreign companies increased from 31 in 1985 to 78 in 1986 with more than half of these (25 and 47 respectively) occurring in the United States. The majority of the deals, however, were small acquisitions, ranging from $1 million to $20 million.

Although hostile takeovers are a customary avenue for acquisitions in the United States, Japanese buyers have rarely chosen this method (the outstanding exception of Dai Nippon Ink is discussed below). Most Japanese companies move into foreign markets slowly and negotiate to buy companies in related industries. Their aim is to reduce production costs (and protectionist pressure) by manufacturing in the United States. In some cases, a foreign acquisition offers the opportunity to diversify away from old-line and unprofitable businesses; in others, foreign acquisitions permit declining industries to reduce their production costs. The biggest companies in the American steel industry, for example, have sold part of their equity to Japanese firms.

Japanese corporations seeking targets for purchase often turn to the domestic banks with which they have had long-term relationships. Traditionally, Japanese banks have functioned as main banks or shareholders when they worked behind the scenes as intermediaries in mergers and acquisitions, but, prior to the 1980's, the majority of Japanese banks were only rarely involved in mergers and acquisitions and none had established a specialist department for the purpose. Osaka-based Sanwa Bank was the first Japanese bank to establish an M&A team (in 1983) and has been Japan's leader in the field, completing twenty deals between 1983 and 1986.

Unlike other banks in Japan, which have ordinarily provided advice and information as a service to clients, Sanwa has charged its cients a fee for its M&A services and has aggressively cultivated a role as an intermediary in, or initiator of, mergers and acquisitions. As a result, the bank earned ¥100 million in commission fees in the first half of 1986.

In 1985, for example, Sanwa (in collaboration with Morgan Stanley), arranged for Fujisawa Pharmaceutical to buy 22.5 percent of Lyphomed Inc of Chicago. In November 1986, Sanwa advised Hitachi Zosen Corp in the $70 million purchase of Clearing Inc (a metal-forming press-maker) from US Industries, Inc (a subsidiary of Hanson Trust PLC). Similarly, in January 1987 Sanwa (in collaboration with Sonnenblick-Goldman, a mortgage brokerage firm) encouraged its client, Kokusai Motorcars Co (Japan's biggest taxicab and livery service), in a $319 million acquisition of the Hyatt Regency Maui from VMS Reality.

## A SAMPLING OF MAJOR CORPORATE ACQUISITIONS IN THE US BY JAPANESE FIRMS, 1984–87

| Us firm acquired | Japanese buyer | equity (%) | Price ($mns) | Year |
| --- | --- | --- | --- | --- |
| National Steel | Nippon Kokan | 100 | 425 | 1984 |
| Bank of California | Mitsubishi Bank | 50 | 292 | 1984 |
| Continental Illinois Leasing | Sanwa Bank | 100 | 64.5 | 1984 |
| Martin Marietta | Nippon Kokan | 40 | 45 | 1984 |
| Scripto | Tokai Seiki | 100 | 38 | 1984 |
| Thin Sheet Metals | Nishan Steel | 100 | 25.8 | 1985 |
| New Hampshire Ball Bearings | Minebea | 100 | 132.9 | 1985 |
| TREA Industry | Toray Industries | 100 | 10.3 | 1985 |
| Sun Chemicals (Graphic Arts Materials Group) | Dainippon Ink | 100 | 550 | 1986 |
| Bell and Howell (Visual Communications Division) | Eiki Industrial | 100 | 25.8 | 1986 |
| Clearing Inc. | Hitachi Zosen | 100 | 70 | 1986 |
| Pyramid Optical | Sokkisha | 100 | 21.2 | 1986 |
| Medasonics (subsidiary of Colgate Palmolive) | Settsu Paperboard | 100 | 19.4 | 1986 |
| Dunlop Tyres | Sumitomo Rubber | 80 | 240 | 1986 |
| CBS Records | Sony Corp. | 100 | 2,000 | 1987 |
| Westin Hotels & Resorts | Aoki Corp (& Bass Group) | 100 | 1,530 | 1987 |
| Reichhold Chemicals | Dainippon Ink and Chemicals | 100 | 540 | 1987 |
| Joseph Horne | Mitsui & Co. | 100 | 150 | 1987 |

Sources: *Nihon Keizai Shimbun, Financial Times, Wall Street Journal*

Since Japanese corporations began to seek overseas acquisitions their traditional banking partners have been steadily drawn into the field. The Long-Term Credit Bank of Japan, for instance, participated in two US acquisitions in December 1986. It advised Sumitomo Rubber Industries, Ltd when it acquired 80 percent of Dunlop Tyre Corporation in a $240 million deal and arranged for a unit of Mitsui and Co to buy the American Acceptance Corporation from Fidelity Bank.

Although the Big Four Japanese securities firms have M&A departments in Japan, they have only recently begun to develop similar capabilities in their overseas subsidiaries. When Japanese corporations seek a US acquisition, they usually turn to a major American investment bank with proven expertise rather that to a domestic securities firm. During the past several years, for example, Morgan Stanley & Co (which has M&A departments in both Tokyo and New York) has advised the Industrial Bank of Japan, Nippon Kokan, Sanwa Bank, and Fuji Bank on transactions worth an estimated $1.8 billion.*

As Japan's banks and securities companies expanded their M&A departments and went scouting for their clients some of them also made acquisitions on their own account. In 1985, for example, Nomura acquired 50 percent of Babcock & Brown, a New York-based real estate leasing firm; subsequently, in December 1986, Nomura Babcock & Brown Real Estate, Inc paid $50 million to acquire a 50 percent stake in New York's Eastdil Realty, Inc, a real estate investment banking firm owned and founded by Benjamin V. Lambert with an extensive Japanese clientele. No sooner was this deal concluded than Eastdil made arrangements for Shuwa Investment Corporation (see below) to buy the Arco Plaza in Los Angeles. Eastdil now functions as the real estate investment banking arm of Nomura's US operations. Under Lambert's guidance, Nomura will engineer complex US real estate deals for Japanese investors.

In 1985, the Industrial Bank of Japan (IBJ) bought 75 percent of J. Henry Schroder Bank and Trust Co from Schroders (the UK banking group). A year later, while Nomura concluded its purchase of Eastdil, J. Henry Schroder Bank and Trust arranged to pay $234 million to acquire Aubrey G. Lanston & Co., one of the few remaining independent primary bond dealers. Before the ink was dry on the legal documents, the IBJ increased its stake in Schroder to 95 percent and changed the name of the institution to IBJ Schroder Bank and Trust company.

A big spender in the American financial market has been Fuji Bank (Japan's most profitable bank) which in 1984 paid $425 million for two finance subsidiaries of Walter E. Heller International. By means of this acquisition, Fuji hoped to provide a majority of Japanese corporations in the US with leasing and factoring services. At the time of the purchase, the two units had aggregate non-performing debts of $400 million. In 1986, Fuji Bank added $300 million in equity to Heller International Corporation, bringing its total commitment to $1.15 billion, the largest single investment in the United States by a Japanese financial institution. Under Fuji management, Heller International has become a major lender in American leveraged buyouts

*See Michael R. Seist, 'Japanese Seek Role as Takeover Advisers,' in *The Wall Street Journal*, 4 May 1987, p. 6.

(financing more than $1 billion in 1987) and after four tough years will finally move from the red to the black in 1988.

In 1985, Sanwa Bank bought Continental Illinois's leasing subsidiary (the thirteenth largest leasing unit in the United States) for $50 million. Now the major component of Sanwa Business Credit Corporation, this was the first US leasing operation to be purchased by a Japanese company. In the expectation that all US interstate banking regulations will disappear, Sanwa Bank has plans to convert the leasing offices into part of a broad network of national banks.

Following on from this, Sanwa bought Lloyds Bank California (a unit of London-based Lloyds Bank PLC) in 1986, paying $263 million. The acquisition was then merged with Golden State Sanwa Bank to create the sixth largest bank in California. Continuing its acquisition strategy in 1987, Sanwa agreed in principle to buy a primary bond dealer, Brophy, Gestal, Knight and Co L.P. (formerly Refco Partners) for about $75 million. Although the deal will not be concluded until the political climate is favourable, it is likely that Sanwa will soon join the Industrial Bank of Japan as owner of a primary dealer subsidiary.

Rumours that one of the Big Four was contemplating acquisition of a US broker with an extensive retail network wafted through the streets of New York's financial district throughout 1986 and 1987. There can be little doubt that such an acquisition will be made when the political climate is favourable.

Meanwhile, Nippon Life, Sumitomo Bank and Yasuda Mutual Life have each paid tidy sums ($538 million, $500 million, and $300 million respectively) for pieces (13 percent, 12.5 percent, and 18–25 percent) of premier Wall Street investment banks. In a more conservative fashion, Sumitomo Life bought 2 million shares (1.5 percent) of the British merchant bank holding company, Kleinwort Benson Lonsdale.

Japan's financial institutions, like her industrial corporations, realize that it is usually more economical to buy a foreign unit (with customers and foreign staff in place) than to create a foreign subsidiary from scratch. Because of their massive equity capital, Japan's securities companies, banks, and insurance companies are well positioned to buy anything they want from the Atlantic to the Pacific.

A leveraged buyout involves the purchase of a controlling interest in a company through the use of borrowed funds. Because the funds are borrowed against the assets of the acquisition, the lender usually gets an equity share in the acquired company. Ordinarily, the loans are repaid by selling a portion of the acquired company's assets and by using its cash flow. It was the technique of financing corporate takeovers through leveraged buyouts which gave birth to the junk bond market in the United States.

### JAPANESE FINANCIAL INSTITUTIONS BUY PIECES OF WALL STREET

| US investment | Japanese buyer | equity (%) | Price ($mns) | Year |
| --- | --- | --- | --- | --- |
| Babcock & Brown | Nomura Securities | 50 | *n.a.* | 1985 |
| Henry Schroder Bank and Trust | Industrial Bank of Japan | 95 | n.a. | 1985 |
| Eastdil Realty | Nomura Securities | 50 | 50 | 1986 |
| Aubrey G. Lanston | Industrial Bank of Japan | 100 | 234 | 1986 |
| Goldman Sachs | Sumitomo Bank | 12.5 | 500 | 1986 |
| Shearson Lehman | Nippon Life Insurance | 13 | 538 | 1986 |
| PaineWebber | Yasuda Mutual Life Insurance | 18–25 | 300 | 1987 |

In June 1987, Prudential Asia Investment of Hong Kong (a newly-created merchant banking subsidiary of Prudential Insurance of America) concluded a leveraged buyout of Simmons Japan (a US-affiliated bed manufacturer with a 70 percent share of the Japanese market for Western beds). Arranged by the Industrial Bank of Japan, the ¥4 billion ($26.7 million) acquisition was the first leveraged buyout to occur in Japan and one of the first in East Asian history.

The deal, which involves a combination of long-term loans and subordinated debt as well as equity, is noteworthy because it could point the way for Japanese companies to arrange similar deals at home. As a result of the buyout, a US subsidiary company became an independent Japanese company under foreign ownership.

It is highly likely that during the course of the next several years, a Japanese market will gradually develop for the unsecured, subordinated paper that is generally used in leveraged buyouts. Thus, medium-sized Japanese corporations may soon undertake leveraged buyouts of Japanese firms. This, in turn, may lead to a new Japanese market in yen-denominated high-yield low-grade securities.

Japan is a patrilineal society in which the family name and property pass from father to sons; sometimes, a man with a daughter and no sons will 'adopt' his daughter's husband. In such cases, the son-in-law legally takes his wife's surname and becomes his father-in-law's heir.

Shigekuni Kuriyama spent part of his childhood in California and graduated in 1958 from New York University's Graduate School of Business. In 1959, he married the daughter of Katsumi Kawamura, the second-generation owner of Dainippon Ink and Chemicals, Inc. Kawamura had no sons and arranged for his daughter's husband to adopt his surname and made him his heir. Thus Shigekuni Kuriyama became Shigekuni Kawamura and, in 1978, assumed the presidency of Dainippon Ink.

Dainippon (which means 'great Japan'), the largest printing company in Japan, produces printing inks, synthetic resins, paper and plastics. In 1976, the firm purchased Kohl & Madden Printing Ink Corp, a small US maker of printing inks. A similar, though smaller, Indonesian company was acquired the following year. In addition, joint ventures with domestic and international companies were arranged in order to expand Dainippon's marketing capability and product lines.

In 1986, ten years after these acquisitions, the firm earned pretax profits of $363.9 million (¥255.32 billion) on $2.7 billion in annual sales. Every year for the past 38 years, Dainippon has posted growth in pretax profits and its yearly dividend of ¥6 (about 4 cents) has been very high by Japanese standards.

With the encouragement of his father-in-law, Kawamura has embarked upon an increasingly aggressive programme of mergers and acquisitions in order to establish an international network in printing inks and specialty chemicals.

In 1979, Dainippon became engaged in a bitter bid battle to acquire Polychrome (a US producer of ink and printing plates) from Rhone-Poulenc (a French chemical firm). In 1986, under Kawamura's direction, Dainippon negotiated to buy several companies in the West German Hartmann Group. At the same time, it undertook discussions to buy the profitable graphic arts materials group of the American firm, Sun Chemical Corp.

When the talks with Sun Chemical failed, Dainippon shocked the American firm's management by making a hostile bid to buy the entire company. Faced with the possibility of a hostile takeover, Sun Chemical quickly capitulated and sold the division for $550 million, a price which analysts considered to be quite high.

In 1987, Dainippon again initiated merger discussions with a US company, this time with New York based Reichhold Chemicals, a producer of adhesives and polymers used in plastics, photography, and various industrial processes. In June, the discussions broke down because Reichhold wanted $70 per share while Dainippon offered less than $60.

In a repetition of its strategy with Sun Chemical, Dainippon launched a hostile tender bid, offering $52.50 per share (about $473 million) for control of the American firm. The move angered Reichhold's management, which rejected the offer out of hand and unsuccessfully sought another buyer. Finally, two months later, Reichhold agreed to a $60 per share offer worth about $540 million.

## MAJOR ACQUISITIONS BY DAINIPPON INK

| Date | Company | Amount ($m) |
|---|---|---|
| May 1976 | Kohl & Madden Printing Ink | 6.00 |
| September 1977 | P.T. DIC Indonesia | .42 |
| March 1979 | Polychrome | 6.26 |
| September 1986 | Several Hartmann Group firms | 3.00* |
| December 1986 | Part of Sun Chemicals | 550.00 |
| August 1987 | Reichhold Chemicals | 540.00 |

*5.5 million deutsche marks
Source: Damon Darlin and Masayoshi Kanabayashi, 'Dainippon Ink Takes Another Bold Step'. *The Wall Street Journal*. 29 June 1987 p. 18.

Decision-making power at Dainippon Ink is far more centralized than in other Japanese companies. Kawamura, as a third-generation corporate president, wields considerable authority and does not need to rely upon the consensus of his corporate directors. This makes Dainippon one of the few firms in Japan in which decisions can be rapidly implemented.

The American education and American management philosophy of the company's president are in no small part responsible for Dainippon's distinctly foreign strategy of expansion through acquisition. Dainippon Ink is, in this respect at least, a Japanese company that acts like an American company.

Many Japanese corporations are studying Dainippon Ink's overseas acquisitions. The smooth integration of a group of foreign companies into a single Dainippon global network will be analyzed not only by Dainippon's domestic competitors but by major corporations throughout Japan. In addition, the M&A departments of Japanese banks and securities houses will assess the success of Dainippon Ink's rapid expansion in the hope that it can provide Japanese companies with an example to emulate.

If Dainippon's corporate profits continue to grow, and if no political problems (trade friction) develop from the foreign purchases, then sooner or later another Japanese company will attempt a hostile acquisition in the United States. The outcome of *that* attempt will also be carefully watched. If a pattern of successful Japanese hostile takeovers in the United States gradually emerges, the stage will be set for a flood of Japanese tender offers for foreign companies large and small.

Because Japanese corporations are patiently watching and waiting, it will be some years before Japanese acquisition is a major factor in the United States and Europe. However, by the early 1990s Japanese corporations will have become active practitioners of the strategy pioneered by Dainippon Ink's Shigekuni Kawamura.

## REWRITING THE RECORD BOOKS: THE CASE OF JAPANESE INVESTMENT IN US REAL ESTATE

Because of its position, Hawaii has long held a special appeal and prestige for Japanese honeymooners and investors. Hawaii is a familiar place for the Japanese and capital investment, not surprisingly, has been flowing steadily from Japan to Oahu (the island dominated by Honolulu) for nearly a quarter of a century.

In the late 1970s Kenji Osano, the Japanese billionaire and power-broker, bought the Waikiki Beach Hotel, the Royal Hawaiian and a number of other similar resort properties in Oahu. A variety of Japanese investors continued to buy Hawaiian hotels during the 1980s, including Azabu, a Tokyo retailer, who bought three hotels, including the Hyatt Regency Waikiki, for a total of $270 million in 1986. As a result, about 85 percent of the roughly 20 ocean-front hotels on Waikiki Beach are currently owned or controlled by Japanese investors. In addition, Japanese interests have acquired shopping centres, condominiums, and office buildings in Honolulu and major resort properties on the islands of Kauai and Maui.

Other portions of Pacific America have also been attracting Japanese real estate investment for a long time. Los Angeles, home to an estimated 1,000 Japanese companies, is a familiar hunting ground and an estimated 25 percent of the downtown district is controlled by Japanese interests.

By 1986, even the conservative Japanese real estate buyers were looking far beyond the Pacific, to New York, Boston, and Washington, and by the end of that year the Japanese had surpassed the British as the largest foreign investors in America's $2.5 trillion commercial real estate market. Their reasoning is not hard to follow. Japanese institutional investors have limited domestic opportunities to invest their excess cash and they have long been hungry for foreign investment opportunities; the US real estate market offers them an economical meal. There are some sound reasons for this:

1 LOW PRICES

The prices of US office buildings have been depressed. By comparison, land prices in central Tokyo increased by 75 percent in 1986. In Japan the ratio of the cost of land to the value of the building standing on it is usually about 3:1 – in the United States the ratio is reversed.

Because of high land prices, profits from renting a new Tokyo office building do not begin to appear for at least 10 years, while it takes about 30 years for returns on Tokyo real estate investments to match the annual capital gains on Japanese stock investments.

Japanese companies can borrow yen at low interest rates in Japan (using their domestic real estate and securities holdings as collateral) and convert the borrowed yen to dollars at a rate which has improved by 100 percent since the yen's low against the dollar in mid–1985. Many real estate investors borrow dollars at Japanese interest rates from the American branches of Japanese banks.

### 2 LOW TAXES

As in the United States, land in Japan is not depreciable for tax purposes. However, a US real estate investment yields a far larger tax deduction than one in Japan because the bulk of the cost of the US investment is in the building rather than the land.

Japanese depreciation schedules on commercial property, at 60 years, are far longer than in the US.

### 3 HIGH YIELDS

Japanese real estate is far more expensive than comparable US properties and can provide a return of only one-third to one-fourth of the return available in the US.

With 100 percent financing (from a bank loan), an 8 percent return (from rental income) will enable a Japanese buyer to repay the principal and interest on a loan in 20–25 years. This means that a Japanese buyer can own blue-chip American property *without using its own capital.*

### 4 LOW POLITICAL RISK

The United States has the best ratings for political risk in the world.

Japanese investment in US real estate totalled $5.5 billion in 1986, a rise of 366 percent over the level of the preceding year, and the figure is expected to double again in 1987. While all of Japan's major financial institutions, real estate firms, and construction companies have been active in the market, the big insurance and real estate companies accounted for 35 percent and 27 percent, respectively, of all Japanese real estate investments in America. More than half of these have been office buildings in a few US cities (such as Manhattan and Los Angeles) where Japanese investment in the best buildings (fully leased with blue-chip tenants) were so significant in 1986 that, according to some estimates, it boosted prices for prestigious office towers by 8–15 percent.

Japan's leading life insurance companies, which together constitute the nation's biggest bloc of institutional investors, have been internationalizing their investment portfolios. While their purchases of foreign bonds grew by 60 percent between the end of 1985 and December 1986, their investments in foreign real estate doubled during the same period.

Although Japan's Ministry of Finance has permitted overseas real estate investments for some time, it has advised institutional investors (through 'administrative guidance') to limit their exposure and temper their lack of experience by engaging in joint ventures. The life insurance companies' real estate purchases require special ministry approval which is granted on a 'case by case' basis, and total real estate investments, as a proportion of investment funds, are limited to 20 percent. But with aggregate industry assets growing by 15–20 percent per year, Japan's institutional investors have billions of dollars earmarked for real estate investment. A hefty portion of this money is destined to flow abroad.

Dai-Ichi Life Insurance Co, for example, operates a special division for overseas real estate investments. The division's joint ventures with Japanese and foreign partners have included the AT&T Centre in Los Angeles and the Citicorp Centres in San Francisco and New York. Sumitomo Life Insurance bought an approximately $300 million convertible mortgage on a major New York office building in late 1987. Still under construction, the 650,000 square foot building (425 Lexington Avenue) was not scheduled to open for nine months. Under the terms of the mortgage, Sumitomo will have the option of converting the mortgage into 49 percent of the equity in the building.

Convertible mortgages offer a special appeal to conservative Japanese investors. After buying such a mortgage, Japanese managers can look forward to an appreciation in the rental value of the property; but if the rental market stagnates they still retain the option of deciding not to convert the mortgage. This strategic advantage is likely to make convertible mortgages ever more popular among Japanese buyers.

Sumitomo Life and Dai-Ichi Life, like other Japanese life insurance companies, book (that is, record on their balance sheets) foreign real estate investments as stocks. This apparent sleight of hand is justified by the argument that the newly purchased buildings are owned by subsidiaries whose stock is wholly owned by the insurance companies. As a result of the accounting convention, the real estate investments become just one component of securities investments. If the investments are successful, they can be used to balance foreign exchange losses in the bond market; if they are unsuccessful, the losses can be concealed within the firms' total overseas securities portfolio.

Since 1986 Japanese buyers of American property have demonstrated their willingness substantially to outbid other investors. The strength of the yen against the dollar, windfall profits from the Tokyo bull stockmarket and opportunities to borrow at lower interest rates in Japan than in the United States have encouraged Japan's investors to pay prices that have stunned American real estate brokers. Because Japanese investors analyze US market prices in terms of Tokyo real estate valuation, they willingly make purchases that yield 1–1.5 percent less than those expected by American investors.

The most aggressive Japanese buyer in the United States has been the family-owned Shuwa Investment Corporation, which has already spent $2 billion on US real estate and plans to continue to spend $1 billion per year on American property. Shuwa (which means 'excellent harmony') owns 45 buildings (4.8 million square feet) in Tokyo, where it ranks with the major *keiretsu* real estate companies (Mitsubishi, Mitsui, Sumitomo) as one of the biggest office landlords.

The owner of closely-held Shuwa, Shigeru Kobayashi, has commented that he wants to buy a building in every American state. To date, Shuwa has purchased office buildings in New York, Boston and Washington, DC, and has become a major landlord in both Los Angeles (where it owns about 12 percent of the downtown area) and the San Francisco Bay area (where it owns many condominiums and commercial properties).

The prices paid by Shuwa have set records in the US real estate industry. In a cash deal in September 1986, for example, Shuwa bought Arco Plaza in Los Angeles for $620 million. This was the biggest all-cash real estate transaction in US history. Later that year, Shuwa bought Capital Cities/ABC Inc's New York headquarters for $174.2 million and the PaineWebber building in Boston for $100 million. In a July 1987 leaseback agreement, Shuwa bought the Washington, DC, headquarters building of *US News & World Report* magazine for roughly $80 million. At $480 per square foot, this was by far the highest price ever paid for office space in the US capital. Three months later Shuwa acquired a full city block in downtown Los Angeles (paying $76.7 million – a record California land price) which it will develop into a $650 million hotel, office, and retail complex.

Shuwa has not been the only Japanese firm to set records in the US real estate market. In November 1986, Dai-Ichi Real Estate paid $94 million for Manhattan's famous Tiffany Building. This set a record as the highest price ever paid per square foot of retail space in the United States. The following month, Mitsui Real Estate Development Company Ltd (*Mitsui Fudosan*) paid $610 million for the Exxon Building in New York's Rockefeller Centre. This was a record payment for a Manhattan office property. During the same month, the family-owned Kato Kagaku Co (a major producer of glucose) bought Manhattan's Tower 49 for $303.5 million, setting a new record for US office buildings in terms of the price per square foot.

Sumitomo Realty and Development Co (*Sumitomo Fudosan*), which had already made enormous investments in Tokyo office buildings for leasing, simply extended its strategy to the United States. In June 1987, for example, the firm bought one of the best-known buildings in Manhattan, 666 Fifth Avenue, for $500 million (about $365 per square foot).

The Sumitomo approach exemplifies the current preference of Japanese investors for landmark buildings, famous hotels and fully leased rental properties in prime locations. This obviates the many risks involved in undertaking a new real estate development and assures an immediate yield on the investment. But although the majority of Japanese buyers who come to the US market currently prefer to buy existing office buildings or hotels, this strategy will gradually change.

An indication of future trends was provided by Mitsubishi Estate Co (*Mitsubishi Jisho* – the largest office building leasing company in Japan) which in late 1986 began a $1.4 billion (¥200 billion) joint venture housing and resort development near Palm Springs, California. The five year project will involve the construction of 2,500 housing units, a convention centre, five eighteen-hole golf courses and a number of hotels.

Like Mitsubishi, Mitsui Real Estate, a pioneer in Japanese real estate development, has also purchased a California site (in San Diego County) where it will build an industrial estate. Similarly, in Hawaii, Japanese investors are engaging in joint development ventures with local partners. These developments mark the beginning of a significant trend in Japan's American real estate development.

Other Japanese investors have also begun to look beyond buying famous buildings in famous cities. The strategy of Sumitomo Life Realty offers an example. In 1985, Sumitomo Life purchased the Boston headquarters of Wang Laboratories; two years later it put up $145 million for the construction of an office block in central Los

Angeles. Shuwa Corporation will soon buy buildings in such American cities as Atlanta, Dallas, Phoenix, and Seattle.

During the next several years, Japanese buyers will diversify their investments from blue chip properties to higher-return second-tier investments scattered throughout the United States. Japanese construction companies will help to build new buildings with money provided by Japanese investors and Japanese banks will become a leading source of real estate financing in the US.

Although a high portion of Japanese overseas commercial real estate purchases have been in the US, Japanese buyers have also begun to consider central London, which, after central Tokyo, boasts the highest rents in the world.* In June 1987, Ohbayashi Corp, one of Japan's Big Five civil engineering groups, paid an astounding £3,575 per square foot for Bracken House, the headquarters of *The Financial Times*. This was by far the highest price ever paid for a property in The City. Similarly, across the Channel in Paris, Kowa Real Estate Investment Co invested FFr2.5 billion ($435 million) in a property development project on the left bank near the Montparnasse railway station.

After central Tokyo and central London, the highest rents in the world are paid in Hong Kong. Not surprisingly, Japanese investors know Hong Kong, the gateway to China, quite well. Japan has been one of Hong Kong's three most active traders (along with the United States and China). Japanese investors have spent an estimated $700 million on Hong Kong real estate and own major office blocks in the central business district as well as extensive holdings in Kowloon.

Not content with joint ventures alone, Shimizu Construction Co (*Shimizu Kensetsu* – the biggest of Japan's civil engineering contractors) bought a minority stake in California-based Dillingham Construction Corp. The other big Japanese construction firms are likely to follow the Shimizu initiative and undertake acquisitions of American (or British, or Hong Kong) construction firms.

Joint ventures between Japanese and foreign companies will also proliferate. Kumagai Gumi, for example, which is Japan's sixth largest contruction firm, has joined Zeckendorf Co in a number of hotel and residential projects in New York. In Hong Kong, the firm has set up a partnership with a local firm, Cheung Kong, and is developing a vast industrial and residential complex. In addition, the Hong Kong arm of Kumagai Gumi is building the new Bank of China headquarters, the second cross harbour tunnel, and a building for China International Trust and Investment. In London, Kumagai is

---

*In 1986, rents in The City of London were roughly 40 percent of the rents in central Tokyo and double the rents of downtown Manhattan.

renovating office buildings for the Nomura and Daiwa securities companies.

Soon, the Ministry of Finance will permit trust banks and life insurance companies to invest corporate pension funds directly in offshore real estate. This will result in a further growth of Japan's overseas real estate investments. Japanese buyers will expand their ventures in London, Hong Kong and elsewhere. Japan's financial institutions will become the number one foreign buyers in the US real estate market – and will hold that position for a long time to come.

They will not be alone. Japanese real estate firms and construction companies, together with wealthy individuals, will select their investments with care and will outbid all-comers. From mansions in Monterey, California, to shopping malls in Indiana, to the most prominent Manhattan towers, the names on the deeds will be Japanese.

## THE FLOOD GATES SLOWLY OPEN: THE CASE OF JAPANESE INVESTMENT IN FOREIGN SECURITIES

The Japanese like to save money, indeed, they save more money than any other nation in the world (about 17.5 percent of disposable income in 1986). These accumulated savings find their way into bank accounts, securities investments, and insurance policies.

For example, at the end of 1986 the outstanding value of life insurance contracts reached $6.4 trillion (¥967.4 trillion). This represents an average of $53,000 (¥7.95 million) for every Japanese citizen – the highest in the world. As a result, Japan's life insurance companies have become the biggest and richest investors in history. With total assets of about $430 billion (¥60 trillion), Japan's 23 life insurance companies have more money than a great many sovereign states.

Nippon Life, the biggest insurance company in the world, holds assets of $105 billion, a total which includes 3 percent of all listed equity in Japan and the nation's second largest private real estate holdings. When Nippon Life casts its gaze abroad foreign brokers snap to attention and foreign markets respond. The mere rumour that Nippon Life and a few of its pals may stay away from a particular auction of US Treasuries is enough to depress the market. On the other hand, in 1986, when the top ten Japanese life insurance companies increased their foreign investments (mainly US securities) by 35–40 percent, the Dow Jones stock average soared.

Financial power on this scale, if wielded in a coordinated fashion, can be awesome. The biggest life insurance companies, prohibited by Article 65 from raising funds through debt issues, are major participants in the foreign exchange markets. It is generally believed that, through trading on the Tokyo foreign exchange market, the insurance companies often move, and occasionally manipulate, the yen-dollar exchange rate.

Collectively, Japan's financial institutions hold a cash pool of vast proportions. At the end of March 1987, Japan's personal savings totalled nearly $4 trillion (¥554 trillion). The surplus funds held by corporations exceeded $1.5 trillion (¥200 trillion), and corporate pension funds, already worth $140 billion (¥20 trillion), were growing at the rate of 22 percent per year. There were, in addition, the investment trusts (¥35 trillion) and special funds in trust termed *tokkin* (¥27 trillion). For several reasons, only a tiny portion of this ocean of capital has so far found its way into overseas investments.

### WHERE SOME OF THE DOMESTIC MONEY IS

| Type of institution | percent share of funds | | | |
| --- | --- | --- | --- | --- |
| | 1965 | 1975 | 1980 | 1986 |
| City and regional banks | 40.8 | 32.5 | 29.6 | 29.0 |
| Finance Ministry trust fund | 10.0 | 15.5 | 19.6 | 20.4 |
| Mutual & credit unions | 14.0 | 14.2 | 13.2 | 12.1 |
| All insurance companies | 5.2 | 5.8 | 6.3 | 8.3 |
| Farm banks | 7.1 | 7.3 | 7.5 | 7.4 |
| Trust accounts of all banks | 7.2 | 7.3 | 7.2 | 7.3 |
| Long-term credit banks | 5.4 | 5.1 | 4.4 | 4.4 |
| Postal life insurance fund | 2.5 | 2.4 | 3.0 | 3.7 |
| Trust banks | 1.8 | 1.5 | 1.2 | 1.2 |
| Other | 6.0 | 8.4 | 8.0 | 6.2 |
| Total | 100.0 | 100.0 | 100.0 | 100.0 |
| ¥ trillion | 50.0 | 276.5 | 509.3 | 888.4 |
| $ billion* | 357.1 | 1971.4 | 3637.9 | 6345.7 |

\* $1 = ¥140
Source: *The Economist*

Japanese portfolio managers have traditionally been strongly averse to overseas markets. Part of their reluctance to buy foreign securities can be attributed to conservative investment principles which favour the home market where conditions are familiar and there is no foreign exchange risk. Managers of pension and trust funds have been content to seek a modest 8 percent return which they have been able to secure by investing in domestic loans, stocks, and government bonds.

Japanese portfolio managers – like their American counterparts – also have a distrust of all things foreign and, until recently, saw little need to study foreign issues or to journey abroad. Thus, they lacked the expertise required to follow foreign securities markets.

A further disincentive to overseas investment has been the policy of the Ministry of Finance, which maintains strict limits on the proportion of trust and pension funds which can be invested abroad. In March 1986, these limits were raised. Insurance companies and trust banks were authorized to invest as much as 25 percent of their portfolios in foreign securities and real estate. Nevertheless, at the end of 1986 Japan's biggest single group of investors, the 23 domestic life insurance companies, had only 11 percent of their assets (about ¥7.3 trillion compared to total assets of ¥62.5 trillion) in foreign securities. As this percentage grows, the market-moving power of Japan's financial institutions will increase dramatically.

The domestic reservoir is already beginning to feed foreign markets. Net purchases of foreign stock by Japanese investors in 1986 totalled $7.048 billion – a figure 138 times higher than that for 1984. Nearly half of these equity investments ($3.3 billion) were in blue-chip issues listed on the New York Stock Exchange. The appreciation of the yen against the dollar, together with the US bull market, made American equities seem cheap and desirable while the yields were not unappealing. As a result, the Japanese became the second largest foreign holders in US stocks after the British. In 1987 Japanese investments in overseas equities are expected to more than triple while the proportion directed to US issues will rise to more than 80 percent, or about $20 billion.

Investments in foreign stock were small, however, compared with Japanese investment in foreign bonds which in 1987 exceeded $72 billion. About half of this amount was spent on US Treasury issues. Japanese purchases of foreign bonds, like foreign equity investments, have grown considerably. The case of the insurance companies surveyed in the table below illustrates this.

### JAPANESE LIFE INSURANCE COMPANIES' INVESTMENT IN FOREIGN SECURITIES

| Year* | ¥ billions | percent of total portfolio |
|---|---|---|
| 1975 | 13 | 0.1 |
| 1980 | 669 | 2.5 |
| 1985 | 4,668 | 8.7 |
| 1986 | 7,307 | 11.7 |
| 1987** | 10,340 | n.a. |

* Fiscal year ending 31 March.
**At 31 May.
Source: Nippon Life Insurance Co.

By the end of March 1987 roughly 60 percent of Japanese foreign bond holdings were dollar denominated, primarily in the form of US Treasury issues. The big investors in the US Treasury market have been the trust banks, the life insurance companies (led by the two giants, Nippon and Dai-Ichi), and the Norinchukin Bank. (The Norinchukin, which collects deposits from all of the agricultural cooperatives, is overall, the sixth largest bank in Japan and, in terms of domestic deposits taken alone, the biggest.) Norinchukin currently holds roughly one sixth of all US Treasuries purchased by Japanese institutions. Foreign securities purchased by the life insurance companies represent about 30 percent of all Japanese foreign holdings and a roughly comparable share is taken by the seven trust banks.

As a result of the yen's appreciation against the dollar, unrealized foreign exchange losses on Japanese institutional holdings of American securities were considerable. The 23 life insurance companies, for example, collectively wrote off foreign exchange losses totalling $14.8 billion (¥2.238 trillion) for the year ending 31 March, 1987. However, these paper losses have not discouraged Japan's institutional investors from diversifying their portfolio holdings into foreign, particularly US, markets. The decline of the dollar has simply reduced the foreign currency expense of buying dollar assets while simultaneously reducing the chances that the holders will incur exchange rate losses in the future.

FROM LITTLE BUYER TO BIG INVESTOR:
JAPANESE NET PURCHASES OF
FOREIGN SECURITIES
$ millions

| Year | Bonds | Stocks |
|------|-------|--------|
| 1980 | 4,285 | −344 |
| 1981 | 5,808 | 240 |
| 1982 | 6,066 | 151 |
| 1983 | 12,507 | 658 |
| 1984 | 26,773 | 51 |
| 1985 | 53,517 | 995 |
| 1986 | 93,024 | 7,048 |
| 1987 | 72,890* | 16,870* |

* Nearest ten million
Source: Ministry of Finance

During the course of the next five years the percentage of the total assets of the life insurance companies and the trust banks which is invested in foreign securities will double. The current level of about 11 percent will begin to approach the ceiling of 25 percent established by the Ministry of Finance. Such an increase will involve a flood of Japanese money moving into the major world capital markets.*

Because the foreign offices of the trust banks and life insurance companies have been small, active trading in foreign securities has been modest. Securities investments have often been treated like real estate investments which are acquired and held for decades. But many of the insurance companies and trust banks are now expanding overseas operations and giving their foreign offices greater autonomy in making investment decisions. As a result, trading activities are growing. At the same time, these financial institutions are beginning to train a new generation of fund managers in the intricacies and subtleties of international securities markets.

In March 1987, Nippon Life paid $538 million for a 13 percent stake in Shearson Lehman Brothers (the third biggest Wall Street securities firm in terms of capital and subordinated debt). Three months later, 28 Nippon Life trainees boarded Japan Air Lines flights for New York. They were to study the securities business at Shearson Lehman for a period of one to two years. Some of these trainees will eventually become fund managers in Tokyo where they will use their knowledge of the American securities industry to manage portfolios which will include foreign, primarily US, issues.

Following the example of Nippon Life, Yasuda Mutual Life Insurance Company (Japan's fifth largest insurer) paid $300 million for an 18 percent voting share of the PaineWebber Group Inc. One component of the agreement reached between the two companies allows Yasuda to send up to 150 trainees to PaineWebber.

For the remainder of this century, Japanese financial institutions will continue to invest heavily in the United States because it represents an oasis where Japanese funds can flourish. The US bond and stock markets are deep wells which can absorb huge capital infusions from Tokyo with little more than a ripple. At the same time, they yield some of the best long-term returns in the world and provide a safe haven for the enormous dollar earnings derived from Japanese trade. Furthermore, because of its 'quality, liquidity, and marketability', the dollar itself is seen as an indispensable receptacle for Japanese assets.

The life insurance companies and trust banks, which hold a vast

---

*Part of this investment results from current Japanese accounting rules which prohibit insurance companies from using capital gains to pay out dividends on the portfolios which they manage. As a result, the insurers have a strong motive for exposing some of their assets to the higher returns available in overseas markets. The Ministry of Finance is expected to change accounting regulations in 1988, permitting total return on assets (yield plus capital gains) to be used in paying dividends. Although this modification of accounting practice could reduce the need to seek higher returns abroad, the overall effect is not likely to be significant.

segment of Japan's liquidity, will become ever more influential participants in the US and other major capital markets. But, it is, above all,
the Japanese securities companies which are in the ideal position to
direct the flow of Japan's domestic savings into international
investments.

## THE BIG FOUR SECURITIES COMPANIES

The Italian stockmarket, in terms of capitalization, is less than 3
percent the size of the Tokyo or New York markets. Trading volume
is minuscule by American or Japanese standards, and it has been of
negligible interest to international investors. Most foreign securities
firms have curtailed operations in Milan because of disappointing
brokerage business. Nonetheless, in the autumn of 1986, Daiwa and
Nomura, the two biggest securities companies in the world, set up
representative offices in Milan. Eight months later, Nikko and
Yamaichi followed suit.

At one level, the Big Four are attempting to get closer to the Italian
government bond market where a massive public debt has resulted in
high yields. They also hope that the presence of representative offices
in Italy will improve their chances of securing underwriting opportunities with Italian companies. For the short-term, the Big Four
are concentrating on a private competition to be the first Japanese
securities company to arrange the listing of an Italian firm on the
Tokyo Stock Exchange. Although little profit is likely to accrue from
such participation, the rival companies believe that domestic prestige
and the promise of future underwriting justify the efforts.

None of these considerations, however, could fully justify the cost
of setting up representative offices. At a deeper level, the Japanese
securities firms are seeking to establish a blanket presence in every
major financial market. From this perspective, Milan is just one
instance of a general expansion into all global securities markets.
Short-term benefits are of little concern and the representative offices
are expected to lose money for many years. Eventually, Milan will be
one unit in the multinational networks which each of the Big Four is
now constructing at great expense, but with high hopes.

Japanese securities firms were born in the early twentieth century
and originally dealt largely in bonds. When Japan's stock exchanges
reopened in 1949, these firms were a minor component of Japan's
financial sector. But the Big Four securities companies (Nomura,
Daiwa, Nikko, and Yamaichi) grew rapidly under the protection of
Article 65. At the same time, hundreds of smaller, second- and third-
tier securities firms also thrived as the growth of the Japanese stockmarket during the 1960s, which paralleled Japan's double digit econ-

omic expansion, generated big revenues for the securities industry as a whole.

The first foreign office of a Japanese securities firm appeared in New York in 1953, one year after the end of the Occupation. However, prior to the enactment of the new foreign exchange law in 1980, the securities companies were almost exclusively domestic affairs.

By 1987 the Big Four together maintained more than 40 wholly-owned overseas units (representative offices or foreign subsidiaries) located in eleven countries. Nomura and Daiwa opened new banking units in London in late 1986 and Nikko and Yamaichi followed a year later. Each of the firms had plans to expand its international business still further and the funds to do so were readily available.

The bull stock market of 1985–87 gave the Big Four record profits and astounding stockmarket capitalization. In 1986, for example, their aggregate net income was 2.5 times higher than the comparable figure for the four biggest firms on Wall Street.

By 1987, Nomura, the biggest securities firm in Japan, had grown to vast proportions. It had 155 offices, serviced roughly 4 million clients and had customer assets of $237 billion – more than any commercial bank in the world. At the end of September 1987, Nomura's stockmarket capitalization was roughly $58 billion, more than triple the *combined* value of Salomon, Merrill Lynch, Shearson Lehman, and Goldman Sachs.

Initially, the Big Four's foreign operations specialized in the sale of Japanese equity to foreign investors and foreign equity to Japanese investors, and these operations continued to lose money for many years. Undeterred, each of the Big Four was determined to establish itself in leading American, European, and Asian financial centres in order to carve out and protect a long-term share of Japanese overseas securities business.

Competition for market share ensured that Nikko and Yamaichi would scramble to compete when Daiwa and Nomura began swiftly to expand their London and New York operations in 1985. Between 1985 and 1987, Nomura increased the staff of its US subsidiary from 180 to 700, Daiwa from 150–400, Nikko from 70 to 260 and Yamaichi from 45 to 275.

In fiscal 1986, each of the Big Four claimed to have derived about 10 percent of its pretax profits from overseas operations and Nomura has announced that it expects 50 percent of its profits to come from foreign markets by the turn of the century. Like a barbershop quartet, the Big Four sing in harmonious optimism about their swiftly expanding international business.

In October 1986 London's 'Big Bang' marked the abandonment of fixed commission rates on bonds and equity transactions. The traditional distinctions between jobbers (who execute trades) and brokers (intermediaries between the public and the jobbers) was eliminated and outside institutions were allowed to buy members of the stock exchange.

Even before the Big Bang itself, the anticipation of a new and vital financial environment in London led to a major reshuffle in the course of which brokers and jobbers merged or were acquired by foreign and domestic interests. More than fifty mergers and acquisitions of this type occurred in London during the period 1984–86, with leading banks from the United States, Canada, Switzerland, Belgium, France and Hong Kong acquiring London brokers or jobbers.

Japanese financial institutions were notably absent from the orgy of buying. Instead, the Japanese securities companies and commercial banks substantially expanded their London subsidiaries, watched as events unfolded, and waited to see the outcome. They had little choice. The Ministry of Finance unofficially advised Japan's financial institutions to refrain from buying into the British financial service sector lest such investments exacerbate trade friction between Japan and the United Kingdom.

With the coming of the Big Bang, 27 firms became market-makers in gilt-edged securities. Competition within both this market (about 20 percent the size of the US Treasury market) and the London stockmarket was intense. Many of the new-comers found that they had overestimated the market share which they could procure and hold.

In March 1987, Greenwell Montagu Securities, the stockbroking arm of Midland Bank, decided to abandon equity market-making. Two months later, Lloyds Bank gave up trading gilts and, not long afterward, Morgan Grenfell reduced its gilts staff by 50 percent. Other market-makers in the gilts market followed suit and reduced their trading staff. In September 1987, the London branch of Shearson Lehman Brothers (the third largest investment bank in the United States) fired 150 employees and reduced the number of stocks in which it made markets from 400 to 200.

These cutbacks by major players were the result of excessive competition within the severely constrained British financial markets. Based in an economy about one-seventh the size of the United States and one-third the size of Japan, Britain's indigenous financial markets cannot offer the depth of opportunity available in New York and Tokyo. Within this environment, British financial institutions (including those acquired by foreign firms prior to Big Bang) have insufficient capital to compete easily with their better-capitalized foreign rivals.

It is against this background that the Big Four decided to become market-makers in British equities and, eventually, primary dealers in gilt-edged securities. Nomura, usually the leader of the Big Four, began making markets in shares in September 1987. By that time, it had expanded its London staff to more than 800 – compared to 400 in 1986 and just two in 1964. It also announced plans to increase its staff by an additional 75 percent by mid–1988.

Soon, the Big Four will be able to serve their domestic customers as market-makers in British equities and as primary dealers in London. Of course, it will be quite some time before Japanese brokers are selected by significant numbers of British investors in preference to local firms. However, with overseas securities investments growing, Japanese clients will provide the Big Four with a respectable volume of broking business. Their short-term goals demand no more.

It is, however, worth noting that within one year of becoming primary dealers in New York, Nomura and Daiwa had developed close relationships with a number of state pension funds (which deal only with primary dealers). Eventually, the Big Four will establish similar relationships with British and other European clients.

By the end of 1987, the London subsidiaries of the Big Four employed several thousand British citizens and were engaged in local broking, banking, and underwriting. These activities are important as components of the total set of products, services, and capabilities which will serve to define the Big Four's market scope in the twenty-first century.

Because of superior rates and easier issuing requirements, Japanese corporations have increasingly preferred to borrow in the Euromarkets rather than at home. Japan's Big Four securities companies and two long-term credit banks have become the lead underwriters for the plethora of Japanese issues floated in Europe.

Of all Japan's financial institutions, only Nomura ranked among the top ten bookrunners in the prestigious Eurobond market league tables in 1985. In 1986 three of the Big Four securities firms were there. One year later, four of the top six positions were filled by the Big Four, with three Japanese banks placed among the top 20. Together, Japanese institutions accounted for roughly 25 percent of all Eurobond underwriting. By comparison, Merrill Lynch fell from ninth place in 1986 to twenty-sixth place in 1987.

The sudden ascendancy of Japanese institutions in the Euromarkets (displacing entrenched firms such as Goldman Sachs and Morgan Stanley) bore a striking resemblance to the powerful growth of the Japanese semiconductor industry in the 1980s. Domestic profits were used to cut margins to the bone; predatory overseas pricing was common; and established domestic relationships seemed to assure the newcomers of a minimum market. At the same time, hundreds of Japanese corporations, flush with cash, turned to their familiar brokers to arrange Euroyen offerings. The money borrowed in this way was used for *zaitek*.

After securing impressive beachheads in the Eurobond market, Japan's Big Four securities firms set their sights on UK equities, big block stock trading in New York, venture capital, leveraged buyouts, mergers and acquisitions and (last but not least) the US Treasuries market.

In 1985, Nomura and Daiwa decided to expand the government bond trading departments of their New York subsidiaries and apply to the New York Federal Reserve Bank for primary-dealer status. Nikko and Yamaichi hastily followed suit. Each firm invested tens of millions of dollars to rent space, create trading rooms and hire expensive local talent. Nikko, for example, hired the Fed's top ranking staff official in 1986 and a vice president of the Federal Reserve Bank of New York a year later.

Virtually overnight, the Big Four became market movers in the US government bond market, where by the end of 1987, they accounted for roughly 18–20 percent of long-term trading in US Treasuries. While continuing to function as conduits channelling Japan's domestic liquidity into the hungry maw of the US government, the securities firms have also grown to be leading traders of American debt.

Despite objections in Washington, the US subsidiaries of the two biggest firms, Nomura and Daiwa, became primary dealers at the Fed in late 1986. Primary-dealer status brings with it special advantages and privileges in the $100 billion-a-day US Government securities market.

Although bidding at US Treasury auctions for new issues is unrestricted, the Federal Reserve Bank of New York deals only with primary dealers when it trades government securities in the secondary market to implement monetary policy. While secondary dealers number more than 400, there are currently just 40 primary dealers. Primary dealer status also involves great prestige and many companies will do business only with a primary dealer.

Eventually, Nikko and Yamaichi will also become primary dealers and a growing proportion of the Big Four's US Treasury bond transactions will be with US rather than Japanese customers. The Big Four will have risen, within a period of just a few years, from being insignificant traders representing Japanese clientele to become powerful forces in the Treasury market serving US customers.

As with Treasuries so with stocks. Although Japanese investors have been net buyers of foreign equities for many years, their total trading in such equities was never great and their annual net purchases never rose above $1 billion. In 1986, however, all of this began to change and Japanese institutional (and individual) investors began transacting a substantial number of small-lot and large-block trades in New York. By 1987, the Big Four accounted for an estimated 8 percent of all trading on the New York Stock Exchange (the bulk of it for Japanese customers) and had set their sights on making markets in British equities.

As the traditional underwriters for Japan's biggest corporations, the Big Four control about 80 percent of Japan's underwriting business. Together, they account for roughly 40 percent of all bond trading in Japan and for nearly half of all equity trading. This dominant position has allowed them to ride the crest of the wave created by Japan's industrial success and its recent stock market boom. With pretax profits of $3.5 billion (¥450 billion) for the fiscal year ending September 1987, Nomura, for example, was the most profitable corporation in Japan.

The Big Four's burgeoning importance in international finance is not due to net income alone. These firms have become the primary agents in the recycling of Japan's vast wealth; together with the leading Japanese banks and insurance companies, the Big Four have become instrumental in directing the deployment of Japan's overseas assets.

Overseas subsidiaries of the Big Four in leading world financial centres are growing like amoebae and are becoming an organic part of the national financial systems in which they participate. In some quarterly auctions of US Treasury bonds, for example, Nomura alone has purchased more than 10 percent of the entire issue while the Big Four together have acquired one-third of the total. Like the insurance companies, the Big Four can move the market through their participation in Treasury auctions.

From Beijing to Bahrain, from Seoul to Singapore, from London to Luxembourg, the Big Four are expanding their influence. Their vast equity capital, rich and loyal client base and long-term strategy for international expansion enables them to disregard short-term return on investment and focus instead on market share. The companies' know – from the example of Japan's manufacturing sector and from their own experience in Japan's financial markets – that securing a share of a market eventually yields stable profits. On the other hand, profits from a short-term situation are as evanescent as cherry blossoms.

## THE CITY BANKS

Japan's biggest national banks, thirteen in number, are termed city banks. The strong yen has made them enormous in terms of assets, capital, and stock market capitalization. Despite a declining demand for loans, the elimination of interest rate ceilings on large deposits and the strongest domestic banking competition during the whole postwar period, the city banks have recorded unprecedented profits (although revenues have been flat). For the year ending 31 March, 1987, pretax profits increased by an average of 40 percent (to ¥1.6 billion).

Beginning in 1985, US and British banks began to fall rapidly behind the top Japanese banks in their capacity to compete in international financial markets. While the money centre banks in Britain and America have been progressively weakened by their insufficient reserves against loan losses to problem credits in the Third World, the Japanese banks have grown stronger.

The bull stock market in Japan caused the city banks' enormous holdings in stock to more than triple in value in dollar terms. Although traditionally concerned primarily with domestic business, the city banks began expanding their international activities during the 1980s.

As early as the 1960s, Japan's banks purchased shares in international investment banks such as ADELA in Latin America and SIFIDA in Africa.* During the 1970s the banks set up joint venture financial subsidiaries throughout Europe and as Japan's global banking presence expanded steadily during the 1980s they bought out their partners.

By 1986, the thirteen city banks had overtaken US and UK banking institutions in terms of the volume of international lending. As the result of the sharp appreciation of the yen which occurred during the period 1985–87, the banks' reserves for overseas loan losses were drawn. At the same time, the city banks seized a major portion of the burgeoning domestic credit flows being intermediated in the international financial markets. By fiscal 1987, an estimated 50 percent of the city banks' profits were derived from international business.

By 1985, Japanese banks had marginally surpassed those of the United States to become the world's leading international bankers. In 1986, Japan's city banks established a clear lead. According to the Bank for International Settlements, foreign lending by Japanese banks reached $1.1 trillion at the end of 1986, representing one-third

*F.N. Burton and F.H. Saelens, 'The European Investments of Japanese Financial Institutions,' *Columbia Journal of World Business*, 1986 (Winter), p. 29.

of all international loans extended by banks in the major industrial countries (by contrast, the comparable statistics for the US were $601 million and 18.6 percent, respectively). In 1987, Japan's banks provided most of the new international lending to the world's non-banks and about 75 percent of the loans to banks.

There are a number of reasons for Japan's emerging strength in international banking:

(1) *High levels of liquidity in Japan,* resulting from the nation's high savings rate and large surpluses (for trade and the current account), have helped the city banks to increase international lending activities aggressively.

(2) *Japanese banks have a far lower overhead* than their US or European counterparts. A major cause of the low overhead is that only a small portion of total bank lending is to individuals. (Corporate lending requires far fewer staff than individual lending.) As a result, the top city banks, for instance, employ between 60 and 80 percent fewer staff than the leading US commercial banks.

(3) *Low capital adequacy requirements* (discussed below) have helped Japan's banks to provide cheap loans in the global markets, so under-cutting other money centre institutions. The average ratio of equity to assets for the city banks was 3.14 percent at the end of March 1987 (this compares with ratios of 5–6 percent for many US and UK banks).

Japanese banks are swiftly becoming the largest single foreign presence in every major financial centre in the world. Since 1985, Japan's regional and specialized banks, determined to join the city banks and long-term banks, have been busy opening overseas branches and representative offices in New York and London. As a result, there were 36 Japanese banks in New York and 40 in London at the end of 1986.

During the 1980s, Japanese banks became increasingly aggressive participants in the American and British banking sectors. By under-pricing local banks, they swiftly acquired substantial market share.

In the United States, Japanese banks have succeeded in replacing the UK as the biggest foreign banking presence, with roughly 8 percent of total banking assets, representing more than half of the foreign sector's share. At the end of 1986, Japanese banks provided 9 percent of all American business loans and controlled half of the market for municipal letters of credit.

Similarly, Japanese banks are now the biggest foreign presence in the UK, accounting for 23 percent of the total assets held by banks and 40 percent of foreign currency lending in London (and about 5

percent of sterling lending).* (By contrast, the foreign banking presence in Japan – 79 foreign banks – accounts for an aggregate share
of just 3 percent of total yen lending, a negligible portion of foreign
currency loans, and less than 2 percent share of total deposits.) Meanwhile, leading Japanese banks have been expanding their overseas
branch networks to include Atlanta, Chicago, Dallas, and a number
of medium-sized European cities.

Japanese banks have been expanding operations throughout the
Pacific Basin as well as in America and Europe. In Hong Kong,
Japanese banks are now the largest foreign presence in the banking
sector, with 24 full banks and 28 registered deposit-taking companies.
In 1986, Dai-Ichi Kangyo bought a controlling interest in Hong Kong-
based Chekiang First Bank.

In Australia, the Bank of Tokyo, Mitsubishi Bank and the Industrial
Bank of Japan were among 15 foreign banks granted licences
following the deregulation of the financial system in early 1985.
Despite terrible profit margins, the three Japanese banks will remain
in Australia in anticipation of long-term growth.

Japan's major corporations, once vital customers of the city banks
and long-term banks, now seek funds directly in the capital markets,
though Japan's cash-rich manufacturing corporations have little need
to borrow funds. Most Japanese industries have, moreover, vastly
reduced their investments in plant and equipment.

As a direct consequence of this permanent structural change, the
leading Japanese banks now hold a disproportionate share of 'problem'
credits in the nation's sunset industries. This, combined with troubled
loans to the Third World (discussed below), has led some observers to
suggest that the leading banks, despite their powerful global stature,
may have an Achilles heel.

Certainly the quality of the assets held by Japan's major banks has
been declining as they have moved aggressively into international
markets. Bank profitability (the return on assets), which has always
been low for Japanese banks, has become lower. Increased participation in the foreign exchange markets and the world's financial
markets has increased the vulnerability of Japanese banks to interest
rate instability and global financial market volatility.

Deregulation in Japan and throughout the world is enabling
borrowers to bypass the banking system in their efforts to raise funds.
This means that Japan's banks will be obliged to compete with investment banks, which have far more experience in the securities industry.
Japanese banks have reacted by placing increasing emphasis on non-

*These banking statistics are from *The Economist*, 4 April 1987, p. 72.

asset related sectors – particularly bond and foreign exchange dealings as well as the promising mergers and acquisitions business (discussed above). The future strength of Japan's biggest banks will be determined by their ability to adjust to a changed world in which the lion's share of their profits are derived from new business areas in overseas capital markets.

With international business accounting for more than a third of their operating profits, the city banks will vigorously oppose any decision that could impair their foreign lending opportunities. On the other hand, they are now obliged to confront the inevitable need to make provisions for a portion of their non-performing loans to the Third World. Japanese banks hold an estimated $35 billion of loans to fifteen major Third-world debtors, giving Japan the world's second largest Third World debt exposure after the $90 billion of the United States.

West German banks have set aside funds to cover 60–70 percent of their Third World debt exposure in order to offset the risk of default. West German tax laws permit the banks to offset these funds against tax. American and British banks have set aside 25–30 percent of outstanding loans to problem Third World debtors. By contrast, Japanese banks have established reserves for only a minuscule portion of their loans to high risk countries.

Japan's tax laws allow little opportunity to offset loan loss provisions against tax. For many years, the International Finance Bureau of the Ministry of Finance has been at loggerheads with the Ministry's Tax Bureau. The conservative Tax Bureau, which has sole authority to revise tax laws, has firmly opposed any change that would reduce tax revenues. A compromise solution was reached in 1987. Just before the end of the fiscal year, the city banks (along with fifteen other major Japanese banks) set up IBA Investment.

Incorporated in the Cayman Islands, IBA is a shell company designed to take over some of the Japanese banks' loans to the less developed nations. The banks sold roughly $6 billion of Mexican loans to IBA at deep discounts and subsequently took tax deductions from the resulting losses.

In addition, the Ministry of Finance announced plans to increase the ceiling on the taxable loan-loss reserves for financial institutions from 5 percent to 10–20 percent. It also indicated plans to increase the minimum volume of taxable loan-loss reserves from 1 percent to 5 percent.

Meanwhile, Japan's banks have placed most debt from Peru, Ecuador and Costa Rica (all hopelessly impoverished small borrowers) on a non-accrual basis. The February 1987 announcement by the Brazilian government that it would suspend interest payments on $67 billion of foreign bank debt will eventually force Japanese banks (which have loaned Brazil an estimated $9 billion) to place Brazilian debt in the same category. If the resulting losses are not counterbalanced by new earnings, then the leading Japanese banks will suffer some decline in profitability at the end of March 1988.

Despite their considerable exposure to risky loans and their paltry reserves, Japanese banks are not worried – although they pretend to be. Each bank could offset the losses by selling a portion of its securities holdings and so converting hidden assets to realized gains. Thus, while Third World debt has been a spectre haunting American banks (which have 40 percent more exposure than their Japanese colleagues), it is a minor headache for Japan's institutions.

LOANS TO THE THIRD WORLD BY THE LEADING CITY BANKS*

| Bank | Amount (¥ billions) |
| --- | --- |
| Bank of Tokyo | 638 |
| Sumitomo Bank | 410 |
| Dai-Ichi Kangyo Bank | 406 |
| Mitsubishi Bank | 346 |
| Sanwa Bank | 330 |
| Fuji Bank | 326 |

*At 31 March, 1987
Source: Ministry of Finance

As the world's financial markets become increasingly integrated, the need for uniformity grows proportionally. Just as futures contracts must be identical in order to be traded, banking regulations among the major nations will inevitably be forced from their current national diversity into the straightjacket of homogeneity.

This is but one instance of a global trend which has characterized the 'age of information'. Socio-cultural features which have developed over decades and centuries are supplanted, almost overnight, by a narrow, predominantly Western, tradition which is loosely shared by all of the free world's nations. This new standardization, which will be a central feature of twenty-first century international finance, could increase global harmony; it could also lead to the dull, grey tyranny of a handful of giant financial conglomerates.

In 1986 and early 1987, considerable European pressure on the Ministry of Finance to increase the capital adequacy ratios (the level of shareholders' equity and reserves) of Japan's banks led to intense discussions. Ministry of Finance officials met frequently with representatives of the city banks to debate the necessity for raising the ratio of capital to assets.

A bank's capital is a significant expense and a crucial reserve against bad debts. Because Japan's banks maintain lower capital adequacy ratios than their leading global competitors, they have the advantage of a very cheap cost of funds. American and British banks have complained bitterly about their Japanese rivals' low capital and international banking authorities have expressed concern that, in the event of a crisis, the global banking system could be undermined by the insufficient capital of Japanese banks.

In February 1987, in a lengthy joint proposal, the US Federal Reserve System and the Bank of England urged commercial banks throughout the world to raise their minimum capital adequacy ratios. This proposal was the result of the sober recognition that loans to the Third World had lost a substantial proportion of their value. Meanwhile, many American and European banks insisted that the 4 percent capital to asset ratio approved by the Japanese Ministry of Finance in May 1986 was not high enough.

Japan's banks baulked at the suggestion of higher ratios. Banking losses in Japan are covered by the liquidation of equities rather than by reductions in capital (the differences between the market value and the book value of portfolio holdings are applied to cover losses). Therefore, the banks argued, if 70 percent of their hidden reserves were taken into account, the average ratio for the city banks would more than triple, to 9–11 percent. Indeed, if 70 percent of the hidden assets of the trust banks were taken into account, *their* capital ratios would more than quadruple.

Furthermore, Japanese bankers pointed out, many US banks (some of New York's money-centre banks for example), had suffered severe declines in their capital ratios as a result of their big reserves against loans to Latin America. Manufacturers Hanover, Citicorp, and Chase Manhattan (three of America's biggest money-centre banks) all had equity to assets ratios of less than 3 percent at the end of August 1987 (prior to their new stock issues).

American and European bankers participating in the Cooke Committee of bank supervisors meeting in Basle (where the Bank for International Settlements is located), responded to these claims by arguing that the valuation of hidden assets at 70 percent of their market value was unreasonably high in light of market volatility. In 1986, Japan's stock and real estate markets had reached exceptionally high levels. Land prices in Tokyo, for example, spurred by excess liquidity and speculation, rose by an average of 85.7 percent, during the twelve months to 30 June, 1987, with residential land prices soaring by 93 percent.*

---

*According to National Land Agency statistics. Land in the Ginza, the most expensive area, was valued at ¥32 million (about $220,000) per square metre.

The Ministry of Finance countered that the figure of 70 percent took into account *all* likely fluctuations in the market values of real estate or securities. At the end of March 1987, for example, the four biggest city banks held invisible assets of roughly ¥14 trillion (about $10 billion). These hidden assets would cushion loan losses, even if the stock and real estate markets lost 70 percent of their current market values.

Moody's Investors' Service, a leading US credit rating agency, did not agree with the Ministry of Finance's optimistic assessment. In June 1987, Moody's placed the Bank of Tokyo, the Long-Term Credit Bank of Japan, Mitsubishi Trust and Banking, and Sanwa Bank under review for possible downgrading. Moody's indicated that these institutions suffered from weaknesses and might not be able to deal successfully with a drastic downward swing in domestic or international markets.

In late 1987, under administrative guidance from the Ministry of Finance, Japan's leading banks began reviewing their total assets in the expectation that 40–50 percent of their hidden assets would be approved by the Cooke Committee as applicable towards total banking capital. Through such asset reviews, the banks intended to cut their assets and raise their capital to asset ratios to the international standards determined by the banking regulators of the industrial world. One result will be that the city banks will be obliged sharply to curtail their practice of taking short-term deposits in the Euromarket (far in excess of necessary funds for loans) and managing the funds in the domestic short-term markets.

More importantly, they will be forced to restrain the practice of extending loans at thin profit margins. Instead, they will be driven to pursue high returns from high-return businesses. Consequently, potentially profitable overseas companies (such as the Walter E. Heller subsidiaries mentioned above) will be purchased and exploited.

Many leading banks have also sought to strengthen their capital ratios by issuing new shares or convertible bonds. In 1987, Dai-Ichi Kangyo, Sanwa, Sumitomo, Mitsubishi, and three long-term banks issued new securities. The biggest new stock issue, floated by the Industrial Bank of Japan, was worth roughly $1.5 billion (¥218 billion). Such issues will raise the banks' capital adequacy ratios by at least 0.5 percent.

At the same time, the Ministry of Finance, in an effort to tighten curbs on overseas loans and other foreign assets, reduced the maximum ratio of foreign assets to foreign net worth from 3.5 times to 2.5 times. This decision will temporarily impede the city banks' efforts to increase overseas market share.

In the course of improving their capital adequacy ratios, however, the banks will be forced to reduce the growth of low quality assets. While short-term growth may be impeded, this will result in greater rationalization of banking operations over the long-term. Indeed, if Japan's banks raise the levels of their capital adequacy to international standards with only modest recourse to hidden assets, they will emerge as the world's most creditworthy banks. Ultimately Japan's banks, by becoming more efficient, will become stronger global competitors.

#### EQUITY TO ASSETS RATIOS
#### OF THE THIRTEEN CITY BANKS
#### ALTHOUGH LOW,
#### WILL IMPROVE STEADILY

| Institution | Equity to assets ratio | |
| --- | --- | --- |
| | 31 March 1986 | 31 March 1987 |
| Dai-Ichi Kangyo Bank | 2.04 | 2.87 |
| Fuji Bank | 2.56 | 3.31 |
| Sumitomo Bank | 2.62 | 3.11 |
| Mitsubishi Bank | 2.43 | 3.22 |
| Sanwa Bank | 2.26 | 3.02 |
| Tokai Bank | 2.09 | 2.92 |
| Mitsui Bank | 2.07 | 2.97 |
| Taiyo Kobe Bank | 2.02 | 2.77 |
| Bank of Tokyo | 2.57 | 3.53 |
| Daiwa Bank | 1.51 | 3.59 |
| Kyowa Bank | 2.02 | 3.81 |
| Saitama Bank | 2.31 | 3.09 |
| Hokkaido Takushoku Bank | 1.98 | 2.59 |
| AVERAGE | 2.19 | 3.14 |

Source: Ministry of Finance

## ALL ABOARD!

Japan's general trading companies (*sogo shosha*) were one of the pillars supporting the pre-war *zaibatsu*. Later, during the postwar period, they functioned as vital intermediaries, trading commodities and capital goods in large quantities with low margins. The *sogo shosha*, involved in every area of production and sales, grew to enormous proportions during the era of Japan's rapid economic growth. The biggest (Mitsui Fudosan, Mitsubishi Shoji, Marubeni, C. Itoh, Sumitomo, and Nissho Iwai), became some of the largest corporations in the world.

Today, the *sogo shosha* are in decline because of structural changes in the Japanese and world economies. Japan's demand for raw materials has decreased as the service sector has grown and, simultaneously, many Japanese manufacturers have begun to bypass their traditional *sogo shosha* linkages. As a result of these changes, the trading companies have been forced to develop new business areas in order to survive. They have become international project managers, overseeing every aspect of major undertakings from financing of plant and equipment to final sales. Recently, the trading companies have also tried their hand at third-country trade (trade excluding Japan), countertrade (barter), biotechnology, telecommunications, and *financial services*.

Between 1984 and 1986, the big *sogo shosha* set up finance subsidiaries in New York, London and a number of offshore banking centres. They hope to use their expertise in risk management and their well-established global networks to trade in financial services just as they have traditionally traded in goods. In 1987, overseas *sogo shosha* financial subsidiaries offered a broad range of financial services which included leasing, export finance, project finance and the handling of many financial instruments.

Although still at an early stage of development, these subsidiaries promise to make the trading companies into financial service vendors. Before the turn of the century, it is likely that Japanese domestic regulations will no longer prevent the *sogo shosha* from functioning as domestic bankers and brokers; when that day arrives, the trading companies will be ready. Meanwhile, they are positioning themselves to compete with the overseas financing operations of the securities companies and commercial banks.

Like the *sogo shosha*, a broad range of leading Japanese manufacturers have also recognized the advantages of diversification into financial services. Matsushita Electric Industrial Co created New York-based Panasonic Finance in 1985. Like hundreds of similar Japanese corporate subsidiaries in New York and London, Panasonic Finance sells its parent's commercial paper to foreign buyers.

Many of these financial companies participate in the securities markets in order to maximize the return of an assigned portion of the parent's cash assets. At the end of 1986, the Ministry of Finance counted 3,196 overseas financial subsidiaries belonging to Japanese financial institutions and corporations. During the next five years these subsidiaries will grow and multiply.

## JAPAN VERSUS WORLD FINANCE?

By 1986 Japan's six major city banks had achieved notoriety within the world's club of international bankers. If the 1988 Olympic Games had included a banking competition, Japan's Club of Six would have ended up with a rich collection of medals dangling from its collective neck, including at least six golds:

The biggest five in the world in terms of assets.
The biggest six in the world in terms of equity capital.
The largest international lenders to final borrowers.
The biggest national group of international lenders.
The largest foreign currency lenders from London.
The biggest foreign banking presence in the United States and the
United Kingdom.

Like all Japanese businesses, Japan's banks have focussed their attention on the acquisition of market share at the expense of short-term
profitability. Because of their size and powerful collective presence
in the world's leading international banking centres, some financial
commentators have expressed anxiety (occasionally panic) that
Japanese banks will soon establish dominance of world banking, so
matching the startling success of Japan's auto and semiconductor
industries.

Japan's big banks, particularly Sumitomo and the Industrial Bank
of Japan, have looked to America's Citibank as the international
grandmaster of banking strategy. Citibank has shown the world how
daring innovation and aggressive retailing can conquer world
markets. Japan's big banks are determined to do the same. *Will they?*

Some Western financial specialists point out that while these banks
have the biggest assets and capitalizations in the world, scarcely any
of their employees are the proud owners of undergraduate degrees
from Oxford University or of parchment from the Harvard Business
School. In the world of international finance, flawless English and
Western marketing etiquette are *de rigueur*. Japanese businessmen
have been notoriously weak at marketing their international financial
services. How can they hope to compete over the long term with the
leading banks of America and Britain?

Japanese banking was, until very recently, a domestic and heavily
protected business. Furthermore, Japan's banking leaders, and the
army of deal-makers and planners who carry their briefcases, began
their careers as banking clerks. They rose through the ranks in a
system which offers no battlefield promotions – indeed which positively discourages individuality and daring decisions. Do they have
the imagination, the cunning and the independent flexibility to excel
in an ultra-competitive field with shrinking margins?

The same question could be posed about Japan's Big Four securities
companies. Yes, they have money. Yes, they are determined. They
have decided to move swiftly into the international sector and like
the city banks they are planning to derive half of their total revenues
from international operations well before the year 2000. But can

money and determination together buy a durable share of the global financial services industry? Are Japanese bankers and brokers such brilliantly innovative financiers, such suave marketers, that they can permanently take significant portions of market share away from the Morgan Stanleys, the Citibanks or the S.G. Warburgs of this world?

Those who would without hesitation answer these questions with a confident 'nay' should pause for a moment. Consider, for example, the rise of the Big Four securities firms to the top of the Eurobond underwriting league tables. Consider Nomura and Daiwa's status as primary dealers in the US Treasury market and their new banks in London. Consider Industrial Bank of Japan's purchase of Schroder Bank & Trust and its acquisition of Aubrey G. Lanston; or Sumitomo's purchase of a Swiss bank (Banca del Gottardo) and its investment in Goldman Sachs; or Nippon Life's share of Shearson Lehman, Yasuda Mutual Life's share of the PaineWebber Group, Fuji's ownership of the Heller subsidiaries and Sanwa's leasing operations in Chicago and its likely purchase of a primary dealer in New York. Consider that five of the eleven biggest banks in California are Japanese and that in 1986 Japanese banks accounted for 16 percent of California's total banking assets.

Japanese financial institutions are at the beginning of a decade-long process of slowly buying what they do not have – overseas business. Many of the ventures and acquisitions mentioned in the preceding paragraph are now losing money or are only marginally profitable. The parent institutions are preparing to absorb losses for as long as necessary. They are hiring high-quality foreign executives and, simultaneously, they are training (often in foreign institutions) a new generation of Japanese employees who will devote their lives to international business.

These new Japanese denizens of the world of international finance will be as capable as their Western counterparts at contriving new products. The whiz-kids of Nomura and other Japanese securities firms have already developed a few innovative instruments for the Euromarkets. In far less than a decade they will master the financial theory and market timing so vital to success in the new world of finance. It would be foolhardy to assume, that because Japanese investment bankers and commercial bankers lack *chic* today, that they will not be inventing the fashion of tomorrow.

Of course, the international financial services industry is not comparable to the auto industry. It is not as inevitable as sunrise that the strategy of Japanese manufacturers can be applied to global banking, investment and securities. There is, however, little persuasive evidence to suggest that Japanese institutions will fail in their plan to become the world's leading providers of financial services.

It has been alleged that money cannot buy lasting love. It has on occasion. It has been argued that money cannot buy a durable and substantial share of global financial services. It can and it will.

# 6 'THE FUTURE BELONGS TO US'

'The war fleet will still be in Japan but we will have more cruisers and destroyers abroad.'

Tsunehiko Ishizuka,
Managing Director,
Sony Corporation (1986)*

## A VAGUE BUT MEANINGFUL RESEMBLANCE
Long ago, the observation that certain aspects of business resemble war became trite. Although, of course, the scrutiny of classic works of military strategy may improve business acuity, in most countries the relationship between war and business is a metaphoric. Associating business strategy with military strategy may help to improve tactical thinking, but a direct, correlative relationship between the two does not exist.

In Japan, however, the parallels between military structure and martial attitudes, on the one hand, and business corporations and business attitudes, on the other, are particularly pronounced. Japanese corporations, perhaps more than the corporations of other nations, resemble the military in a number of respects: recruitment (mentioned in Chapter 2), strong hierarchical structure (individual status and behaviour are rigidly defined), stability (only mercenaries,

*Quoted in Kevin Rafferty, 'Japanese Corporate Finance Goes Global'. *Institutional Investor*, November 1986, p. 293.

who are social deviants, move from army to army or job to job) and impenetrability (discussed below).

## IMPERVIOUS

When a military force is garisoned outside its national borders (whether as an occupier or as an ally) it does not hire local nationals as generals, colonels or even as privates. Foreign embassies may hire local staff, but not the army or navy. Nor does the military attempt to imitate local customs. Learning a foreign language is always useful and speaking the language of an occupied country is vital to maintaining security. Soldiers, however, are discouraged from adopting native garb, native cuisine and native spouses. The military protects its interests, and if those interests cease to exist in one location, the military goes away. It goes to wherever its interests can be served best.

Like the military, the Japanese corporation which sets up units in overseas markets remains impervious to the environment. Unlike Western corporations which view themselves as immigrants in new markets, Japanese companies do not 'go native'. The managers sent by the parent company, like officers sent overseas, give key commands and report to headquarters.

The citizens of a democracy own the military, but have remarkably little authority in relation to it. In much the same way, the shareholders own a public Japanese company but have virtually no *de facto* control of its management.

Although a special arm of the military can be discontinued, reduced in size, or merged with other units, it cannot go bankrupt. Similarly, large Japanese corporations have been heavily protected by MITI from the oblivion of insolvency.

## MANAGERS AND GHOSTS

Like the army, Japanese corporations have not traditionally established local subsidiaries with high ranking foreign staff. Japanese management is exported by the parent company to the overseas units as a matter of course. And just as career soldiers are routinely moved from post to post, limiting the duration of their exposure to a foreign country, so the average tour of duty overseas for a Japanese businessman is also limited.

In order to maintain maximum control of those foreign workers who must be hired, every effort is made to avoid establishing factories in areas where labour unions are strong. Whenever possible, young non-union employees are hired.

Increasingly, Japanese subsidiaries in the United States and the European Community have created high-ranking positions for 'local hires'. Foreign senior executives close to retirement are often hired as 'senior executive vice presidents' and 'vice chairmen'. A small number of Japanese manufacturing firms have installed Americans and Britons as chief executive officers of a local subsidiary. The presence of these individuals creates the appearance of foreign management within the Japanese overseas unit. Needless to say, none of these 'top executives' has risen through the ranks.

However, these 'foreigners' (with one recent exception) do not have executive positions with the parent company. In nearly all instances, the parent corporation regards 'local hires' as a component of a subsidiary's operating expense rather than as a part of the corporation. The authority of the foreign employee extends only to the foreign aspects of the overseas unit. Japanese citizens who are recruited locally also fall into the 'foreign' category (they are not part of the parent organization).

Take the example of a 57-year-old American senior executive vice president at the overseas subsidiary of a Japanese company. He may be dissatisfied with a 27-year-old Japanese assistant vice president who reports to him, but under no circumstances will he have the authority to fire or even reprimand his subordinate. The Japanese employee, although officially employed by the subsidiary corporation, has actually been seconded by the parent company to the subsidiary. Thus, every effort is made to avoid giving foreign employees authority over Japanese (parent company) staff.

From the perspective of the parent corporation in Japan, foreign executives have form without content. They are ghosts. They are employed to act as an interface between the foreignness of the overseas market and the Japanese management of the subsidiary.

In Japanese folklore, ghosts have no feet. This missing attribute is significant. These unwholesome and disturbing apparitions do not walk on the land of Japan and thus are not connected to it. Like foreigners, ghosts are not Japanese people and acquire much of their repugnance from that irreversible fact.

Similarly, the Japanese overseas subsidiary is itself a ghost. It appears at first glance to be an accurate replica of comparable subsidiaries of other multinational companies, just as a ghost appears to be a living person. However, its management (consisting of expatriate Japanese and foreigners) is not grounded abroad. Its feet are in the parent company; it has no feet of its own.

### THE FOREIGN EMPLOYEES OF SOME MAJOR JAPANESE CORPORATIONS*

| Corporation | Number of foreigners | Number of total employees |
|---|---|---|
| Sony | 30 | 15,000 |
| NEC | 30 | 38,364 |
| Kobe Steel | 30 | 26,151 |
| Marubeni | 29 | 7,678 |
| Nikko Securities | 25 | 8,637 |
| Dentsu | 19 | 5,760 |
| Toyota Motor | 18 | 62,530 |
| Nippon Kokan | 17 | 31,660 |
| Ricoh | 15 | 11,358 |
| Fuji Bank | 14 | 15,000 |
| Mitsubishi Corporation | 13 | 8,820 |

*Data refer to the Japan-based parent corporation only.
Source: *Japan Economic Joiurnal*, 5 September 1987.

## FOREIGN SUBSIDIARIES: WHERE ARE THE FEET?

The majority of the West's multinational corporations have established overseas subsidiaries in dozens of nations. Each of these subsidiaries is generally based upon a local management structure which transforms it (in essence if not in fact) into a national company. These 'overseas nationals' must contend with the demands of their workers' unions and the exigencies of the local markets which they serve. The greater the obligations to local employees, local conditions, and local markets the less free is the subsidiary to pursue the international strategy of the parent organization.

As a result, the overseas operations of multinational corporations usually compromise their greatest asset: the potential to allocate the corporation's total resources *freely*. In effect each of a multinational's overseas units becomes embedded in its local market. Instead of rising above a particular domestic market, the subsidiary becomes a provincial unit. It is as though Marco Polo had journeyed to Cathay only to settle there permanently and set up shop. Rather than being a component of an international marketing structure, the overseas subsidiary is a foreign business. Instead of becoming part of a galaxy, each overseas operation becomes a lone star.

In the case of Japanese corporations, by contrast, the overseas subsidiary never ceases to be a local production unit fully integrated into the parent organization. Top (and sometimes middle) management is predominantly Japanese and the total activities of the unit are directed towards the fulfilment of the parent's international goals. This means that the product being produced or marketed takes precedence over the subsidiary. This distinction between Japanese and Western overseas subsidiaries may appear to be vague and inconsequential, but it is not.

Although Japanese corporations sometimes claim that their overseas subsidiaries are separate profit centres, such an attitude is, at best, equivocal. Employees of Japanese companies, including those in overseas subsidiaries, do not traditionally receive bonus payments based upon their performances and a subsidiary is not awarded new equipment on the basis of its profitability. The total pre-tax profits of the overseas subsidiary belong to the parent company and can be directed by the home office to other overseas units or to domestic operations. Unprofitable subsidiaries can therefore float indefinitely on the profits of the parent corporation or its other subsidiaries.

Some of the most successful foreign corporations bear close resemblances to their Japanese counterparts in many respects. International Business Machines Corporation (IBM), for instance, has been identified as one example of Japanese organizational structure in a non-Japanese company.* IBM Japan, however, is a Japanese corporation with a Japanese president, Japanese management and Japanese staff.

When, in 1987, the US Defense Department vetoed the sale of an IBM computer by IBM Germany to Transnautic, a Soviet-owned West German corporation, West German diplomats in Washington objected that the Pentagon exceeded its authority by prohibiting a transaction between two *German* entities. The fact that West German representatives could make such a claim is indicative of the extent to which subsidiaries of multinational corporations have become national companies.

By contrast, the Japanese overseas subsidiary is *subsidiary* in the literal sense – its essential purpose is to *support* the parent company. It also exists to assist or supplement the creation and distribution of products. It is *always* subordinate or secondary to the product and to the parent company. Unlike Western multinational corporations, or British social anthropologists, Japanese companies do not go native when they go abroad. Their feet as well as their heartbeats remain in Japan.

## PRODUCTS WITHOUT COUNTRIES

Western firms, like dairy farmers, give priority to the cow – its health, its feed, its barn. They assume that if the cow is given the best possible conditions its milk production will be outstanding. Conversely,

---

*See for example William G. Ouchi *Theory Z. How American Business Can Meet the Japanese Challenge*, New York: Avon Books, 1982, p. 58.

Japanese corporations give primary attention to the milk (the product) and only secondary attention to the cow (the local production unit). If the cow does poorly, others can be purchased in the same country or elsewhere.

Although Japanese corporations scour the world for the best and most economical equipment, raw materials and unskilled labour, management remains a domestic component of production. Even if the overseas subsidiary is operated on a day-to-day basis by a local (foreign) president and managing director, the native management remains a puppet. The strings are controlled by puppet masters at the parent company in Japan.

Just as troops can be pulled out of a foreign base, so Japanese management can be pulled out of a troubled overseas subsidiary. The product can then be produced by the means and in the place offering maximum efficiency. Thus, it is the product *not the producer* that is truly international. While Western corporations invest heavily in the creation of global networks, Japanese corporations focus on the creation of global products.

Of course, a general product line may be adjusted to a particular local market. Sony Corporation, for example, produces different *models* of its Walkman for markets in Japan, the United States, West Germany and France. However, the creation of these country-specific models does not *necessarily* involve local-level manufacture. Much the same could be said about other Japanese industries.

Japanese manufacturers devote their research and development programmes to the creation of products which are tailored to the needs, expectations and tastes of foreign markets.* Just as soldiers are equipped in accordance with the terrain and climate where they will be deployed, the global product is finely tuned to match the characteristics of each marketplace. The child of the parent corporation is *not* the subsidiary company, it is the product.

Given the preeminence of the product over all other factors in the Japanese corporate world-view, it is easily understandable that long-term strategic goals *always* override short- and medium-term costs and obstacles in Japanese corporate culture. The month-to-month and year-to-year losses of a particular subsidiary are viewed within the total context of the creation and marketing of particular products.

---

*Many Japanese corporations are able to utilize their total resources in order to efficiently maximize the effectiveness of their production and marketing functions far more flexibly than the corporations of other nations. As a result, certain corporate sectors (such as research and development) are more closely integrated into their central corporate structure than other sectors (such as overseas marketing).

## THE FUTURE BECKONS

Gradually, the world's markets for manufactured goods will come to resemble the global financial markets. Just as a Japanese bond futures contract can be purchased on the Tokyo Stock Exchange in the morning and sold on the London International Financial Future Exchange the following night (afternoon in London), goods will increasingly become as interchangeable as raw commodities and will transcend national borders. Hence Kenichi Ohmae's observation:

Today, new products circle the globe with the speed of a satellite. It no longer holds that innovations trickle down like a cascade or waterfall from the most to the least technologically advanced countries.*

What will distinguish the future from the past is not the development of 'companies without countries' but rather the evolution of *products without countries*. Like today's incipient 24-hour financial markets, where uniform products are bought and sold independently of geography and politics, tomorrow's electronics or auto markets will not be based on location.

The supreme measure of the manufacturing industries of tomorrow will be product quality and universality. The arrangement or placing of the source of production will become irrelevant to the global manufacturing market of the future in which success will hinge upon product selection, design, price, and financing. Recall from the previous chapter that Honda Motors intends to export 70,000 automobiles per year from the United States by 1989; or that Aiwa Corporation now produces 50 percent of its total output in Singapore and exports more than half of Singapore production to Japan; or that the Toshiba Corporation imports into Japan microwave ovens and colour televisions manufactured by its United States unit, Toshiba America.

Soon the proliferating overseas units of Japanese corporations will routinely export a significant portion of their production. Before long, Japanese cars made in Tennessee or Wales, for example, will be more threatening to European manufacturers than was General Motors in its heyday.

Japan's third-country ('triangular') trade will steadily become ever more predominant and will serve to deflect protectionist outcries. Gradually, too, Japan will become a major importer of its own foreign-produced goods. This, in turn, will stabilize its growing current account surpluses. The potentially destabilizing influence of the excessive accumulation of money will be ameliorated. The hurricane,

*Kenichi Ohmae *Beyond National Borders*, Homewood: Dow Jones Irwin, 1987, p. 84.

travelling from ocean to land, spends its force and becomes a gale wind.

As a direct result of overseas production, pressure on the yen (which will drive the currency higher during the next several years) will relax. The yen, following Japan's surpluses, will rise to a plateau in a range which, today, Japanese manufacturers equate with death: 100–115 yen to the dollar. In this new world, which resolutely approaches, Japan's manufacturers will reside abroad – but few will become expatriates.

## THE YEN AS A WORLD CURRENCY

Although foreign exchange traders and central banks are loath to admit it, exchange rates are impossible to forecast. In early 1985, for example, when the dollar traded at $1.03 to the pound sterling, many experts predicted that the dollar and pound would soon attain parity. They were wrong, of course, and the dollar stabilized in the range $1.60–1.75 to the pound. No forecasters predicted in early 1985 that within two years, in terms of purchasing power parity, the overvalued dollar and the undervalued yen would have become an undervalued dollar and an overvalued yen.

Traditionally, central banks (which hold the nations' banking reserves) have been responsible for intervening in foreign exchange markets in order to stabilize the foreign exchange value of their national currencies. But the internationalization of world markets has inevitably reduced the power of the individual central banks. As a result, or partly so, the world's major central banking establishments (the Fed, the Bundesbank, and the Bank of Japan) have intervened significantly over the past few years only when forced to do so by the threat of severe imbalances.

The agreement reached at the Plaza Hotel (in September 1985) and the later Louvre agreement (in February 1987) have become landmark examples of today's central bank approach to intervention. These agreements, reached by the major industrial nations, resulted in coordinated intervention* designed to force the dollar down from its overvalued level and subsequently to maintain it within an undisclosed range of stability. Measured against many major currencies, the dollar fell 40–50 percent during the period between the Plaza Hotel and Louvre agreements.

The swift decline of the dollar in 1985–87 was more than Japan bargained for. From its trough of ¥263 to the dollar in February 1985, the yen appreciated to a postwar high of ¥120.5 per dollar in late

---

*During the first three quarters of 1987, for example, the dollar was prevented from tumbling by the weight of $90 billion of central bank interventions.

1987.* Subsequently, Japanese industry revealed (to the chagrin of its overseas competitors) that not only was adjustment to a strong yen possible but that it could be achieved quickly. Can the yen strengthen further during the next five years? Will Japanese companies adjust (rationalize) successfully to an even stronger yen?

Japan has been reluctant to adopt a significant role in financing world economic growth. Domestic demand for manufactured goods has been modest and aid to the Third World unimpressive (recall the discussion of aid in Chapter 1). Within this context, the yen has been a provincial currency. In fiscal year 1986 only 35.5 percent of Japan's exports and 9.7 percent of her imports were denominated in yen.

Foreign holdings of yen have been primarily confined to the Euro-bond market and the Japanese stockmarket. Yet the Euroyen bond market is functionally a segment of Japan's domestic capital markets.† (Nonetheless, the supranational World Bank, a leader in yen financing, now raises 20 percent of its funding requirements in yen.) Meanwhile, although foreign investors have been drawn to Japan's stockmarket, they have since 1983 been net sellers of Japanese equities and incremental increases in their holdings have been due to share price appreciation.

As a result, the world's central banks make only marginal use of the yen as a reserve currency. The member countries of the International Monetary Fund hold 70 percent of their foreign exchange reserves in dollars, 13 percent in deutsche marks, and only 7.6 percent in yen. Given Japan's role in the global economy (in which it is the biggest creditor nation and represents about 15 percent of the free world's GNP‡ and about 9.5 percent of *all* world trade), the yen should constitute at least 25–30 percent of currency reserves while the over-represented, and now weak, dollar should decline to about 40–50 percent. As a result, an imbalance has arisen between the role of the dollar in the global monetary system and the US role in the world economy.

Japan and West Germany cannot permit such an imbalance to continue for long. It is therefore likely that a multi-currency system, which has already been proposed by central bankers, will be established. In such a system, the US dollar would cease to function as the

---

*In April 1949, the official Japanese exchange rate was set at ¥360 to the U.S. dollar. (On December 20, 1971 the yen was revalued to ¥308 to the dollar.) As this book goes to press, this was the highest level reached by the yen since April 1949.

†However, because yen raised in the Euroyen bond market are usually swapped into floating rate dollar securities, the Euroyen market is a technical extension of the dollar-based international capital markets.

‡By contrast, in 1984 the United States and Germany accounted for 34 percent and 6 percent respectively of the free world's GNP.

primary unit of value in international trade and would be replaced by a systematic combination of the dollar, the yen and the deutsche mark.

For reasons already explained, the yen will remain strong and will gradually achieve stability. A strong and stable yen will pressure Japan to internationalize its currency. The steady opening of Japan's financial markets will contribute to an increased use of the yen as a reserve currency.

Suppliers of vital commodities (such as oil) will someday demand that Japan pay them in yen. Expectations that the yen will appreciate against the dollar over the long term should further encourage producers to seek payment in a currency that may gain in value. This, in turn, would lead to an accumulation of yen assets abroad (and yen liabilities in Japan). Under such circumstances the yen will remain strong indefinitely.

The stronger the yen, the greater is the pressure on Japanese industry to produce abroad. Thus, the inevitable trend of the strengthening yen will involve a steady emigration of production facilities and marketing organizations from Japan to all of the world's major markets.

## THE EMERGING POWER OF JAPANESE MONEY

Tributary streams of dollars, pounds, deutsche marks and other currencies now flow steadily from the Western nations to Japan. These rivers of money pour into corporate treasuries. The treasuries direct a large portion of the flow of funds to Japan's commercial banks. Japan's individual savers do the same thing.

About half of Japan's surplus stays at home, contributing to the world's greatest reservoir of liquidity. The other half is 'recycled', forming 'distributaries' which flow out to the United States, Europe and Hong Kong. A tiny brook even meanders its way to the governments of the Third World in the form of development assistance.

During the next decade, these distributaries will grow deeper as Japan's surpluses increase and domestic funds seek higher returns (and greater diversity) abroad. Japan's financial industry will be the corps of engineers that determines how these brooks, streams and rivers will flow – fast or slow, deep or shallow, East or West. Their decisions, in turn, will be largely determined by overseas interest rates, foreign exchange markets and, perhaps, protectionist legislation.

That hackneyed phrase, 'money is power', may be as old as Croesus. But while money can certainly be used to promote ascendancy, authority or influence, it does not, in and of itself, embody power. Money, like the financial services that help to deploy it, is only a means to an end – a medium of exchange, a unit of account, or a store of value that facilitates the production of real goods and services but does not create them.

Today, money is flowing among financial institutions and across national borders with an increasing velocity, and the rate of flow promises only to accelerate further. Throughout the free world, interest rates, securities prices and asset valuation are becoming ever more volatile. Foreign exchange rates – if the trading activities of Japan's life insurance companies are any indication – have become susceptible to the trading practices of private companies as well as central and commercial banks.

Japan's accumulation of domestic liquidity, the strength of the yen and the consequent growth of overseas assets do not necessarily imply a parallel increase in Japanese power. It is, however, inevitable that the importance, authority and influence of Japanese investors will grow as their actions increasingly affect overseas markets and the pattern of the flow of funds. Toshiba Corporation's likely deflection of some sanctions under the Omnibus Trade Bill is a demonstration of how the *penetration of foreign markets carries with it the distinctive power to influence events abroad*. Therein lies evidence of the truth embedded in the old cliché.


Ongoing developments in the world's financial markets are gradually encompassing Japan. Regulations inhibiting the development of domestic futures and options are being revised while, simultaneously, restrictions excluding Japanese participation in the derivative securities of overseas markets are being demolished.

Meanwhile, as new financial instruments proliferate throughout the world, some are percolating into Japan's tightly regulated markets. The birth of global futures and options markets has brought about a shotgun marriage between the financial and commodity markets. Commodities trading (traditionally the country's sleaziest market sector) will grow in importance. The global trend favouring automation will also encourage Japanese investors to play a bigger role in new markets and to participate in the trading of new vehicles.

Global financial competition will increase in intensity as the integration of financial markets and financial systems becomes more complete. The ongoing process of the 'globalization', or standardization, of finance is the product of financial deregulation in each nation. As legal and regulatory barriers fall in one country the likelihood of parallel changes in other nations increases.* Japan's Ministry of Finance, the most powerful arm of the Japanese government, has traditionally opposed financial innovation. But under the pressure of precedents set elsewhere, the Ministry (with Japan at its heels) is changing.

Two powerful cultural forces within Japan have begun to merge. On the one hand, a centrifugal force that excluded foreign incursions with xenophobic zeal has been forced to compromise while, on the other hand, a centripetal force which has stressed internal conformity has reached outward. In a process that began with the Meiji Restoration, pressures inside and outside Japan have precipitated a drive to conform to foreign financial market patterns and practices.

Global financial deregulation will lead Japanese institutions to move directly and swiftly into the future. They will become increasingly proficient in their overseas participation in securities trading, mergers and acquisitions, joint venture investments, real estate investments and project finance.

In parallel with these changes, Japan's Ministry of Finance will change its policies in step with the structural transformation of the US financial system – a product of the dramatic modification of the Glass-Steagall Act and other restrictive legislation. Already, American banks have been authorized by the ministry to set up securities subsidiaries in Tokyo and Japanese banks have been actively engaged in investment banking in foreign markets.

In the near future, banks and securities companies will be permitted by the Ministry of Finance to encroach on each other's domestic territories through subsidiaries. Key distinctions between long-term credit banks, trust banks and commercial banks will disappear. During the next several years, financial reforms will transform Japan's highly segmented and rigid financial world into a new, fluid system. The Chinese walls will crumble and foreign barbarians will travel freely across Japan's financial borders.

The realignment of the world's currencies, which has resulted in a sharp appreciation of the yen against the dollar and other major currencies, enhances the current ability and motivation of Japanese investors to engage in foreign investments. Simultaneously, official ceilings inhibiting overseas investments are being raised.

Today, Japanese investors are scrutinizing the investment universe

---

*Thus, for instance, the impending 'Petit Bang' in Paris (scheduled for 1992) is a direct result of London's 'Big Bang' of 1986. Faced with the deregulation of markets in New York, London, Tokyo and Toronto, Paris was *forced* to deregulate in order to become competitive. As in London, France's financial markets will be opened significantly, enabling foreign and domestic banks, insurers, as well as other companies to buy into French brokerage firms beginning in 1988.

with single-minded absorption. As Japan's portfolio managers master new investment techniques they will become like astronomers with ever more powerful telescopes. Japanese knowledge and understanding of overseas markets will become increasingly sophisticated. Thus, by being obliged to internationalize (in order to keep in step with global financial markets) Japan will benefit immeasurably from the transformation which has been occurring in the world of finance. As a direct result, the incipient power of Japanese money will grow.

As a result of the changes that have already occurred, and the changes yet to come, the institutions which control Japanese money have acquired considerable power. Were Japan's leading investors to sell most of their US securities holdings simultaneously, for example, American interest rates would rise like a hot air balloon, while the black curtain of recession would fall on America's financial stage.

Of course, the consequences of a US recession and spiralling dollar inflation would devastate Japan's economy too. But the mere fact that a handful of Japanese institutions has the power to ravage the American economy is awesome. It means that the motivations of Japanese investors have become a key factor in global economic and political stability. The complex psychology and opportunistic philosophy that inspired these motivations cannot be ignored.

Today, there are few indications that the US current account deficit (which measures the deficit in trade in goods and services) will decline significantly during the next five years from its level of about $150 billion (or 3 percent of GNP) in 1987. Meanwhile, the proportion of American debt owned by foreign interests is likely to soar steadily and will exceed 20 percent of GNP by the early 1990s, up from less than 10 percent in 1986. Japanese institutions will control the lion's share of this foreign-owned debt.

Concurrently, the magnitude of Japanese overseas investments will rise in parallel with Japan's growing surplus. Japan was a net creditor to the tune of nearly $100 billion in 1986, and her surplus is likely to at least triple by the early 1990s. The increase in Japanese overseas investments will keep pace with this growth, and they will certainly double before the end of 1990.

Japan's towering surplus is being created primarily by the private sector, and it will be managed by financial institutions within the private sector. Because big institutional investors in Japan tend to reason along similar lines (and thus to act in concert without collusion), a decision to shift a portion of foreign investments from one country to another often affects the vast holdings of many big institutions. Already the inclinations of a small number of Tokyo- and Osaka-based fund managers can have an instantaneous impact, not only on specific markets, but also on national economies. During the next five years, this influence will expand in magnitude and scope.

The strong Japanese penchant for bond investments in preference to the stock or money markets has caused a large proportion of overseas investments to be positioned in fixed income assets, particularly government issues. It is precisely these issues that help to determine the entire spectrum of interest rates – from mortgages to consumer credit. Thus, as Japan's increasingly sophisticated portfolio managers begin to manoeuvre their holdings, shifting funds from nation to nation according to global trends, domestic pressures, and inflationary concerns, economic growth in particular countries will be promoted or inhibited by Japanese decisions.

At the same time, Japan's trust banks, life insurance companies and other asset managers have initiated new policies intended to improve overall portfolio performance. A traditional focus on yield is shifting to a concern with total return.* This shift has been prompted by complaints about poor performance from the clients of the managing institutions. It also has been stimulated by a recent change in regulations which permits trust banks to trade for their own accounts. In 1986, bond dealing became a meaningful contributor to the pretax profits of the trust banks.

As a direct result of a shift in emphasis from yield to total return, Japanese institutional fund managers have been steadily increasing the turnover of their bond portfolios. This has triggered a significant growth in bond trading volume in Tokyo, New York and London. The volume of the Tokyo dollar bond market, where US Treasury issues are traded while New York sleeps, has grown enormously and will continue to increase. And, of course, the greater the overall Japanese trading volume, the more volatile the world's major bond markets will become, and the greater the influence of Japanese traders.

Finally, Japan's burgeoning investments in the US stock market and commercial real estate market will result in increased Japanese influence on those markets. Prices at the high end of the commercial real estate market in New York and Los Angeles are already believed to have risen from 8–15 percent because of aggressive Japanese buying.

Although they are far smaller than US markets, the stock and bond markets of the UK, West Germany and Australia will also be the objects of increased Japanese buying and, thus, increased Japanese influence. The Big Four securities companies have branches near all

*See Chapter Five above. See also, Aron Viner, *Inside Japanese Financial Markets*, Homewood, Illinois; Dow Jones-Irwin; 1987, pp. 284, 290–2.

of the world's leading stockmarkets. Their role as brokers and investors can only grow.

## THE CONSOLIDATION OF FINANCIAL POWER

Both the government and major financial institutions in Japan have a powerful and durable commitment to global economic stability. From their perspective, Japan is a nation with few natural resources and no natural allies. Japan's dependence upon exports of its goods and its equal and parallel dependence upon imports of food, render the nation perpetually vulnerable to trade sanctions. Furthermore, the recent growth of Japan's investments in overseas assets has heightened the country's concerns regarding foreign exchange and interest rate stability (as well as protectionist legislation).

During the next five years, Japan will consolidate its position as the world's greatest capital exporter. Unlike that of OPEC, Japan's surplus is controlled by Japanese institutions. Thus, while capital surpluses strengthened OPEC *governments* during the 1970s, Japan's surplus is serving to strengthen Japanese *financial institutions* and to extend *their* power. Japan's multitude of private financial firms have far more flexibility and far greater skill at handling money than do the handful of OPEC governments which had barely entered the twentieth century when their great windfall occurred.

The deregulation of Japan's domestic banking and securities sectors will result in insolvencies (or mergers to avert them) and acquisitions that will increase the size of the major banks and securities firms. Sumitomo Bank's decision to merge with Heiwa Sogo (a beleaguered mutual savings bank) in 1986 foreshadowed this trend.

As a result, Japan's banks and securities companies will find themselves in a position of outstanding strength at the beginning of the twenty-first century. By then there are likely to be no more than three or four dozen fully international 'banks' in the global arena. It is probable that within twelve years, Japanese and American financial institutions will have been permitted to evolve into financial department stores. Thus, by the end of the 1990s, a small number of Japanese and American universal financial institutions will compete among themselves and with the Big Three German banks, the Big Three Swiss banks together with a few London, Paris, and Hong Kong-based establishments.

Diversification into foreign markets (through the creation of new businesses as well as acquisition) will continue hand-in-hand with the concentration and liberalization of Japan's financial sector. A relaxation of tensions between Japan and her British and American trade partners will enable the Ministry of Finance to approve further acquisitions of American financial firms and their more vulnerable British counterparts.

## TO THE VICTOR BELONG THE SPOILS

In less than a decade, Japan's share of world trade will surpass that of the United States. Within Japan, pressures to improve infrastructure will inexorably lead to improvements in the standard of living. Not only will Japan boast the world's highest *per capita* income, but she will eventually provide her citizens with a 'quality of life' comparable to the best of Western Europe. Holding more foreign assets than any nation in the world, Japan will be swathed in a twenty-first-century version of twentieth-century American affluence.

Japan's sudden rise to global financial ascendancy during the late 1980s took the nation by surprise. Despite the country's importance within the world economy, Japan's bureaucratic, industrial, and financial leaders were unprepared and unwilling to assume international leadership roles.

Japan has long provided modest contributions to the major supranational organizations. However, with the sole exception of the Manila-based Asian Development Bank (which Japan has been seeking to dominate), no Japanese representative has publicly expressed a willingness to accept a major role in the governance of a multilateral institution such as the World Bank.

Although Japan is the largest supporter of the World Bank after the United States, for every Japanese on the World Bank's professional staff in 1986 there were eighteen Americans. The limited Japanese participation in international organizations has long been regarded as an indication of Japan's reluctance to assume a leading role in global finance.

Unable to choose its own direction and not fully in control of the developments that have drawn it into international financial markets, Japan has failed to apply its skills at long-term planning to its political and economic destiny. With the future in the palm of its hand and 'internationalization' a popular buzzword for all imported ideas (and people), Japan remains wrapped in the cloak of Tokugawa-era provincialism.

A first, massive wave of modernization that began in 1868 raised Japan from feudal economy and technology to the highest levels of technological development within seventy years. The wave then spent itself on war. Beginning in the 1950s, another wave raised Japan to economic and financial power unprecedented in modern Asia. How much higher the crest will mount and how long it will last are questions that will be decided by the Japanese themselves.

## THE POWER OF MONEY IN THE TWENTY-FIRST CENTURY

Weapons are at a standoff. In the nineteenth and early twentieth centuries, concentrations of arms served to assure power. The most heavily armed nation was the mightiest. Paradoxically, perhaps, nuclear weapons have negated the sheer power of accumulation. The superpowers cannot gain supremacy through military means without mutual destruction.

Manufacturing has ceased to stoke the fires of the developed nations' economic growth. The post-industrial era is now at mid-day. The free world's industrial leaders represent economies that derive the largest portion of their GNP from the services sector. Within this area, financial services are growing.

The industrial revolution once enabled Great Britain to rule the waves. During the twenty-first century, new leaders with a new basis of power will call the shots. Money will replace weapons as a vital means of wielding influence, *making capital a crucial strategic asset*. The nation with a surplus of money will use the money to attain political and military aspirations by influencing the integrated world economy.

Although glib and perfunctory, this quick appraisal is not devoid of immediacy. Recent economic reforms initiated by Deng Xaoping and Mikhail Gorbachev are expressions of a vital realization: in the twenty-first century, international power will be the *direct* outcome of an economic strength which in turn will rest upon the prosaic capitalist activities of universal banking.* Within this new environment, Japanese financial influence will hold the world in a tight embrace.

---

*These ideas will be expanded in my next book which discusses global strategies and the political ramifications of financial competition.

# BIBLIOGRAPHY

Abegglen, James C. *et al. US-Japan Economic Relations.* Berkeley: University of California Institute of East Asian Studies, 1980.

Abegglen, James C. and George Stalk, Jr. *Kaisha, The Japanese Corporation.* New York: Basic Books, 1985.

Adams, T. F. M. and Iwao Hoshii. *A Financial History of the New Japan.* Tokyo: Kodansha, 1972.

Allen, G. C. *A Short Economic History of Modern Japan.* Fourth Edition. New York: St Martin's, 1981.

Azumi, K. *Higher Education and Business Recruitment in Japan.* New York: Columbia University Press, 1969.

Ballon, R. J. (ed.). *The Japanese Employee.* Tokyo: Sophia University Press, 1969.

Ballon, Robert J. And Eugene H. Lee (eds.). *Foreign Investment and Japan.* Tokyo: Sophia University, 1972.

Befu, Harumi. *Japan: An Anthropological Introduction.* San Francisco: Chandler, 1971.

Behrman, J. N. *Some Patterns in the Rise of the Multinational Enterprise.* Chapel Hill: University of North Carolina, 1969.

Robert N. Bellah. *Tokugawa Relgion, The Values of Pre-Industrial Japan.* Boston: Beacon Press, 1970.

Benjamin, Roger and Kan Ori. *Tradition and Change in Postindustrial Japan: The Roles of the Political Parties.* New York: Praeger, 1981.

Bergsten, C. Fred. and William R. Cline. *The United States-Japan Economic Problem.* Washington, DC: Institute for International Economics, 1985.

Bisson, T. A. *Zaibatsu Dissolution in Japan.* Berkeley: University of California Press, 1954.

Burks, Ardath W. *Japan, A Postindustrial Power.* Second Edition. Boulder, Colorado: Westview Press, 1984.

Castle, Emery N. and Kenzo Hemmi (eds.). *United States-Japanese Agriculture Trade Relations.* Baltimore: Johns Hopkins University Press, 1982.

Caves, Richard E. and Uekusa, Masu. *Industrial Organization in Japan.* Washington, D.C.: Brookings Institution, 1976.

Christopher, Robert C. *The Japanese Mind: The Goliath Explained.* New York: Simon and Schuster, 1983.

Clark, Rodney. *The Japanese Company.* New Haven: Yale University Press, 1979.

Cole, R. E. *Work, Mobility and Participation: A Comparative Study of American and Japanese Industry.* Berkeley: University of California Press, 1979.

Crocker, Olga L, Syril Charney, and Johnny Sik Leung Chiu. *Quality Circles, and How We Can Make It Work For Us.* New York: Methuen, 1984.

De Vos, George. *Socialization for Achievement: Essays on the Cultural Psychology of the Japanese.* Berkeley: University of California Press, 1973.

Dore, Ronald. *Aspects of Social Change in Modern Japan.* Princeton, N. J.: 1971.

——*British Factory-Japanese Factory, The Origins of National Diversity in Industrial Relations.* Berkeley: University of California Press, 1973.

Goldsmith, Raymond W. *The Financial Development of Japan, 1868–1977*. New Haven: Yale University Press, 1983.

Hadley, Eleanor M. *Antitrust in Japan*. Princeton, N. J.: Princeton University Press, 1970.

Hanabusa, Masamichi. *Trade Problems Between Japan and Western Europe*. Farnborough: Saxon House, 1979.

Hasegawa, Nyozekan. *The Japanese Character, A Cultural Profile*. Trans. John Bester. Tokyo: Kodansha, 1966.

Havens, Thomas R. H. *Farm and Nation in Modern Japan*. Princeton, N. J.: Princeton University Press, 1974.

Hayashi, Shuji. *Culture and Management in Japan*. Tokyo: University of Tokyo Press, 1986.

Higashi, Chikara. *Japanese Trade Policy Formulation*. New York: Praeger, 1983.

Hirschmeier, J. and T. Yui. *The Development of Japanese Business*. Second Edition. London: Allen & Unwin, 1981.

Ho, Alfred K. *Japan's Trade Liberalization in the 1960s*. New York: International Arts and Science Press, 1973.

Hollerman, Leon. *Japan's Dependency on the World Economy: The Approach toward Economic Liberalization*. Princeton, N J: Princeton University Press, 1967.

Hori, Ichior, *Folk Religion in Japan, Continuity and Change*. Edited by Joseph M. Kitagawa and Alan L. Miller. Chicago: University of Chicago Press, 1968.

Hyoe, Murakami and Johannes Hirschmeier (eds), *Politics and Economics in Contemporary Japan*. Tokyo: Kodansha, 1983.

Japanese Ministry of Finance and the United States Department of the Treasury Working Group on Yen/Dollar Exchange Rate Issues. *Report by the Working Group on Yen/Dollar Exchange Rate, Financial and Capital Market Issues to Japanese Minister of Finance Noboru Takeshita [and] U.S. Secretary of the Treasury Donald T. Regan*. Tokyo, May 1984.

Japan External Trade Organization (JETRO). Staff, ed. *White Paper on International Trade: Japan*. Tokyo, 1981.

Johnson, Chalmers. *MITI and the Japanese Miracle, The Growth of Industrial Policy, 1925–1975*. Stanford, Calif.: Stanford University Press, 1982.

Kahn, Herman. *The Emerging Japanese Superstate*. Harmondsworth: Penguin Books, 1973.

Kahn, Herman and Thomas Pepper. *The Japanese Challenge*. Harmondsworth: Penguin Books, 1973.

Kaplan, David E. and Alec Dubro. *Yakuza, The Explosive Account of Japan's Criminal Underworld*. Reading, Mass.: Addison-Wesley, 1986.

Kaplan, Eugene J. *Japan: The Government-Business Relationship*. Washington, DC: US Department of Commerce, 1972.

Lincoln, Edward J. *Japan's Industrial Policies*. Washington, DC: Japan Economic Institute of America, 1984.

Lockwood, William W. *The Economic Development of Japan*. Princeton, N J: Princeton University Press, 1954.

McCraw, Thomas K. (ed.). *America Versus Japan*. Boston: Harvard Business School Press, 1986.

Magaziner, Ira C. and Thomas M. Hout. *Japanese Industrial Policy*. Berkeley: University of California Institute of International Studies, 1981.

Marsh, R. M. and H. Mannari. *Modernization and the Japanese Factory*. Princeton, N J: Princeton University Press, 1976.

Marshall, Byron K. *Capitalism and Nationalism in Prewar Japan: The Ideology of the Business Elite, 1868–1941*. Stanford: Stanford University Press, 1967.

Mayer, Fanny Hagin (trans. and ed.). *The Yamagita Kunio Guide to the Japanese Folk Tale*. Bloomington, Indiana: Indiana University Press, 1986.

Morishima, Michio. *Why Has Japan 'Succeeded'? Western Technology and the Japanese ethos*. Cambridge: Cambridge University Press, 1982.

Nakamura, James I. *Agricultural Production and the Economic Development of Japan, 1873–1922*. Princeton, N J: Princeton University Press, 1966.

Nakane, Chie. *Human Relations in Japan*. Tokyo: Ministry of Foreign Affairs, 1972.

——*Japanese Society*. Berkeley: University of California Press, 1972.

Nakane, Fukio (trans. and ed.). *Japanese Laws Relating to Banks*. Tokyo: Eibun-Horei-Sha., 1977.

Nishikawa, S. (ed.). *The Labor Market in Japan*. Tokyo: University of Tokyo Press, 1980.

Nitobe, Inazo. *Bushido, The Soul of Japan*. Rutland, Vermont: Tuttle, 1969.

Norman, E. H. *Origins of the Modern Japanese State, Selected Writings*. Dower, John W. (ed.) New York: Random House, 1975.

Okimoto, Daniel I. and Takuo Sugano, and Franklin B. Weinstein (eds.). *Competitive Edge, The Semiconductor Industry in the U.S. and Japan*. Stanford, Calif.: Stanford University Press, 1984.

Ouchi, William G. *Theory Z, How American Business can Meet the Japanese Challenge*. New York: Addison-Wesley, 1981.

——*The M-Form Society*. New York: Addison-Wesley, 1984.

Ozawa, T. *Multinationalism, Japanese Style: the Political Economy or Outward Dependency*. Princeton, NJ: Princeton University Press, 1979.

Pascale, R. T. 'Zen and the Art of Management,' *Harvard Business Review*, March-April, 1978.

Pascale, Richard Tanner and Anthony G. Athos. *The Art of Japanese Management*. New York: Simon and Schuster, 1981.

Passin, Herbert (ed.). *The United States and Japan*. Second Edition. Washington, DC: Columbia Books, 1975.

Patrick, Hugh. *Japanese Industrialization and its Social Consequences*. New York: Columbia University Press, 1976.

Patrick, Hugh and Henry Rosovsky, eds. *Asia's New Giant, How the Japanese Economy Works*. Washington, DC: The Brookings Institution, 1976.

Perrin, Noel. *Giving up the Gun, Japan's Reversion to the Sword, 1543–1879*. Boulder, Colorado: Shambhala, 1979.

Petri, Peter A. *Modeling Japanese-American Trade: A Study of Asymmetric Interdependence*. Cambridge, Mass: Harvard University Press, 1984.

Reischauer, Edwin O. *The Japanese*. Cambridge, Mass: Harvard University, Press, 1977.

Roberts, John G. *Mitsui: Three Centuries of Japanese Business*. New York: John Weatherhill, 1973.

Rohlen, T. P. 'Spiritual Training in a Japanese Bank,' *American Anthropologist*, Vol. 75, 1973.

Rohlen, T. P. *For Harmony and Strength*. Berkeley: University of California Press, 1974.

Sansom, G. B. *The Western World and Japan*. New York: Knopf, 1950.

Sasaki, N. *Management and Industrial Structure in Japan*. Oxford: Pergamon, 1981.

Schonberger, Richard J. *Japanese Manufacturing Techniques, Nine Hidden Lessons in Simplicity*. New York: The Free Press, 1982.

Shirai, Taishiro (ed.). *Contemporary Industrial Relations in Japan*. Madison, Wis: University of Wisconsin Press, 1983.

Smith, Thomas C. *The Agrarian Origins of Modern Japan*. Stanford: Stanford University Press, 1959.

Sperelakis, N. 'Electrical Properties of Embryonic Heart Cells.' In Demallo, WC (ed.), *Electrical Phenomena in the Heart*. New York: Academic Press, 1972.

Spindler, J. Andres. *The Politics of International Credit, Private Finance and Foreign Policy in Germany and Japan*. Washington, DC: The Brookings Institution, 1984.

Stone, P. B. *Japan Surges Ahead: the Story of an Economic Miracle*. New York: Praeger, 1969.

Tatsuno, Sheridan. *The Technopolis Strategy, Japan, High Technology, and the Control of the 21st Century*. New York: Prentice Hall, 1986.

Tokyo Metropolitan Government (ed.). *Financial History of Tokyo: A Century of Growth Amid Change*. Tokyo: Tokyo Metropolitan Government, 1972.

Toyo Keizai Shinposha (The Oriental Economist). *Japan Company Handbook*. Tokyo: annual.

Trevor, Malcolm. *Japan's Reluctant Multinationals, Japanese Management at Home and Abroad*. New York: St Martin's, 1983.

Tsunetomo, Yamamoto. *Hagakure* (Trans. William Scott Wilson). Tokyo: Kodansha, 1979.

Vernon, R. *Storm over the Multinationals: The Real Issues*. Cambridge, Mass.: Harvard University Press, 1977.

Viner, Aron. *Inside Japanese Financial Markets*. Homewood, Ill: Dow Jones-Irwin, 1987.

Vogel, Ezra (ed). *Modern Japanese Organizations and Decision Making*. Berkeley: University of California Press, 1975.

——*Japan as Number One*. Cambridge, Mass: Harvard University Press, 1979.

——*Comeback, Building the Resurgence of American Business*. New York: Simon and Schuster, 1985.

Wildes, Harry Emerson. *Typhoon in Tokyo: The Occupation and Its Aftermath*. New York: Macmillan, 1954.

Yoshino, M. Y. *Japan's Managerial System: Tradition and Innovation.* Cambridge, Mass: The MIT Press, 1971.

——*Japan's Multinational Enterprises.* Cambridge, Mass: The MIT Press, 1976.

Yoshino, M. Y. and Thomas B. Lifson. *The Invisible Link, Japan's Sogo Shosha and the Organization of Trade.* Cambridge, Mass: The MIT Press, 1986.

Young, Alexander K. *The Sogo Shosha, Japan's Multinational Trading Companies.* Boulder, Colorado: The Westview Press, 1979.

# INDEX